Valentine's Day

Valentine's Day

Women against men:
Stories of revenge

Introduction by Alice Thomas Ellis

Duck Editions

Second impression August 2000
This collection first published in February 2000 by
Duckworth Literary Entertainments, Ltd.
61 Frith Street, London W1D 3JL
Tel: 0207 434 4242
Fax: 0207 434 4420
email:DuckEd@duckworth-publishers.co.uk

A CIP catalogue record for this title is available from the British Library.

ISBN 0 7156 3006 7

Typeset by Derek Doyle & Associates, Liverpool
Printed and bound in Great Britain by
Redwood Books Ltd, Trowbridge

Contents

Acknowledgements

The Publishers would like to thank Victoria Field for her invaluable research, and the following authors and publishers for granting copyright permission:

Eating Vic © 2000 Shelley Weiner
The Cat's Whiskers © 1994 Alice Thomas Ellis. Originally a radio play. First published in the collection *The Evening of Adam* (1995) Viking, London.
Pot Luck © 2000 Patrice Chaplin
Accident © 1934 Agatha Christie Mallowan. Taken from *The Listerdale Mystery*, by kind permission of the Estate of Agatha Christie.
Down There Undercover © 2000 Judith Amanthis
Widow's Peak © 1997 Sylvia Petter. First published in New Zealand in the Southern Ocean Review (#4, Winter 1997), P.O. Box 2143, Dunedin, New Zealand.
Stitch and Bitch © 2000 Jane Barker Wright
The Mole Trap © 2000 Norma Meacock
Sitting Pretty © 1995 Pauline Holdstock. First published in Canada in the collection *Swimming from the Flames* (1995), Turnstone Press, #607, 100 Arthur Street, Winnipeg, Manitoba R3B 1H3.
The Father © 2000 Jean Pickering
Escape Artist © 2000 Vicky Grut
Beware the Gentle Wife © 2000 Deborah Bosley
Leda and the Swan © 1995 Fay Weldon. First published in the collection *Wicked Women* (1995), Flamingo, London.
The French Boy © 1997 Amanda Craig. First published in *She* magazine.
The Sound of the Horn © 2000 Clare Colvin
I Was in Love © 1970 Joyce Carol Oates. Originally published in the *Ontario Review Inc*. Taken from *The Wheel of Love* (1970), Vanguard, NewYork.
Before the Change © 1998 Alice Munro. Originally published in *The New Yorker*. Taken from *The Love of a Good Woman* (1988). Used by kind permission, Chatto & Windus, London, and McClelland & Stewart Inc, Canada.
Larry's Words © 1997 Carol Shields. Reprinted by kind permission of Fourth Estate Ltd, London, from *Larry's Party* by Carol Shields.
Set in Stone © 2000 Pat Knight

Introduction

Lord Byron wrote, 'Vengeance is sweet – especially to women,' a distortion of the truth, since bloody vengeance has almost without exception been the province of the male. Yet few have ventured to question the proposition. The feminists have not objected to it nor complained that it is misogynistic or unjust, and modern feminism, which could be seen as a collective act of revenge on men, celebrates female acts of retribution, sometimes elevating the concept to an art form. While the murderous tribal vendettas that constantly erupt all over the world are deplored by the *bien pensant*, the woman engaged in getting her own back is now frequently the object of approval, not unmixed with amusement; a psychological stratagem which perhaps has the effect of minimising the fear and loathing once inspired by the Erinyes.

The perception of woman as Angel in the House, so dear to the Victorians, has been largely dissipated but there is still a widespread sense that violence and unrestrained anger are not natural to women and that when they behave badly the overall effect is more comical than alarming. This holds true only in their reaction to the healthy, stalwart male: women who abuse children or the helpless are still seen as inhumanly horrifying. Mothers and nurturers, sooner and later, have us all at their mercy. We must trust them to meet our expectations, or, by extension, lose sight of the parameters of our own identities. The female, despite the ideologies that would deny any difference between the sexes, is not as innately destructive as the male. Even the dreaded spider who eats her mate immediately after intercourse does so not from any hostile motive or urge to supremacy but since, now she is pregnant, she needs the protein and he provides the nearest accessible source. The female of the species is more deadly than the male usually only when her offspring are in need or threatened, not from innate cussedness.

Lord Byron's dictum is not borne out by nature nor by history. There have always been cruel, nasty and indeed murderous women but their evil acts have more commonly been inspired by greed, irritation or expedience rather than the urge to vengeance. The saying 'Hell hath no fury like a woman scorned' does not hold up to examination. A woman scorned, again until recently, would as often as not be found sobbing on the bosoms of her female friends, whereas a man whose prowess – be it sexual, sporting or financial – has been denigrated, will indeed be in a devilish mood. (Those women who are impelled by wounded vanity or spite to make false declarations of rape or sexual harassment are beneath our notice, deserving only of inclusion in a work on petty criminality or psychiatric disorder: they lack the tragic status of the victim turned avenger and are merely contemptible.) It is perhaps that women are of necessity, since so much depends on them and contrary to the popular view, less romantic, less idealistic and also less narcissistic than men and seldom turn to violence unless there is something of practical value to be gained: freedom, wealth, the peace of mind that results from definitively ending an unsatisfactory situation, and occasionally, or so they claim, because some man has demanded their complicity.

Not all women necessarily shrink from violence even in the ordinary course of events. There have been instances of female warriors; the fabulous Amazons, the bodyguard of the King of Dahomey, our own armed and police forces, while in a less elevated context the scold's bridle, the ducking stool, were designed to restrain brawling women who terrorised the neighbourhood. It has been said, by way of excuse, that those Red Indian women who contributed enthusiastically to the torturing of prisoners were motivated by feelings of frustration and vengeance on behalf of their dead warriors, but the assignment of contemporary mores to peoples of the past is a fruitless and misleading exercise. A contemporary European observer, after describing in detail the ingenious and frightful discomforts that were inflicted on captives, writes, 'The women, forgetting the human as well as the female nature, and transformed into something worfe than furies, even outdo the men in this fcene of horror ...' He adds, however, 'What is the moft extraordinary, the fufferer himfelf, in the little interval of his torments, fmokes too, appears unconcerned, and converfes with his torturers about indifferent matters.' It is pointless to attempt to explain such behaviour from the perspective of a different set of rules and beliefs.

Then there are those well-known heroines of history and myth: Judith, who took advantage of Holofernes by dressing in her best and getting him drunker than 'he had ever been before' in preparation for decapitating him (Artemesia Gentileschi, who painted this scene, might, one speculates, have found the exercise a relief to her feelings, for she had been raped by the artist Agostino Tassi who, adding insufferable insult to injury, claimed he had been trying to teach her the rules of perspective at the time of the alleged rape: a lamentable variant on the 'come up and see my etchings' theme and an unforgiveable slur on her artistic capabilities); Salome, who demanded the head of John the Baptist on a meat plate at the behest of her mother, who had taken umbrage at his rejection of her advances; Delilah, who is a heroine to the more dedicated feminists since, even if she was on the wrong side, she did render a male impotent; and Clytemnestra, who undoubtedly had cause for grievance since her husband had sacrificed their daughter in order to raise a wind and enable his fleet to set sail and do battle with the Trojans, and who on his return had brought as a trophy the unfortunate Cassandra. Nevertheless, men in particular find Clytemnestra's actions reprehensible, since she slew Agamemnon in his bath, when he was naked and vulnerable, during what should have been a welcoming rite. And she *had* taken a lover of her own, but then she was only human. Many people, including judges, have reservations about women who slay men who are in the bath, at table, asleep, temporarily out of their senses or otherwise disadvantaged. This was not done in the heat of the moment, they say of the woman in the dock, ignoring the obvious fact that few women are able to take on a powerful aggressor, man to man as it were, and must needs have recourse to stealth if they find it advisable to murder him. Others – Boudicca, the Maid of Orleans,

Charlotte Corday (another bath-murderess) – who, like the above, took an active part in affairs, performed their rough deeds in the interests of the people, the tribe, or, as some would say now, 'the community', as partisans, freedom fighters, rather than through any sense of personal affront. They are revered for their courage and enterprise, unlike those female monsters who arouse only revulsion: Lamia, the Libyan Queen who was beloved of Jupiter and robbed of her offspring by the jealous Juno and, in consequence 'vowed vengeance against all children whom she delighted to entice and devour'; Lilith, according to the Talmudists, Adam's first wife, who refused to submit to him, left Paradise to haunt a region of the air, and is especially dangerous to children and pregnant women; Medea, who killed her children in order to spite her faithless husband; Lucretia Borgia, once represented as 'outside the pale of humanity by her wantonness, vices and crimes', but who was probably, in her youth, only the rather too pliant instrument in the hands of Alexander and Caesar Borgia; and the possibly apocryphal Empress of China who cut off the arms and legs of a rival and kept her in a large jar as a diversion for the amusement of the court. Somebody once remarked of this episode that it had an awful kind of *style* and it may be that retaliation against a female rival seems less threatening to the intrinsic fabric of society than aggression against the male. A plea to a museum of witchcraft for examples of magical revenge for those crossed in love elicited the information that most spells of this kind were aimed at the Other Woman rather than the Faithless Man. It must be the result of modern feminism and notions of sisterhood that have changed the emphasis and largely shifted the blame from Her to Him. Of course, many women remain uninfluenced by the trend and continue to hold the trollop responsible, but cattiness is out of vogue and seldom makes the headlines. It is usually the Love Rat who draws opprobrium on himself and is held up to public scorn, and it is a strange twist in the 'empowerment' of women that encourages us to applaud the wronged one when she takes a decisive role in the drama, while in many cases perceiving the third (female) party as passive, free of malice afore-thought and, it must be said, of any hint of autonomy or intelligence.

The exceptions test the rule, and the scheming hussy revealed is still the object of particular opprobrium. (It is interesting that the adulteries of the late Princess of Wales, who could be undeniably devious, went unrebuked, while her husband's one, earnestly single-minded, infidelity has called down the disapproval of the nation and his unremarkable mistress was, until recently, widely disliked.)

Helen of Troy is an ancient example of the inert object of desire, no more capable of settling her own destiny than a ping-pong ball; a prize, a fairground coconut, deserving of neither praise nor blame as reprisal and counter-reprisal rage about her. Early films often centred around a Helen, usually a blonde wearing incapacitating clothes (tight bodice, voluminous skirts) or very little, who was required to do no more than was called for by the standards of the time – to wring her hands and assume an anxious expression, as the hero and villain wrecked the furniture in the battle to decide her fate. Much of the audience must, even then, have wondered exasperatedly why she didn't *do* something. Invariably if she did attempt to take a hand in the proceedings she would make matters worse; hovering uncertainly, holding aloft the Ming vase, she would mistime her move and bring it down on the head of the hero. Women were too charmingly daffy to challenge the aggressor with any hope of victory and it was safer for all concerned to leave her on the sidelines. Underlying this convention was the unacknowledged suspicion that a woman giving free vent to her feelings would be an uncontrollable and ugly force: bad for the box-office and a destabilising example to society. There was a feeling that women could not be trusted to abide by the Queensbury rules: 'A woman may act like a man but can never behave like a gentleman.'

Nor has the overtly vengeful woman been much in evidence in literature. Bad women abound – stepmothers, adventuresses, poisoners, witches, schemers, jealous women – but few who have dedicated themselves to full-scale vengeance in the way that men have done. The 'ruined' woman was a reproach to her menfolk and they reacted accordingly. It was not her well-being that was in the forefront of their minds as they sought to rectify the wrong done to her, but the insult to *their* dignity: they took an injury to a female of the family as a personal offence, and if the female in question was actually quite happy to be 'dishonoured' that was beside the point. It was men who pursued the vendetta and few women took an active part in the bloody machinations. It could be argued that this bias towards uniquely male involvement in vengeance is evident partly because men wrote most of the books, but the lady-novelist has been with us for some time and until latterly has not much addressed herself to the subject. Here it could be claimed that she had better things to think about and did not suffer from the obsessive urge to vengeance evident in her male counterparts, but this would not be entirely accurate.

One subtle but satisfying route open to the avenger is to put the villain in a book, rather than run him through or blow his brains out, while the heroine, in her quietly impeccable way, can be seen as not only triumphant but virtuous. The Brontë sisters, to take one example, were aware of this: Lucy Snowe, Jane Eyre, Helen Huntingdon, come out on top while the men in their lives are, in their various ways, all losers. The impartial reader might think that to be subjected to the company of any one of these grimly self-righteous females would be punishment enough, but it cannot be maintained that this was the intention of the authors, who were chiefly concerned with establishing the moral superiority of their heroines and were unworried by the effect they might, in truth, have on those around them. The doubtless gratifying sense of being in the right sustained many Victorian women and was heartily encouraged by the society of the time. No *lady* would sully her purity with anything so vulgar as a loss of temper or self-control – a view which stood Lizzie Borden in good stead, for few, including the jury, could believe that a young woman, well brought up and neatly dressed, could be so rude as to murder her parents with an axe.

Poisoning, both accidental and deliberate, was once rife, and it will never be known how many family members were dispatched by this means. Those women who were apprehended were mostly of the lower classes and suspected only after they had finished off improbable numbers of their loved ones in order to claim the insurance money, their meagre belongings or simply to rid themselves of extra mouths to feed. The middle-class woman who aspired to wealthy and uncluttered widowhood had usually only to dispose of one hindrance, and here again it was seldom the urge to vengeance that moved her, but the rational, if regrettable, desire to better her circumstances and remove an inconvenience. There have been virtual epidemics of murder committed by women, usually by poisoning, although at one time, in several places round the Mediterranean, the bones of a surprising number of missing husbands were found at the bottom of dry wells. Their wives had explained their absence by saying they had emigrated. It seems that nothing was ever proved, though certain widows had an apparently inexplicable habit of throwing flowers down these wells: a prettily pious touch. In a village in Hungary in 1929 the local midwife, who ran a sideline in procuring abortions, extended her activities to include poisoning to order. Most of her customers were female and their motives various. It is said that one woman murdered her son because his increasing age was an unwelcome indication of her own. She sat, or so it is rumoured, on his bed, singing elegiac hymns as he expired, an oblique and desperate response to the remorseless passing of the years.

But it was not until the 1970s that the idea of the avenging female became chic and seized the popular imagination. Women who could acquit themselves well in a rough-house became not merely acceptable but admirable. Nor did they need to sacrifice glamour as they mastered the complexities of the martial arts. The female detective and private eye came into vogue, doing their bit to clean up those 'mean streets', although they are not such a remarkable innovation as is generally supposed. Around the turn of the century Baroness Orczy's Lady Molly was employed at Scotland Yard, unravelling the motives behind crimes that no mere male could be expected to comprehend. She seldom, however, got her frock torn or dirty.

Then came the anecdotes, some true and some urban legends. Kathy Lette's prawns in the curtain pole of her faithless lover; Lady Moon's original approach to the altering of clothes, and the distribution of her husband's vintage wines to the doorsteps of neighbours; the bunny-boilers who proliferated as the film-makers realised the possibilities inherent in the new attitudes. Tales of women who telephoned the speaking clock in Australia from the homes of their erstwhile partners and left the phone off the hook, who soaked his carpets and sowed them with the seeds of mustard and cress, who alerted the Inland Revenue to discrepancies in his accounting methods. There was a gleeful explosion of tales of retribution as notions of modesty, humility, forbearance and all the old-fashioned virtues were put aside as inappropriate in the life of the modern female. We may be sure that similar, if possibly less imaginative, petty vengeances have been practised throughout history, but it was not considered nice, nor was it prudent, to boast about them or flaunt your triumph.

Men still, even in the teeth of the latest evidence, prefer to think of their women as gentle and harmless. One man, on being told that his ex-mistress had been receiving lewd and threatening phone-calls but had bought a powerful whistle and planned to burst the caller's eardrums next time he rang, said, shocked, that she would never do anything so unkind. He will be surprised by the stories in this collection.

Some illustrate the possibilities of reprisal available in the kitchen, another aspect of vengeance which has been curiously under-explored in literature – perhaps again because it is too uncomfortable a subject to be openly confronted. Those who abuse their positions of trust, who should be all comfort and welcome, with, ideally, a smudge of flour on their noses and an aura of freshly baked bread about them, are too frightening to contemplate. The bedroom may be regarded as a legitimate area of conflict, but she who reigns in the kitchen (or holds the soap or strygil, as the case may be) should be in a pacific frame of mind, at once generous and hygienic. (I, I hasten to add, have never given anyone a cat's meat sandwich, but it is sometimes refreshing to brood on the possibility.)

The more violent tales are also, one hopes, the result of sublimation, mere wistful flights of fancy and divorced from reality, while the more realistic stories are sadder and illustrative of the dangers inherent in the blind search for revenge. Witches, when engaged in maleficent practices, used to chant incantations to protect themselves against any ricocheting effect, and for all I know still do.

Clare Colvin's cleverly titled 'The Sound of the Horn' shows the helplessness of a rightly intentioned child in the face of adult misbehaviour and injustice, how she ends up somehow in the wrong, while Joyce Carol Oates in 'I Was in Love' writes of the resentment of a small child at his mother's actions, her inability to cope with it and the terrible consequences; the inverted effects of lust and anger. The woman in Alice Munro's 'Before the Change' avenges herself on her lover by telling him the truth, things he would not want to know, but remains miserably affected by both him and her father, their insensitivity and self-absorption. Amanda Craig writes of a minor revenge, that of a mother on her children who have relegated her to the background, while the other more cheerful stories tell of revenge by the exercise of the attainment of superiority. 'Larry's Words', the saddest story of them all, is, as one reader put it, 'sympathetic to men for once', and shows revenge as arbitrary, cruel and destructive.

'Vengeance', so the saying has it, 'is a dish best eaten cold,' but perhaps from the point of view of both morality and prudence it is rather a dish best imagined, and we should hearken more attentively to the injunction of the Lord, 'Vengeance is mine.' Still, reading about it can be, to our fallen human nature, not only salutary but sometimes deplorably satisfying.

Alice Thomas Ellis, August 1999

Eating Vic

Shelley Weiner

It's not like I'm a bad sort. On the contrary, as my best friend Denise keeps telling me, I'm much too soft for my own good. Toughen up, Marleen, she goes. Get real. It's high time you stood *up* to Vic, let him know who's who, stop giving in to the bugger like that. But what does Denise know, married to old Martin Van Niekerk who can't tell his elbow from his arse any more, so she can spend till the cows come home with nothing asked of her at all?

With Vic it's different. He wants his pound of flesh. And fair's fair, no one's arguing with that, an arrangement's an arrangement. I can't say I went into it with my eyes closed, and I've certainly got my share. Quid pro quo, as he'd put it, in his most lawyerish way – assuming of course that I won't understand what the hell he's talking about. I do though. I understand the lot. And even if there are things I slightly regret, I'm not the type to go back on a deal. Even Sandra Jackson, who basically hates my guts, admits that I'm a sticker – when Marleen gets her teeth into something, she told Denise who told me, she holds on tighter than a Rottweiler. Which is all very well for a Rottweiler, but certainly gives *me* jaw-ache – hanging in there and smiling, agreeing to whatever he wants within reason, making sure everything's as smooth as smooth can be. Knowing I shouldn't really complain, since he's stuck to *his* side of the bargain – an eye for an eye, a tooth for a tooth, if one can measure his goodies against my sexual favours like that. I won't go into details, but for example the remuneration required for my two-carat diamond was, to put it mildly, off the wall. I'm hardly a prude, but – as Denise agrees – there are limits. The thing is, though, I adore the trappings: the clothes, the house, the ring, the fact of being Mrs Victor Arenson, and of course the prospect of being widow of the late Victor Arenson. Not that I'd dream of speeding up this ultimate outcome – never ever, unless absolutely pushed – but it's nice to think about, isn't it? And I must admit that the more outrageous his demands become, the more I think about how fabulous it'll be one day to be rich and free. So that by the time we arrive in Malawi …

You heard it. *Malawi*. Not exactly my sort of place. How he twisted my arm to get me there, God only knows. Mind you, it's almost as much of a mystery why Vic himself would want to go there, with all his pickiness about personal hygiene and uncontaminated food. Tarzan and Jane we are not. So picture my horror when, here we are on our patio on a peaceful Johannesburg autumn eve – his beer, my Cinzano, my slight worry about having splashed out on an extremely extravagant little number that morning but what the hell – when out pops his plan. I'm shocked, almost dumbstruck. I mean there's Paris, London, New York, the Caribbean if the guy wants close to nature, he's not short of a bob or two …

But no. His mind's made up. Some bloke, the mayor of Blantyre or whatever, has somehow convinced him that there's something special about the place. More than special – *irresistible*. Vic's eyes are shining, he's hardly able to swallow his beer, he's so excited that I'm half expecting him to have his coronary right there on the spot. Easy easy, I say, thinking *my* what a bargaining position I'm in – and not ready to submit yet, not by a long shot. It's the future, Marls, he says, going on about our ethnic neighbours and economic co-operation and pragmatism and all the stuff he hears about at his Chamber of Commerce meetings. Bullshit. What's in it for me, I ask. Polluted water, wild animals, dirty food, not to mention Vic's unbroken attention and all *that* means for two bloody weeks on end. Not on your life.

I give in, of course. Every girl has her price, some higher than others, and I'm not too unhappy with the final reckoning. Plus it's a bit of a coup to be able to report to Denise (and along the grapevine to Sandra) that we're off to darkest Africa like adventurers of old, repeating all Vic's crap about the lake and the palm trees and how Malawi's the holiday destination of the future and how the Arensons are trailing the blaze. She's impressed. Didn't know I had it in me. Next thing, I'll be joining the Black Sash and holding placards outside the City Hall. Like hell. Politics and me don't mix, and whatever Vic says about his multi-racial meetings, I know that deep down all he cares about is where he sticks his willy. That's the truth of it, the only certainty, the one thing that'll outlast apartheid ...

Mind you, the way he's putting it about even at the *prospect* of a fortnight with his Marls in seclusion in the sun, one would think it'd be showing at least some sign of wear and tear. No such luck. Once a night, twice a night, three, four, five times a night, this way, that way – by day I've hardly got the energy even to shop. But I do. Splash out, Marls, he urges me (as if I need urging). Treat yourself to anything you fancy, anything at all. As I tot up my expenditure I'm slightly concerned about the eventual pay-off but so what. I'm euphoric by now, my charge cards are frazzled, my wardrobe has quadrupled, my luggage (three matching pieces) all assembled like I'm off on a royal grand tour. Maybe, I think, as we sit there in the departure hall at Jan Smuts waiting for our flight – maybe it won't be too bad ... ?

But something warns me that it will. As I glance at Vic seated opposite me, in his blue jeans and lemon Lacoste shirt and whiter-than-white casual slip-ons, his face as shiny as his balding crown and his hands all twitchy with anticipation, I suddenly get an ache. A sort of clutching feeling deep in the pit of my belly that makes me want to cry. Which is ridiculous, of course, because I never cry, never get close to it, so I swallow hard and smile and remind him to take his airsick pills – and, while he's at it, the various other medications he stuffs into himself each day to keep his heart pumping, blood flowing, lungs puffing and the rest. He smiles back at me in appreciation of my concern and my tits and looks very pleased with himself indeed.

But the ache lingers. Even when we're up in the air and I'm on my third Bloody Mary, my tranquillity's not quite restored. By the fourth, things seem better, and by the time we land at Chileka International Airport, I'm in such a stupor that we may as well be on the moon for all I care. While Vic sees to the suitcases, I stagger to a seat and try to distract myself by reading various notices taped to the wall. No smoking. No spitting. No wearing of dresses and skirts in public that do not fully cover the kneecap when the wearer is standing upright. Bloody hell. Vic, I call, look at this, bloody stupid country, what year do they think we're living in, what will they think of next ... ! He laughs his head off, would you believe, and says there'll be no problems about me being upright since I'll be spending the next two weeks on my back. Ha ha. Sunbathing, of course, he adds, seeing my expression. Then winking and sniggering to himself all the way into the taxi.

Which, as one would expect, turns out to be as filthy and dilapidated as the road that's sign-posted Lake Malawi. Vic burbles on about how, when the place used to be Nyasaland, they called the lake Nyasa, but then after independence ... The car lurches dangerously and I mutter something nasty about the driver, feeling angry and resentful and lonely and trapped. Wishing I hadn't been seduced into this foolhardy venture, wishing I were dead. No, wishing *he* were dead. I shut my eyes to comfort myself with the usual daydream of prosperous widowhood ... how dignified I'll be at the graveside, dabbing my eyes with a handker- chief plucked from a small black Gucci handbag, smoothing the skirt of my charcoal Prada suit. And Vic in a box, his prick at last subdued in its final resting-place ...

But he nudges me back to reality. Look, he exclaims, Marls look, don't sleep now, look at the view! Stop nudging me with your elbow, I grumble – but I must admit I'm startled by the sight of the lake stretched out before us, a sheet of sun-bright blue with palm trees shading a sandy beach. And then a large wooden building flanked by a neon sign. Nkopola Lodge, flashing on and off. Well, he says, isn't this something? Didn't I *tell* you it'd be something? Isn't it *great* over here?

I reserve judgement, allowing myself to be helped out of the car (thinking, *hell* but the place is dusty, my shoes will be wrecked!), and stand there staring at that lake while they sort out our stuff. And as I

gaze out over the water, a kind of peace envelops me. Truly. The ache
seems to melt away and – don't laugh – I lapse into a sort of trance.
Marleen, he yells, come along old girl. Coming, I manage, and make my
way to the reception and it stinks of furniture polish and there's no one
there but an ancient man shining tables. The Hilton it isn't, I mutter, but
Vic doesn't hear, he's pacing back and forth and cracking his knuckles
the way he does when he's impatient, and for a while I quite enjoy the
delay because I know what he's impatient for and quite honestly it's the
last thing I need. Then his knuckle-cracking gets to me. Stop it, I snap,
and try to distract myself with the sight of the lake through the window.
But the window's filthy and I think to myself that someone should tell
that man to move on from the tables ...

Then at last we're in our room and, miracle of miracles, it's not too
bad. A king-sized bed and a bathroom en suite, all moderately clean.
Maybe my expectations have dropped already (even my enemies admit
I'm adaptable), but I don't even object to the odd bit of grime here and
there. It gives the place character, I concede to Vic – but he's already
stripped off and is ready on the bed for our inaugural run. Now look,
I'm not complaining, I've always known what was what when it came
to Vic and me, so it's not as though anything has changed. But something has. I can't even do as they say in the books which is shut your
eyes and think of England. He bumps and grinds and moans and swears,
and I'm just so achy and sad. I try to visualise that lake again, to
summon back its soothing sheen, but it doesn't come ... only Vic does
at last. I sigh. Which, of course, he interprets as a tribute to what a stud
he's been and I can't be bothered to put him right. Instead, I chuck loads
and loads of expensive bubbly stuff into an enormous hot bath and lie
there and talk myself beautiful.

Which I am, as everyone agrees – and have been ever since I was
seven and crowned Junior Miss Klerksdorp. A future Miss South Africa
for sure, if it hadn't been for what most people say was a terrible run of
luck ... the accident, Piet Maartins knocking me up, I don't even like to
think about it. Anyway, there's no doubt that Victor Arenson was my
good luck, you know what they say about Jews. I couldn't believe it. A

lawyer as well. You should have seen his mother's face when he took me home and announced he was to marry me. In truth, I was as stunned as she was, since he hadn't warned me either. In fact if the *real* truth were told I don't think he'd warned himself. But what the hell, a person doesn't argue when her ship's come in and, since any fool knows about breaches of contract, I held him to his word. And now, having wooed him and won him and kept him, I spend most of my time holding on to my good looks. Working bloody hard at it, but the same can be said – in vain – for Vic with his gym and his low-fat diet and the poncy barber he uses for what's left of his hair. Denise is convinced his voracious sexual appetite is compensation, but she's always spouting bullshit like that. Meanwhile ...

He's summoning me back to bed – does he ever get enough? Voracious isn't the word – the bloke's *rapacious*. I put my foot down. Enough's enough. It's almost dinnertime and I'm starving.

So down we go, all dressed to the nines, and I admire my reflection in my slinky purple cat suit and my mood definitely improves. There are a few other guests, mostly young couples, and I note their glances and wonder what they're thinking about my old man and me. The hell with it. I flash my ring and sidle closer to him, which he naturally takes to be a come-on and whispers *later* in my ear. The manager himself serves us, which is nice. Mr Kasonga his name is. Very respectful and respectable, and it feels good to call him Mister. But I'm still so pissed off with Vic for not being Robert Redford and demanding so much you-know-what that I embarrass him by telling this Mr Kasonga very loudly about Vic's dodgy heart and high cholesterol and how he's restricted to a low-fat diet. Mr Kasonga grins and declares he has just the thing for someone in that condition, a dish to satisfy doctor and gourmet alike, a special lake fish they call chambo that is world renowned for its succulent lean flesh. Succulent lean flesh, repeats Vic with relish as he squeezes my thigh, and I quickly order hollandaise for myself and plain grilled for him.

As it turns out, it's delicious. Even Vic, who hates fish, has to agree. Mr Kasonga – who's over the moon about our enthusiasm – introduces us to his wife Pansy the cook. I tell her how much I'd like to pack her in my suitcase and take her back with me to Johannesburg, but I don't think this goes down too well. Altogether, though, it's such a good meal that I decide the hell with the calories and treat myself to pudding as well – not to mention wine *and* a Tia Maria at the end. The biggest bonus is that Vic's so stuffed afterwards that he collapses sans sex into bed. I can't believe my luck.

But that's it. The high point. Little do I know, lying there that first night and counting my chickens, that I've reached the apex. From now on, it's downhill all the way. The next morning he wakes up crack of dawn and it's like he's making up for lost time or something – twice before breakfast, three times during the afternoon siesta and one-and-a-half (even he wears out eventually, thank heavens) in the cocktail hour. And so it goes, day after day, until I want to yell take the diamonds, take the brooches and bangles and designer dresses, take the lot and just leave me alone. To add to my misery, there's the chambo. Once is delicious, twice – three times – is more or less bearable, but day after day, meal after meal ... Chambo Rissoles, Casserole a la Chambo, Chambo Milanese and Chambo Peking ... the *thought* of it is enough to induce severe nausea.

The worst punishment though – for me, much worse than bad food or bad sex – is the fact that I can't get to sleep, and one thing I need without fail is my regular eight hours. Which normally isn't a problem – in fact, Vic teases me like mad about the way I can nod off at the drop of a hat. Out for the count, no trouble. Not here, though. Not at Nkopola Lodge, where the lapping of the lake at night sounds like gunshot and the cries of distant gulls are like screeching old hags. I toss and turn, trying not to waken Vic, and concentrate on summoning soothing thoughts. But even his funeral and my longed-for liberty doesn't placate me – on the contrary, it agitates me. My heart pounds, the lonely ache returns, and with it an anger and resentment that, for me, is something new. I hate it here. I want to be somewhere else, anywhere else, with someone else ...

And that is when, as though in a dream, deliverance arrives.

It's the dead of night, a dark still night, and Vic is soundly asleep. I'm doing the usual insomniac thing, unusual for me, so I count gemstones and grudges, when all of a sudden I hear a piercing scream. That's no gull, I think, going rigid with fright. As sure as I'm Marleen Arenson, that's a human cry. I don't breathe, I'm listening so hard – but all that follows is Vic's snoring which I deal with, as usual, by applying a toe to his ribs. Even then, when all's quiet, I can't forget that yell of terror – for that's what it was, I know it, and my imagination's running riot. I creep out of bed and peep through the window, but can see nothing. Just the lake smoothing out in the gathering dawn.

Then I notice a few people huddled together on the beach. Four of them – their silhouettes are growing clearer – are crouched over something on the ground. What the hell is it? I'm wishing I had binoculars and am about to call Vic to have a look, when the party disperses. Two figures attend to the thing on the ground ... they're carrying it away ... it's a body, I know it's a body, it's the source of that cry. The other pair, meanwhile, approach the lodge – I can hear their crunching footsteps beneath my window. And their voices ...

—*What* a to-do!

—And now, Mr Kasonga? What happens now?

—The main thing – listen to me carefully – the *main* thing is to make sure the guests don't find out. It would be very bad for business.

I'm straining every muscle to make out their muffled words. My God, I think, this is exciting. What a stroke of luck I'm not asleep. Mr Kasonga and his henchman are now directly below my window.

—I'm sure the boy won't talk at any rate. Silly bugger. He should have known better than that. He could have been seriously injured.

—Never mind seriously injured – mauled to death! You know what hippos are like when they get going. It's a *miracle* the boy escaped with a few cuts. The trouble is, a creature like that is very likely to attack again. When a hippo has tasted blood ...

There's further mumbling. I'm too shocked to take it in, too bent on absorbing what I've heard. A hippo? In the lake? A hungry hippo who has already struck once in the placid-seeming waters where I frolic each day with my Vic? Bloody hell.

—At least we know hippos only hunt at night. The guests will be safe, at any rate. I can't see *this* lot going for a midnight swim, can you?

There are gurgles of mirth from Mr Kasonga as two pairs of footsteps recede. I'm not sure if my pounding heart is due to shock or anger. How does the pompous idiot know what I'd do? Does he think Marleen Arenson née Smit hasn't engaged in some judicious skinny-dipping in her time? Does he think she's *past* it? As for Vic, with the promise of some steamy sex, he'd jump into the Bay of Biscay, naked and unafraid ...

Which is when it hits me smack in the middle of my forehead. The idea. The solution. The answer to all my prayers. As I make my plans, Vic doesn't stir. He will, though. He'll be *mightily* stirred in a few hours when I suggest (with a wink and a nudge and a small show of nipple) that the two of us take a moonlight swim. Which, I'll suggest, will be followed by delights beyond even the scope of the *Kama Sutra*. Will he resist? Is the Pope Catholic? There's not a chance in the world that Vic Arenson will turn down a proposition such as this. Together, we'll head for the beach in the darkness. I'll strip then he'll strip, then I'll hesitate at the shore, shivering delicately. You go in first, I'll simper. How I love to watch you diving in! I simply *adore* your manly body ...

The simplicity of it. The sheer brilliance. Who the hell needs to hang about for a chance coronary when there's a hungry hippo waiting in the wings? I tickle Vic's tummy and he groans pleasurably. Not now, I whisper – and regale him with elaborate details of our revels for the night ahead. He's speechless, begs for a preview, just a tiny foretaste – but I resist his advances to keep him hot. Later, I say.

The day drags forever. We can hardly contain our impatience, either of us. Being of a slightly squeamish nature, believe it or not, I try to keep my mind off the prospect of blood and gore and to focus instead on liberation. The funeral, my expensive black suit, my glorious afterlife. Dinnertime comes at last – and Vic suddenly announced he's worried that if he swims too soon after a heavy meal he might get cramp. Managing to keep a straight face (cramp? He should be so lucky ...), I point out that with chambo on the menu again, it's extremely unlikely that we'll overeat. To which he agrees, sniffing appreciatively at the perfume I've dabbed on my most tantalising bits. He can't wait. Anticipation oozes out of his every pore.

When Mr Kasonga approaches us with the menu, I watch him carefully for any sign of unease. Nothing. The bugger's cool as a cucumber, smiling as broadly as ever. *The main thing is to make sure the guests don't find out.* Sneaky bastard. How I want to shock him with my knowledge, to shake his composure ... but that would ruin my scheme. I watch him rubbing his hands together and extending his grin till it almost meets at the back of his head and am astonished to hear him saying he has a wonderful, wonderful surprise for us. A surprise? I narrow my eyes and ask what amazing form tonight's chambo is to take. No, no, he insists. No chambo. Not tonight. Tonight we're going to partake of something new and delicious. I have a bad feeling as he says this. Tonight's not the night for a break with routine. Quickly, I point out my husband's dietary restrictions, but Vic silences me – it's our last night, what the hell, you only live once Marls, et cetera. Mr Kasonga interrupts – he wants to tell us a story. A story? I don't like the sound of it one little bit. He tells us a story about an intruder in the lake, a persistent sort of fellow who's been giving trouble. A story about how the night before, this intruder attacked a young man who, thank goodness, escaped with a fright and a few scratches. A happy, heroic story – Mr Kasonga proudly grips his lapels – about how he and a few of his men went out and caught the rogue ...

—Bang, bang! Dead. *What* a prize, my friends – a *great* prize!

You got it. The hippo copped it ...

—A great big hippopotamus captured in his prime.

Vic is lavish with his congratulations but I seem to have lost my voice. Mr Kasonga, meanwhile, raises his hand and snaps his fingers as though summoning a troupe of dancing girls. And in marches the waiter bearing a huge steaming platter – not, this time, a variation on the theme of chambo, but ...

Hippo meat, I must admit, is delicious. It's also enormously and dangerously high in saturated fat. The one thing that *everyone* agrees about me is that I'm basically a good sport – so I think, the hell with it, I may as well resign myself to fate. And if fate has decreed that instead of the hippo eating Vic, Vic eats hippo, so be it.

Nevertheless, I can't help watching with some anticipation as each cholesterol-laden mouthful passes down his throat ...

The Cat's Whiskers

Alice Thomas Ellis

She woke early, as she always did now. It was one of the signs of age, she told herself. It could not be long before there would be plenty of time to sleep.

'Oh for God's sake,' she said aloud, smiling insincerely at the morning air. Her awareness of the prospect of death depressed her not so much because of its inevitability as because it made her wonder if she was falling prey to self-pity, losing her sense of humour. That would be intolerable. 'When I go,' she said to the cat, 'I will go with all guns blazing. Death will not take me prisoner without a fight.'

I'm glad I only said that to the cat, she thought. What a boring remark. The cat requested its breakfast. Sensible beast. She asked whether it had slept well. It patted her ankle with its paw, not over-demandingly but confidently expectant. 'Such a clever cat,' she said to it.

'Damn cat,' said her husband walking into the kitchen. He had elected himself the cat's enemy, perhaps out of some obscure sense of structure: his wife loved the cat therefore he would not. It made everything neater somehow, more balanced. She turned on the radio and hummed as best she could to the strains of an unfamiliar tune.

'Where's my gun?' he inquired. She had forgotten he was going shooting and her spirits rose. Today would be her own and she would walk in the garden and later sit in the comfortable armchair. She might even watch the dreadful morning television.

'Where you left it, ducky,' she said, wondering as she always did why he asked such odd questions. He frowned at the jug of roses on the table.

'Those are Elizabeth of Glamis,' he said. 'I've told you I wish you wouldn't pick those. Let's have some quiet,' and he turned off the radio. She contemplated turning it on again but he had gone to the bathroom and there would have been no point. She disliked modern music as much as he did.

'I wonder why Elizabeth is sacrosanct,' she mused. 'She grows like a weed.' Her husband's voice came down the stairs, muffled by the sound of running water.

'The water's cold,' he told her. 'Did you see to the boiler?' She straightened up and put her hand to the small of her back, arching it slightly, like a person in a film expressing physical weariness. He didn't really expect an answer.

'No,' she mouthed silently, 'I didn't see to the boiler. Did you see to the boiler, cat? He always sees to the boiler. Why should he suppose I've suddenly taken it into my head to see to the boiler?' She made another gesture more usual on the stage than in real life, holding her head with both hands and rolling her eyes upwards. Such silent, unseen manifestations of unease, of her sense of oppression had become habitual with her. She had become an actress in her own life. As good a way to survive as any.

'Will you ring the boiler people,' he called, 'and fix me a bacon sandwich? I don't want to be late.'

'That would be a shame,' she said. 'All the pheasants got up early, you wouldn't want to keep them waiting.' She hummed under her breath as the bacon began to sizzle.

'Where's my breakfast?' he asked, looking at the frying-pan as he crossed the kitchen.

'It's here, my darling,' she said, and out of old habit she added, 'and for goodness' sake dry your hair or you'll get pneumonia ...' People who have brought up children find it difficult not to make this sort of remark, sometimes even to strangers.

'I've found it,' he said, fondling his gun.

'Well don't point it at me,' said his wife, suddenly pettish. 'I'm not a pheasant. I hate pheasants. They have very small eyes.'

'Fine example of workmanship, this gun,' he observed, peering down the barrels. He sounded defensive, as though she had called him infantile. 'Pow, pow,' he said. 'This for me?' he asked, reaching for the sandwich.

'It was going to be for the Empress of China,' said his wife, and felt briefly ashamed for taking an unfair advantage of his weakness, 'but you're welcome. And for goodness' sake, go and get dressed.'

He went obediently, carrying the sandwich and she knew that if she had told him to sit down and eat it nicely he would have done so. She picked up the gun and said, 'Pow, pow,' handling it curiously. 'I've never liked these things,' she said. 'This is the bit you pull, cat. See? Then it goes bang, and some mother's child is all ruined and spoiled and dead. Blown to bits. Bang.'

'Where the hell are my socks?' inquired her husband from above, where he was out of sight, away from her disconcerting glance.

'Try the drawer,' she shouted. 'Do I ask him where my socks are?' she demanded of the cat. 'What would he say if I asked him where my socks were? Darling,' she whispered, wiping out the frying-pan, 'where is my chiffon blouse? The one with the embroidery and the tasselled fringe? Where are my golden gloves, and the beaded sash my father gave me?'

'Why don't you change your mind and come too,' called her husband, who was pulling on a sock at the time. 'Jane is going and Jenny. You like Jenny ...'

'I've got too much to do here,' she called back. 'I'm too busy.'

'What have you got to do?' demanded her husband boldly. 'You've got a cleaner, haven't you?'

'She's off sick,' yelled his wife, adding, for her own satisfaction, 'she discovered a bubo under her armpit.'

'A what?' he cried.

'Nothing, just nothing at all.'

'What did you say?' He went to the top of the stairs and looked down, straining his ears to hear her.

'I said I had to sort out the linen cupboard,' she said rapidly. 'And polish the spoons and pick the caterpillars off the cabbage and write a letter to your aunt in Australia.'

'What?' He could hear only a muttering and wondered worriedly if he was really going deaf. Such hints of age depressed him.

'Nothing,' she said clearly.

Relieved that he had heard this he buttoned his shirt. 'You're silly,' he said. 'You don't know what you're missing.'

'Oh, I know what I'm missing,' she said, scratching the cat behind its ears. 'I'm missing sitting in a car all day, creeping along the lanes with the women while the men go bounding around in the undergrowth, popping off at those wretched birds. Why does he say I like Jenny? I can't stand Jenny. She wears her waxed jacket to bed and she's losing her hair. I have always been moderately civil to Jenny. I suppose that could be construed as liking – but then I'm moderately civil to everybody. Perhaps he thinks I like everybody. I don't, cat. I don't like everybody at all.' She ran her hand along its back to indicate that however sour she had become she excepted cats from her disapproval.

'Have you seen my club tie?' came a cry.

'No,' she enunciated. 'Of course I've seen his club tie,' she said to her furry friend. 'I've seen it more times than I care to remember – round his neck, hanging over the back of the chair, lying on the floor. I was with him when he bought it. Cat, do you remember the old days before you were spayed? Do you remember those nights in the garden, waving your tail at the gentlemen? Wondering where they were? No? Perhaps it's just as well. I don't really remember the past either.' She sighed. 'I tell a lie. I remember – oh, so long ago – I remember sitting by the telephone and waiting for it to ring. And do you know whose voice I was waiting for?'

'You must have seen it,' cried her husband, his voice plaintive.

'That's it,' she said. 'That's the voice I was waiting for.'

'It's in the tie press on the right of the wardrobe,' she shouted. 'Unless, of course, he's tied up Elizabeth of Glamis with it in an idle moment.' She stopped stroking the cat and stared out of the window, waiting.

'It isn't here,' he cried again.

'Yes it is,' she said calmly. 'Wait for it, cat.'

'No it ... Oh, yes all right, I see.'

She turned on the sink tap. 'There ... Mind you, cat, to be fair, I sometimes do the same thing. Many's the time I've gone looking for the mustard and I can't see it. I'm looking straight at it but I can't see it. I wonder why that is? Some would say I don't want to see it, and I must admit making mustard it boring. Perhaps he's bored with his tie. Sometimes I look straight at him and I don't really see him. Do you know what the greatest release in the world is, cat? It's the release from love. Well, they call it love.'

She turned the tap off and wondered from where the terror arose: the quick terror that came on her unexpectedly, fracturing the light so that she didn't know where to look, disorienting, horrible. Something she couldn't describe, even to the cat, even to herself, for despite its intensity it seemed too trivial to mention.

'When that woman comes you might get her to do something about the state of this wardrobe,' said her husband from the security of the bedroom.

'Why, my darling?' she asked sweetly, almost relieved to raise her voice, to pretend that at one and the same time she had found a focus for her fear and a way of denying it.

'Because it's in a hell of a mess,' he said in reasonable tones.

'Well, of course it is,' she said, almost light-hearted again. 'He's gone through it like a badger. You were so wise, cat, in your unregenerate days, only to meet your mate in the moon shadow, in the gloaming – a little passion, some howling, howling – then, whoosh, you came back to the kitchen to have your kittens; nice little furry, furry kittens; and your mate went loping off. God knows where he went. Did you know, cat? No, of course you didn't. What did you care? You had your babies and your basket and four walls around you. Did you notice that uncastrated tomcats never laugh? They have that air of urgency, as though they felt here was something enormously important they had to do. Did you ever notice that?'

She felt as though she had made a discovery, had contrived to impose some order on, some explanation for, the chaos that threatened her. She went on speaking half under her breath, hurriedly. 'They look very serious and rather worried because they have to impregnate all those females and fight all the males. Serious stuff. No laughing matter. They have to live alone. No one could put up with them in the house – all that sorrowful, pressing importance, the smell, the clawing. You wouldn't want him around much, would you, cat?'

'I still wish you'd come,' called the man upstairs. A different man now: conciliatory, a little plaintive.

Her courage strengthened. The dancing demons, the imps of insecurity receded. After all, her unease was only the human condition. She almost felt as though she could laugh. 'I bet your mate never said that to you, did he, Grimalkin?' she suggested to the cat. 'He didn't want you around. Your tribe hasn't progressed like ours has. You meat eaters. You haven't changed since the – oh, since the ancient Egyptians made gods of you. Now *we* are different. Once upon a time our men – toms to you, cat – would take up their clubs and their bows and arrows and go hunting, but not for little mice. They went out chasing big, hairy, dangerous things with horns and hooves.'

She raised her arms above her head to demonstrate the fearful hugeness of the horns; she widened her eyes to show the awful incomprehension of the hunted beasts. 'Big, fat animals,' she said; 'full of cholesterol and probably infested with parasites. Savage, terrified, dangerous things. Do you see the fun in chasing them? Now the women – queans to you, cat – didn't do that. They stayed put round the cave mouth – I'm afraid to tell you, cat, we lived in holes like mice. Or so they say – but don't let that prejudice you – and they ate the nuts and berries that they picked off the trees and bushes, and they gossiped away among themselves and agreed what fools men were – risking their lives chasing big fat animals – and they laughed a lot. Like this ... ' And now she felt that she could laugh, and she did.

'Darling ...?'

She stopped and uttered a little moan. 'Yes.'

'What are you doing?'

'Nothing.'

'What are you laughing at?'

'Just something I heard on the radio,' she said half in defiance, half in resignation.

'The radio isn't on,' he said sternly.

'Oh, isn't it?' she said.

'You're spending too much time on your own,' her husband explained from above. 'You're going mad.'

'They always say that, cat,' she said. 'When they can't understand you, they tell you you're going mad. I used to believe him – a long, long time ago. When he was angry I trembled. I used to iron his handkerchiefs. That was before I remembered Kleenex. I used to think that he must be right about everything. Just as those women in their caves might have thought it was clever of the men to go and get gored and trampled chasing hamburgers. He went to the office every day and I stayed at home with the children, and every morning before he left he would say, "What are you going to do today, darling?" And every evening when he came home he'd say, "What have you done today, darling?" And I'd say, "Oh, nothing, darling".' She shuddered and began to wash the dishes with naked hands in the hot water. Too late to worry about the skin of her hands. Her fear had changed to regret, for the children were grown up and gone. 'Because I'd only cooked and cleaned and fed the baby,' she continued determinedly. 'And washed the clothes and the children, and sung them songs and pushed them on the swing. Not a lot. You see that's the sort of thing women do, and whatever women do, it isn't work. Not *work*. What men do is work, you see, cat. Even if it's only shooting birds.' She was surprised and annoyed to feel tears in her eyes but there was nothing she could do about it for her hands were covered in detergent.

'Hell, I'm going to be late,' said the father of her children. 'Have you got my lunch ready?'

'Nearly ready, darling,' she lied. She wiped her hands on her dressing gown and went to the fridge, staring at the contents, wondering what she was doing. There was pâté, there was smoked salmon and for a moment she forgot what it was usual to do with these things. Sandwiches, she reminded herself. You wrap them up in bread. She'd done it so often her memory had failed her out of sheer weariness. Making sandwiches was probably the most boring task the housewife could perform.

'Do you want a boiled egg?' she called. Boiling eggs seemed rather more creative. The water moved around at least.

'You forgot to put the salt in last time,' said her husband. 'Tyler said eating a boiled egg without salt was like kissing a woman with a moustache.' He laughed.

'Goodness, how droll,' said his wife.

'What?'

'Nothing.'

'You've started talking to yourself a lot.' He moved again to the top of the stairs and gazed down although he couldn't see her.

'Once upon a time, cat,' she said under her breath, 'when the men were in pursuit of the hairy rhinoceros, I should've had the women of the tribe to talk to. But they've been corrupted by civilisation, taken in by what their mates say. They're all sitting in cars following the chase. Now do you think the cave woman would have wasted her time sitting around on the savannah in a Range Rover? No, of course she wouldn't. Far too much sense.' She watched the water beginning to move and the eggs trying helplessly to get out. Quickly she started whispering again. 'Now you may say, cat, you may want to point out to me that my cave woman also benefited from the slaughter of these animals. Fur coats, you might say to me – although considering your own species it is a delicate matter and perhaps you prefer not to dwell on it – but if you put aside your natural reservations, you just might want to remind me that the skins kept the women warm too. And to this I would answer that if man had left the beasts alone, woman would – with her native ingenuity, which has been suppressed by circumstance and the jealous envy of men – she, as I say, would have invented fake fur long before the animal-rights protestors started fussing about it. And meat? Protein? Remember the nuts. Nuts are simply humming with protein. And remember how all over the Western world men are eating T-bone steaks and dropping dead from heart attacks.'

She emptied away the boiling water and ran the cold tap over the eggs, raising her voice. 'Now, if they'd followed the example of the women and stuck to nuts they'd never have got this problem. The women, you see, never got to eat much meat in the cave – the odd ear or knuckle-bone – because the men needed it all so they could conserve their energy to go and catch more meat. I hope I'm not offending you, cat, with this dismissive talk of meat. I quite understand that it is all that agrees with your digestive system. *Homo sapiens* is different. You can tell by our teeth.' She bent, and by way of demonstration, snarled at the cat. 'See? Omnivorous, we are. That is, we can eat almost anything – from pieces of big dangerous animals, right down through nuts and winnowed grasses to blancmange. I have to confess, cat, I've never fancied mice. The Romans used to eat dormice, but they were given to what became known with the rise of civilisation as *luxuria* ...' She had turned off the tap but forgotten to lower her voice.

'What did you say?' came the query.

'I said the Romans ate mice.'

'Why did you say that? Who are you talking to?'

'The cat,' she said defiantly.

There was a short silence. 'You *are* going mad,' he said, and she thought he sounded resigned but triumphant.

'He is incorrect, you know, cat,' she said, defiance increasing. 'Once I was going mad. Once I was giving dinner parties twice a week and going to them three times a week. Now that's mad if you like. Always the same people and the same food. Marinated kipper fillets I remember were all the rage at one time, and grilled grapefruits. And the men used to talk about the wine, and I may be doing them an injustice but, to the best of my recollection, the women used to talk about the whiteness of their wash. Now there's an interesting thing, cat. Perhaps the poor creatures were expressing an atavistic nostalgia for the days when the women gathered at the river and trampled on the clothes and battered

them with flat stones and talked and talked to each other. The men put
a stop to that. They invented washing-machines. They had to break up
the women, you see. They were frightened of what they were saying.
They feared a plot and also, cat, they knew damn well that what the
women were saying about *them* would not give them comfort to hear.
They could hear them laughing down by the river.'

'I may bring a couple of chaps back for a bit of supper,' said her
husband in the casual tone of a man doing up his tie.

She stopped in the middle of cracking an egg and lifted her head.
'Don't do that,' she said reprovingly as though he had made a childish
but improper suggestion.

'What?'

'I said there isn't any supper. I'm defrosting the freezer and all there
is is a tiny cauliflower cheese and a Cornish pasty.'

'Can't you do some spaghetti or soup or something?' he inquired. He
sounded polite but there was something wrong with the way he phrased
himself.

'I'm not a magician you know,' she retorted, shouting. Her voice fell.
'What I am is a liar. I have a great deal of delicious food, and not one
morsel is going down the gullet of Tyler. Not a scrap. Tyler's missus
would feed them. Tyler's missus is a perfect example of a woman driven
mad by the men. She does what he tells her, and she's stuffed so full of
Valium she doesn't even rattle any more. Do you know what she does?
She tells people what Tyler says. She says, "My husband always says ..."
or "Jim says ..." or "That's what Jim thinks" or "Jim doesn't think
that." It's enough to make a cat laugh. What do you think, cat? Funny,
huh? What's more she's called Edith. Poor thing. Perhaps much should
be forgiven a person called Edith. I don't know whether you've noticed,
cat, but the woman I am now is light years away from the woman I was
then in her Laura Ashley frock ...' There was an old mirror on the wall.
She moved and looked into it.

'Then we'll probably go back to Tyler's place,' he said as one who
against his better nature must needs disappoint.

'OK,' she said.

'What?'

'I said that's a good idea,' she yelled.

'If I was Tyler's missus I would take his gun and blow his head off, but she will take lemons and scoop them out and fill them with mackerel mousse and set them before him and his friends, and she will have freshly ironed napkins, and warmed plates for their goulash, and chilled plates for their ice-cream. It makes me think of butter in a lordly dish. That's what it makes me think of, cat. Jael and Sisera – she banged a nail in his head after tea. Actually I have been less than frank with you. I know when I came to my senses. It was when his father died. I thought then – one day it will be him and I will be glad. Now that's not a nice thing to think of the person with whom you have shared bed and board for many years. Not nice at all. It gave me a nasty shock. Good little women in their Laura Ashley frocks don't think like that. That's when I gave away my Laura Ashley frock to Oxfam. I have to live with myself, you see. Not just with him, but with myself. Somehow there was one too many of us so the frock had to go.'

'Is my lunch ready? Don't forget the salt,' he instructed her.

'I tried to cut down his salt because it's bad for his blood pressure,' she told the cat. Where is it?' She buttered the bread and started slicing the pâté. The cat spoke in the way of a cat who still hasn't had her breakfast. 'Oh cat, I'm sorry,' said the woman. 'I was so interested in our discussion I forgot your breakfast. I must be getting absent-minded.' She cut off a sliver of pâté and held it out between her finger and thumb. The cat ate it, licked the woman's finger and thumb and its own chin, and asked for more. 'Hang on,' she said, 'where's your tin? What have we today? Ah – 'Carefully chosen meaty chunks in a rich gravy with chicken morsels added.' I wonder what that means. They probably dug up some old bison,' she said and paused in opening the tin for the thought of absent-mindedness had given her an idea. She put the pâté on a plate and the plate on the floor. 'Take that,' she said to the cat. She emptied the tin of cat food into a basin and began mashing it up with a fork, breaking up its carefully chosen meaty chunks. It smelled savoury. She drained away some of its rich gravy down the sink, wondering precisely which morsels of chicken had gone into its composition. Then she spread it on the bread and closed the sandwiches. After a moment she opened them again and sprinkled them with salt. 'Now,' she said to the cat, 'I will put them in this useful, hygienic plastic box with the patent seal for the ever-fresh effect and I will arrange some watercress on them as a garnish. Such garnish ...' she told the cat, 'always reminds me of wreaths, of what are known as floral tributes, an attempt to conceal the fact that here in these tender morsels we have mortality.'

'Still talking to yourself,' observed her husband in quite a friendly way as he entered the kitchen, smelling pleasantly of soap and tooth-paste.

'Here's your lunch and here's your gun,' she said handing it to him carefully by the barrel.

'Careful,' he said. 'So what are you going to do today, darling?'

'Oh, nothing, darling,' she said. 'Have you got your scarf? And make sure Tyler tries these sandwiches. They're special.'

When he'd gone she turned on the radio again. 'I know what's going to happen next,' she said to the cat against the noise of modern music. 'After all that pâté you're going to be sick.' She knelt and kissed the cat between the ears by way of apology.

Pot Luck

Patrice Chaplin

Kay stirred the stew, tasted it and added freshly picked herbs from the garden. A stew should not be bland. The dumplings were ready to go in the moment the last grease rose and was skimmed from the gravy.

Kay had long bright hair tied back with a ribbon and a slow smile.

The cleaner, who hated housework, quickly put away the Hoover. 'It all comes down to luck,' she said suddenly.

'Luck?'

'It's lucky you cook so well. Men love women who cook.'

It wasn't what she wanted to say at all. The cleaner thought Kay had breeding in the true sense and a perfect marriage to Joel, a physics professor; she dared to be happy and seemed to believe it would last. The cleaner, for a reason she couldn't explain, thought these very assets would be Kay's downfall.

One of Joel's students dropped off an essay. The girl was untidy, her nails dirty and she looked undernourished. Kay felt sorry for her. 'My name's Paula,' said the girl as she left. A wasp droned brazenly in through the window. Kay killed it. She hated its warning colours, black and yellow.

Joel brought the head of the diagnostic division home for dinner and stroked Kay's hair, proud of her. 'Marvellous meal. I could eat it all over again.' Joel never tired of looking at her. It gave him the same heightened pleasure as eating her food. Everyone said Joel and Kay were lucky. They had a good marriage that their friends clung to like a raft in a sea of divorce.

Was it the next day the untidy student again came round? This time she sat in the kitchen, uninvited. She explained her visit to her tutor's house by saying she needed an extra tutorial. Calmly Kay turned the kitchen mirror to the light and powdered her pale skin. It was then she noticed the girl's expression. She was looking around the kitchen as though it ought to be hers. Kay suppressed a laugh. What was her name? Paula?

'I don't expect my husband back for some time.' Why had she lied? He was due any minute for lunch. She laid out green vegetables for a salad. She loved the colour green. Outside, the sycamore stretched out a branch in the sudden wind and tapped on the window as though with approval.

The girl sat solidly, not moving, her long hair hanging over substantial breasts.

'I suggest you phone and make an appointment,' said Kay.

'Oh he'll be here.' Paula had a common voice and a tough attitude. She didn't bother with any further explanation.

The cleaner brought used laundry down from the bathroom. She glared at Paula. Kay asked her to get some cooking apples from the market and not to be timid about choosing the best. Then Joel was in the room.

He had a sturdy body, exuding energy. He had the yellow eyes of a cat and a small, firm, sensual mouth. He kissed Kay and threw his briefcase onto the nearest chair. If he noticed Paula he didn't show it. In fact he didn't look at her at all. 'Oh, my favourite soup.' He took a spoon and tasted it. Then he decided to acknowledge the visitor on the chair. 'Ah, yes, we'd better have a look at that essay.' He still didn't, Kay noticed, look at her. He went on tasting the soup, a little boisterously, and surprisingly his hand was shaking.

Kay suggested the girl stay for lunch. Joel didn't like that. 'Oh no. We'll just pop over to the pub and run through it.' Without looking at anybody he got his briefcase, then held out his hand in the direction of the girl. 'Come on, then.'

And Kay realised how lovely his hands were, their movements so clever and quick.

When they'd gone, the cleaner furiously wiped the chair the girl had used. Kay had never seen her do anything so odd.

Kay was unscathed by fear or envy. She was good and attracted only good things. She'd never be unfaithful to Joel. Her women friends sometimes asked why. Because no one could be better than him.

That night Joel ran ahead of her up the narrow stairs to their bedroom. 'I'm so lucky to have you,' he said.

She put a hand over his mouth. 'Ssh. Don't give your luck away.'

Suddenly everything was about luck. It had begun with the cleaner. She felt chilled.

She thought he wasn't entirely in the mood as they performed the act they'd succeeded in making satisfactory thousands of times before. At one moment she looked out of the window at the moon, a mere slit of subdued silver in a busy sky, and it reminded her of the student's face. What was her name?

The following Sunday after lunch they stayed in the kitchen instead of going upstairs to watch television. Joel commented on the Sunday papers and she made coffee, adding a touch of cinnamon. A sharp knock and the back door opened and they smelt the perfume, strong and heady. Energetic footsteps clicked along the passageway and Paula was in the room.

She was unrecognisable. Her hair was piled up, she wore substantial make-up. Her skirt was a mere strip across the top of her thighs. Her shoes were scarlet suede with towering heels. She smiled and held out a cheap bunch of mixed flowers. They were apparently meant for Kay. 'You've got such a lovely house. And I really admire—' it was either 'you' or 'it'. Kay couldn't be sure. 'And I think the way Joel has helped me has been wonderful.' She made the 'wonderful' sound like a caress.

He almost looked at her, then couldn't; it seemed forbidden. He turned the pages of his newspaper rapidly. As Kay was pouring coffee she asked if Paula wanted to join them. The pot on the stove fizzed in warning. The clock ticked like gunfire. Joel's private line gave its piercing cheep like a trapped bird.

'No. I just came by.'

And then Joel looked at her face. Kay thought the darkness of the kitchen was deceiving her. No one looked at anyone like that. They both stayed silent as Paula's shoes clicked to the back door. With a breezy 'Bye', she left.

That night Kay excelled herself. Marrowbone jelly, cheese-filled brioche, rack of lamb. She wanted to batter, shake, pound, fry and expel every vestige of the memory of his eyes looking into the eyes of Paula. Inexplicably, she put aside the green vegetables. Green – she didn't like it anymore. Green – the colour of jealousy.

But when Joel came to the table he said he wasn't hungry.

She searched his clothes, his books, his desk. She found the diary finally and, heart pounding violently, had to sit on the floor. The sweat dripped from her face as she turned the pages. And yet they contained accounts of his new research, the progress of his students, the difficulties with the faculty. She hadn't realised he'd been so ambitious and so disappointed.

That night she asked point-blank about infidelity. He had an answer for that. He said he couldn't go with someone else. His reasons were selfish. Someone else would change his view of sex and alter the chemistry between Kay and him. He found their intimacy so compelling he didn't want to lose it. It was his own pleasure he was protecting.

Kay thought it was a lot of words to say 'I'm faithful.'

They made love but she felt his excitement had nothing to do with her. The next day he said, 'Darling, I have to go to Milan.' She heard him say 'lecture' and 'something's come up.' He packed an overnight bag speedily. His hands – again she watched them. How they could give pleasure. She watched him as he hurried up the road, his step lighter and faster, as though off to some splendid adventure. The walk told her one thing: he was happy.

The cleaner found her eating baked beans out of a tin. The next day the cleaner noticed she didn't eat at all. It took a week before she started to look thin and haggard.

Kay found out about Paula. She hadn't gone to the bad. She'd always been there. Joel's friends knew and were appalled by her. 'She's so common. Even her name. She's a Woolworth's shop-girl.'

Wasn't that what he liked, Kay realised? He liked Paula's common touch.

Kay was aware of his return from a place called Milan and then he was off again. He didn't say he was having an affair, not in words, but everything in his behaviour screamed that this was the one total consuming passion in his life, one for which he'd give his life if necessary. Kay knew he'd never felt that about her. They'd got by on sex, his pride in her and her desire for him that had sometimes come near to adoration. Paula wasn't beautiful, couldn't cook, could never be considered an asset. She wasn't someone you'd even notice unless she was stealing your husband. She had the utter ruthlessness of the very young. She was out to get him but also to get him away from Kay. She was settling some past unhappy parent business. Kay was sure about that.

When he came back from the urgent trips into academia he found a different wife and a very different menu. She served him barely cooked frozen peas and indifferent fish fingers. He noticed her thinness.

'Are you on a diet, Kay?'

'Oh yes. That's what it is,' her tone sarcastic.

They lay in bed, side by side, a mere inch between them. It felt like a mile.

'What exactly does she study?'

He dared to say 'Who?'

And as she lay sleepless she could see her life had been murdered. Her trust, her love, her passion, even her cooking, all because she wasn't a tart and the other one was. And she wondered how Paula made love, what vulgar indecent excitements she provided. She could see her breasts large and swinging – until she could only see her breasts.

She discovered one of Paula's previous conquests, who told her the girl was cool in life but the reverse in bed. She could give a man hours of sensation approaching ecstasy. So that was what Joel was getting. Kay's short laugh wasn't altogether sane. The man added that Paula always knew at what point to remove her yielding, greedy body and when not to answer the phone. She would only come back if there was some advantage in it. He thought her real label was 'Homewrecker'.

Kay spent her time finding out all about Paula: what she did, where she lived, and she no longer socialised or bothered with how she looked. Instead of sole meunière, she provided takeaway fish and chips. But no amount of knowledge quietened her heart.

The cleaner got her downstairs and made her something to eat. In her house, eggs always came into it when a soothing dish was required. But the scrambled eggs on toast were left untouched. Kay had never cared for the colour yellow. The eggs had a jaundiced look. The cleaner, now worried, considered phoning Joel. But she knew, hadn't she always known, that that girl brought bad change into the near-perfect house. What she couldn't understand was how a creature like that could usurp a woman like Kay.

Joel phoned from New York and said he needed time to think. Kay thought she heard the girl's mocking laugh. And then she knew she'd divorce him. Take him for everything. The house, the lot. The change in him – it was as though he'd taken to drink. And she, Kay – all her good qualities simply killed off.

She hated Paula but she didn't recognise it immediately. She was still obsessed with what the girl was and what she did and what she meant to her husband. But the mocking laugh stirred the fury. She went to the place called New York, which instinct informed her only too well was a dreary flat in North London. She wanted to throw burning cooking oil in the girl's face, slice off her generous breasts, twist the head off her shoulders until the neck snapped, maim her soft, greedy hands, stuff up her orifices with scorching oven-cleaner.

She knocked loudly on the scuffed door. Silence. Then she heard a shocked girlish laugh, which she, forever the optimist, took to be the television. Another knock brought Paula to the door. She wore a man's dressing gown and a cigarette hung at the corner of her lips.

'I want to speak to my husband.'

Paula shrugged, putting as much insolence into it as she could. 'Why come here?'

'He's here.' Kay started to push past her into the untidy room.

Joel said, 'Let her in, for heaven's sake.'

Paula made a sign of mock helplessness.

Joel came out of the bedroom doing up his trousers. Behind him, the low Japanese bed was unmade. Kay's face as she looked at the bed fell apart like a bad pie-crust. Paula saw it all. She'd won. Joel murmured something about not wanting to hurt her, not knowing what to do. Kay stayed staring at the bed in which he'd enacted a million fantasies. The sheets like traitors were only too willing to give her the whole story. Joel tried to move the duvet to cover the copious stains.

'I really didn't want you to see all this, darling.'

Paula threw off the dressing gown. How proud she was of her body. Her underclothes, tiny wisps of silk, were strewn, making a virtual path to the bedroom. The sex had obviously begun in the living room. Kay saw his underpants and one sock. The girl picked up his sock and held it. It was the most intimate thing Kay had ever had done to her. Joel, furious, said, 'For Christ's sake cover yourself up.'

A glass of brandy was put in Kay's hand as she sat mute, like the victim of a road accident. Joel asked a question which she did not hear. Paula laughed and her breasts joggled about in front of Kay's eyes. They seemed to fill the room. She dressed very slowly, unwilling to cover herself up. Joel sat beside his wife.

'So you do want to hear it. She came into the room and life suddenly made sense. I felt I'd known her from the day of my birth. That well. And yet we'd never touched. I promise you that and—'

Kay got up and did the only thing she knew. She went into the tiny filthy kitchen to see if there was anything to cook. Cooking would give her back an identity.

Paula was amazed. 'You really take it well.' She laughed. A rough, smoker's laugh.

'My wife has a generous heart,' said Joel. His face after making love was younger and smooth, the shadows under his eyes deeper.

Oh, but I don't, thought Kay as she planned to kill him. She would never be at peace until this assault on her heart had been avenged.

Then Paula said, 'We women have it rough. I'm glad you understand. I didn't want your fucking husband. He's all right, Kay, but let's face it, I wouldn't have noticed him but he kept coming after me.'

Not him. Her, thought Kay. No. Both. And she realised the power a woman could have in the kitchen. You nourish a man. You could also kill him. Just outside the open window was a laburnum tree and suddenly she saw the point of yellow. Yellow was the colour of vengeance.

Laburnum seeds. They worked instantly. She'd got the idea from a TV serial. You crushed them with a mortar and pestle and put them in a soft concealing food like marzipan or paella – or an omelette. TV had its uses. There were eggs among the sparse ingredients in the kitchen. She reached out to harvest death and called, 'Come to dinner.'

A wasp buzzed against the dirty window. Instinctively she looked for something to swipe it with. But wait. Wasn't it quite elegant? Yellow and black, nice colours for a modern widow.

Accident

Agatha Christie

'... And I tell you this – it's the same woman – not a doubt of it!'

Captain Haydock looked into the eager, vehement face of his friend and sighed. He wished Evans would not be so positive and so jubilant. In the course of a career spent at sea, the old sea captain had learned to leave things that did not concern him well alone. His friend, Evans, late CID inspector, had a different philosophy of life. 'Acting on information received—' had been his motto in early days, and he had improved upon it to the extent of finding out his own information. Inspector Evans had been a very smart, wide-awake officer, and had justly earned the promotion which had been his. Even now, when he had retired from the force, and had settled down in the country cottage of his dreams, his professional instinct was still alive.

'Don't often forget a face,' he reiterated complacently. 'Mrs Anthony – yes, it's Mrs Anthony right enough. When you said Mrs Merrowdene – I knew her at once.'

Captain Haydock stirred uneasily. The Merrowdenes were his nearest neighbours, barring Evans himself, and this identifying of Mrs Merrowdene with a former heroine of a *cause célèbre* distressed him.

'It's a long time ago,' he said rather weakly.

'Nine years,' said Evans, accurate as ever. 'Nine years and three months. You remember the case?'

'In a vague sort of way.'

'Anthony turned out to be an arsenic eater,' said Evans, 'so they acquitted her.'

'Well, why shouldn't they?'

'No reason in the world. Only verdict they could give on the evidence. Absolutely correct.'

'Then that's all right,' said Haydock. 'And I don't see what we're bothering about.'

'Who's bothering?'

'I thought you were.'

'Not at all.'

'The thing's over and done with,' summed up the captain. 'If Mrs Merrowdene at one time of her life was unfortunate enough to be tried and acquitted for murder—'

'It's not usually considered unfortunate to be acquitted,' put in Evans.

'You know what I mean,' said Captain Haydock irritably. 'If the poor lady has been through that harrowing experience, it's no business of ours to rake it up, is it?'

Evans did not answer.

'Come now, Evans. The lady was innocent – you've just said so.'

'I didn't say she was innocent. I said she was acquitted.'

'It's the same thing.'

'Not always.'

Captain Haydock, who had commenced to tap his pipe out against the side of his chair, stopped, and sat up with a very alert expression.

'Hallo – allo – allo,' he said. 'The wind's in that quarter, is it? You think she wasn't innocent?'

'I wouldn't say that. I just – don't know. Anthony was in the habit of taking arsenic. His wife got it for him. One day, by mistake, he takes far too much. Was the mistake his or his wife's? Nobody could tell, and the jury very properly gave her the benefit of the doubt. That's all quite right and I'm not finding fault with it. All the same – I'd like to *know*.'

Captain Haydock transferred his attention to his pipe once more.

'Well,' he said comfortably. 'It's none of our business.'

'I'm not so sure ...'

'But surely—'

'Listen to me a minute. This man, Merrowdene – in his laboratory this evening, fiddling round with tests – you remember—'

'Yes. He mentioned Marsh's test for arsenic. Said *you* would know all about it – it was in *your* line – and chuckled. He wouldn't have said that if he'd thought for one moment—'

Evans interrupted him.

'You mean he wouldn't have said that if he *knew*. They've been married how long – six years you told me? I bet you anything he has no idea his wife is the once notorious Mrs Anthony.'

'And he will certainly not know it from me,' said Captain Haydock stiffly.

Evans paid no attention, but went on: 'You interrupted me just now. After Marsh's test, Merrowdene heated a substance in a test-tube, the metallic residue he dissolved in water and then precipitated it by adding silver nitrate. That was a test for chlorates. A neat unassuming little test. But I chanced to read these words in a book that stood open on the table: "H_2SO_4 *decomposes chlorates with evolution of* Cl_4O_2. *If heated, violent explosions occur, the mixture ought therefore to be kept cool and only very small quantities used.*"'

Haydock stared at his friend.

'Well, what about it?'

'Just this. In my profession we've got tests too – tests for murder. There's adding up the facts – weighing them, dissecting the residue when you've allowed for prejudice and the general inaccuracy of witnesses. But there's another test of murder – one that is fairly accurate, but rather – dangerous! *A murderer is seldom content with one crime.* Give him time, and a lack of suspicion, and he'll commit another. You catch a man – has he murdered his wife or hasn't he? – perhaps the case isn't very black against him. Look into his past – if you find that he's had several wives – and that they've all died shall we say – rather curiously? – then you *know*! I'm not speaking *legally*, you understand. I'm speaking of *moral* certainty. Once you *know*, you can go ahead looking for evidence.'

'Well?'

'I'm coming to the point. That's all right if there *is* a past to look into. But suppose you catch your murderer at his or her first crime? Then that test will be one from which you get no reaction. But suppose the prisoner is acquitted – starting life under another name. Will or will not the murderer repeat the crime?'

'That's a horrible idea!'

'Do you still say it's none of our business?'

'Yes, I do. You've no reason to think that Mrs Merrowdene is anything but a perfectly innocent woman.'

The ex-inspector was silent for a moment. Then he said slowly: 'I told you that we looked into her past and found nothing. That's not quite true. There was a stepfather. As a girl of eighteen she had a fancy for some young man and her stepfather exerted his authority to keep them apart. She and her stepfather went for a walk along a rather dangerous part of the cliff. There was an accident – the stepfather went too near the edge – it gave way, and he went over and was killed.'

'You don't think—'

'It was an accident. *Accident*! Anthony's overdose of arsenic was an accident. She'd never have been tried if it hadn't transpired that there was another man – he sheered off, by the way. Looked as though he weren't satisfied even if the jury were. I tell you, Haydock, where that woman is concerned I'm afraid of another – accident!'

The old captain shrugged his shoulders.

'It's been nine years since that affair. Why should there be another 'accident', as you call it, now?'

'I didn't say now. I said some day or other. If the necessary motive arose.'

Captain Haydock shrugged his shoulders.

'Well, I don't know how you're going to guard against that.'

'Neither do I,' said Evans ruefully.

'I should leave well alone,' said Captain Haydock. 'No good ever came of butting into other people's affairs.'

But that advice was not palatable to the ex-inspector. He was a man of patience but determination. Taking leave of his friend, he sauntered down to the village, revolving in his mind the possibilities of some kind of successful action.

Turning into the post office to buy some stamps, he ran into the object of his solicitude, George Merrowdene. The ex-chemistry professor was a small dreamy-looking man, gentle and kindly in manner, and usually completely absent-minded. He recognised the other and greeted him amicably, stooping to recover the letters that the impact had caused him to drop on the ground. Evans stooped also and, more rapid in his movements than the other, secured them first, handing them back to their owner with an apology.

He glanced down at them in doing so, and the address on the topmost suddenly awakened all his suspicions anew. It bore the name of a well-known insurance firm.

Instantly his mind was made up. The guileless George Merrowdene hardly realised how it came about that he and the ex-inspector were strolling down the village together, and still less could he have said how it came about that the conversation should come round to the subject of life insurance.

Evans had no difficulty in attaining his object. Merrowdene of his own accord volunteered the information that he had just insured his life for his wife's benefit, and asked Evans's opinion of the company in question.

'I made some rather unwise investments,' he explained. 'As a result my income has diminished. If anything were to happen to me, my wife would be left very badly off. This insurance will put things right.'

'She didn't object to the idea?' inquired Evans casually. 'Some ladies do, you know. Feel it's unlucky – that sort of thing.'

'Oh, Margaret is very practical,' said Merrowdene, smiling. 'Not at all superstitious. In fact, I believe it was her idea originally. She didn't like my being so worried.'

Evans had got the information he wanted. He left the other shortly afterwards, and his lips were set in a grim line. The late Mr Anthony had insured his life in his wife's favour a few weeks before his death.

Accustomed to rely on his instincts, he was perfectly sure in his own mind. But how to act was another matter. He wanted, not to arrest a criminal red-handed, but to prevent a crime being committed, and that was a very different and a very much more difficult thing.

All day he was very thoughtful. There was a Primrose League Fête that afternoon held in the grounds of the local squire, and he went to it, indulging in the penny dip, guessing the weight of a pig, and shying at coconuts all with the same look of abstracted concentration on his face. He even indulged in half a crown's worth of Zara, the Crystal Gazer, smiling a little to himself as he did so, remembering his own activities against fortune-tellers in his official days.

He did not pay very much heed to her singsong droning voice – till the end of a sentence held his attention.

'... And you will very shortly – very shortly indeed – be engaged on a matter of life or death ... Life or death to one person.'

'Eh – what's that?' he asked abruptly.

'A decision – you have a decision to make. You must be very careful – very, very careful ... If you were to make a mistake – the smallest mistake—'

'Yes?'

The fortune-teller shivered. Inspector Evans knew it was all nonsense, but he was nevertheless impressed.

'I warn you – *you must not make a mistake*. If you do, I see the result clearly – a death ...'

Odd, damned odd. A death. Fancy her lighting upon that!

'If I make a mistake a death will result? Is that it?'

'Yes.'

'In that case,' said Evans, rising to his feet and handing over half a crown, 'I mustn't make a mistake, eh?'

He spoke lightly enough, but as he went out of the tent, his jaw set determinedly. Easy to say – not so easy to be sure of doing. He mustn't make a slip. A life, a valuable human life depended on it.

And there was no one to help him. He looked across at the figure of his friend Haydock in the distance. No help there. 'Leave things alone,' was Haydock's motto. And that wouldn't do here.

Haydock was talking to a woman. She moved away from him and came towards Evans and the inspector recognised her. It was Mrs Merrowdene. On an impulse he put himself deliberately in her path.

Mrs Merrowdene was rather a fine-looking woman. She had a broad serene brow, very beautiful brown eyes, and a placid expression. She had the look of an Italian madonna which she heightened by parting her hair in the middle and looping it over her ears. She had a deep rather sleepy voice.

She smiled up at Evans, a contented welcoming smile.

'I thought it was you, Mrs Anthony – I mean Mrs Merrowdene,' he said glibly.

He made the slip deliberately, watching her without seeming to do so. He saw her eyes widen, heard the quick intake of her breath. But her eyes did not falter. She gazed at him steadily and proudly.

'I was looking for my husband,' she said quietly. 'Have you seen him anywhere about?'

'He was over in that direction when I last saw him.'

They went side by side in the direction indicated, chatting quietly and pleasantly. The inspector felt his admiration mounting. What a woman! What self-command. What wonderful poise. A remarkable woman – and a very dangerous one. He felt sure – a very dangerous one.

He still felt very uneasy, though he was satisfied with his initial step. He had let her know that he recognised her. That would put her on her guard. She would not dare attempt anything rash. There was the question of Merrowdene. If he could be warned ...

They found the little man absently contemplating a china doll which had fallen to his share in the penny dip. His wife suggested going home and he agreed eagerly.

Mrs Merrowdene turned to the inspector: 'Won't you come back with us and have a quiet cup of tea, Mr Evans?'

Was there a faint note of challenge in her voice? He thought there was.

'Thank you, Mrs Merrowdene. I should like to very much.'

They walked there, talking together of pleasant ordinary things. The sun shone, a breeze blew gently, everything around them was pleasant and ordinary.

Their maid was out at the fête, Mrs Merrowdene explained, when they arrived at the charming old-world cottage. She went into her room to remove her hat, returning to set out tea and boil the kettle on a little silver lamp. From a shelf near the fireplace she took three small bowls and saucers.

'We have some very special Chinese tea,' she explained. 'And we always drink it in the Chinese manner – out of bowls, not cups.'

She broke off, peered into a cup and exchanged it for another with an exclamation of annoyance.

'George – it's too bad of you. You've been taking these bowls again.'

'I'm sorry, dear,' said the professor apologetically. 'They're such a convenient size. The ones I ordered haven't come.'

'One of these days you'll poison us all,' said his wife with a half-laugh. 'Mary finds them in the laboratory and brings them back here, and never troubles to wash them out unless they've anything very noticeable in them. Why, you were using one of them for potassium cyanide the other day. Really, George, it's frightfully dangerous.'

Merrowdene looked a little irritated.

'Mary's no business to remove things from the laboratory. She's not to touch anything there.'

'But we often leave our teacups there after tea. How is she to know? Be reasonable, dear.'

The professor went into his laboratory, murmuring to himself, and with a smile Mrs Merrowdene poured boiling water on the tea and blew out the flame of the little silver lamp.

Evans was puzzled. Yet a glimmering of light penetrated to him. For some reason or other, Mrs Merrowdene was showing her hand. Was this to be the 'accident'? Was she speaking of all this so as deliberately to prepare her alibi beforehand? So that when, one day, the 'accident' happened, he would be forced to give evidence in her favour? Stupid of her, if so, because before that—

Suddenly he drew in his breath. She had poured the tea into the three bowls. One she set before him, one before herself, the other she placed on a little table by the fire near the chair her husband usually sat in, and it was as she placed this last one on the table that a little strange smile curved round her lips. It was the smile that did it.

He knew!

A remarkable woman – a dangerous woman. No waiting – no preparation. This afternoon – this very afternoon – with him here as witness. The boldness of it took his breath away.

It was clever – it was damnably clever. He would be able to prove nothing. She counted on his not suspecting – simply because it was 'so soon'. A woman of lightning rapidity of thought and action.

He drew a deep breath and leaned forward.

'Mrs Merrowdene, I'm a man of queer whims. Will you be very kind and indulge me in one of them?'

She looked inquiring but unsuspicious.

He rose, took the bowl from in front of her and crossed to the little table where he substituted it for the other. This other he brought back and placed in front of her.

'I want to see you drink this.'

Her eyes met his. They were steady, unfathomable. The colour slowly drained from her face.

She stretched out her hand, raised the cup. He held his breath. Supposing all along he had made a mistake.

She raised it to her lips – at the last moment, with a shudder, she leaned forward and quickly poured it into a pot containing a fern. Then she sat back and gazed at him defiantly.

He drew a long sigh of relief, and sat down again.

'Well?' she said.

Her voice had altered. It was slightly mocking – defiant.

He answered her soberly and quietly: 'You are a very clever woman, Mrs Merrowdene. I think you understand me. There must be no – repetition. You know what I mean?'

'I know what you mean.'

Her voice was even, devoid of expression. He nodded his head, satisfied. She was a clever woman, and she didn't want to be hanged.

'To your long life and to that of your husband,' he said significantly, and raised his tea to his lips.

Then his face changed. It contorted horribly ... he tried to rise – to cry out ... His body stiffened – his face went purple. He fell back sprawling over the chair – his limbs convulsed.

Mrs Merrowdene leaned forward, watching him. A little smile crossed her lips. She spoke to him – very softly and gently ...

'You made a mistake, Mr Evans. You thought I wanted to kill George ... How stupid of you – how very stupid.'

She sat there a minute longer looking at the dead man, the third man who had threatened to cross her path and separate her from the man she loved.

Her smile broadened. She looked more than ever like a madonna. Then she raised her voice and called: 'George, George! ... Oh, do come here! I'm afraid there's been the most dreadful accident ... Poor Mr Evans ...'

Down There Undercover

Judith Amanthis

From the kitchen Prudence walked along the passage to the front door. She opened it, stepped forward and stopped. Sweat ran down the sides of her chest, soaking her clothes from her arms to her waist. She turned round and walked back to the kitchen.

I tried, I really did. Don't ring, leave it another week, please, Sarah. Hello Mum, you'll say, how are you? I'll lie and you'll rattle on about the girls at work. And then. How about the weekend after next, you'll say, I'll take the 6.20 Friday evening and you'll be there to meet me. Won't you.

The kitchen had a high ceiling. It was bare, very clean, pale green. Two stools stood next to the work top under the cupboards which covered one wall. Prudence sat sideways to the work top, her back hunched, and lit a cigarette. She held it near her face. A thread of smoke rose and spread, hanging above her hair. It wasn't dyed. Her thighs bulged over the sides of the stool.

She breathed out, straightened her back and looked round the kitchen. The smoke halo scattered. She noted the spots of grease on the oven, the patch which wasn't shiny on the floor by the fridge, the finger marks on the cupboards. She thought about the specks of dried urine on the toilet seat. Her husband liked to leave his mark. There'd be little bits of shit stuck to the toilet bowl. What was it like down there, further down, where the reptiles lived? She smiled. Terry had done the Saturday morning shopping for two months now. For two months Prudence had been too frightened to go outside the house.

'How've we been today then?' he said. He stamped his feet on the door mat. 'Damn Siberian wind. Everyone wrapped up to the nines today. You should have seen them.'

The sweat soaked her blouse. He unwound his scarf and handed it to her with his coat to hang up.

'Any good news for me?' he said.

'I ...' she said.

He took hold of her forearm, hurting her. 'Well, I'm sure you've kept yourself busy. As long as the kettle's on, eh?'

He put his cup on the saucer. She reached over, picked up his cup and saucer and put them back on the tray. The tray gleamed. He rubbed his hands together in front of the fire. His wife kept his fingers manicured. She made his hands look capable. He was surprised when she pointed out the white hairs among the brown ones on the backs of them.

'Well, well,' he said, 'An irresistible older man at last.'

Later his hands crept to his crotch.

He said, 'These silly young secretaries. Just hopeless. Take Chrissy. I've had her for upward of two months and she still insists on calling a report a preliminary finding. I've told her and told her.'

'These young girls like doing things their own way,' said Prudence, it seems to me.'

'Silly little thing. I don't know.'

He stared into the fire. His hands hung between his legs.

Prudence said, 'I've cooked a steak and kidney.'

'You're an angel. You don't deserve my troubles all evening, do you. Now then,' his voice grew louder, 'you just stay right where you are and I'll get everything.'

The lights were off so the TV was bright and clear. Prudence sat at one end of the sofa, Terry at the other, his hand round a tumbler of whiskey and soda. Prudence smoked. She blinked. The screen made her eyes tired. They followed the cigarette smoke which climbed into a corner above the door, became blurred, dark, and then disappeared. On the TV, car brakes screeched. Terry leaned forward. The smoke reappeared, a haze hovering above the sofa. She looked into the gap between the sofa cushions. It's like that. You know everything's been flushed down there. You can't see much, it's too dark, but you feel it all, all the snotty scraps of tissue and nail clippings and flakes of skin, they're all held together in little clumps of grease, yes, grease, and you wade through, and further down shitty scraps of tissue and swollen pink tampons nudge you. And the smell, sweet clean jesus, the smell. You have to find the way out. But it has to be the right way out.

Terry nudged her, hard. She jumped.

'Aren't you watching?'

'No. Yes. Why?'

'Look.'

'Oh. Yes. Looks ...' her face went red but no one could see '... interesting.'

'Just the thing,' said Terry.

On the TV, a couple, husband and wife she could tell, were sitting on a leather sofa, holding hands. Opposite them, a woman who was prettier and more elegant than the wife leaned forward on another expensive sofa. She had a sympathetic smile and smile lines. '... Back in a few minutes,' said the TV. *Air Your Problem* in sympathetic blue letters came on the screen.

'She's the same,' said Terry.

'Who?'

'The wife. The same as you. We nearly missed it.'

Prudence said, 'There's always the second half.'

'Just as well my film finished when it did otherwise we'd never have known, would we?'

'No,' said Prudence.

'And I bet it's in the paper,' he said. He reached down for the television page. 'There you are. Just what I thought. I don't know. If you can't keep an eye out for these things.'

He thumped the tumbler down on the carpet. Some of the drink spilled. He looked at her. She carried on smoking.

'Leaving it till after, are we?' he said.

She nodded.

He said, 'I don't know why you make such a fuss about the carpet. It's too old anyway.'

A trumpet announced a commercial for the water and sewerage company of southern England. It didn't show the reptiles.

'It seems to me, Joyce,' said the smiling woman, 'that you've made quite a lot of progress. D'you agree?'

'Yes, yes, I do.' Joyce glanced at her husband. He squeezed her hand.

'What about coming back from your son's school on your own? Wouldn't that be something to aim for? Say, by next month?'

'Well ...' For a second, Joyce looked appalled.

'Good.' The woman sat back. 'That's good.' She turned to the husband. 'Brian,' she said crisply, 'I want you to remember that Joyce is trying, and trying very hard, to regain her self-respect, her sense of self-worth. Which means Joyce learning to depend on herself again.' She leaned her cheek on her hand. 'How does that make you feel, Brian?'

'Um. As I see it, what I'm doing, it's my duty as a husband.'

'Of course, Brian. I can see you're a very good husband to Joyce. In fact, she's said so herself. However, I want you to think about the difference between helping Joyce and protecting Joyce. Over-protecting Joyce. Will you think about that, Brian?'

He squared his shoulders.

'Joyce,' the woman leaned forward, softening her voice, 'Can you tell me what you'd most like to be able to do? Can you tell me? Go down to the shops?'

Joyce looked at her husband. She smiled.

She said, 'He's a fucking beast.'

For three seconds there was silence.

She turned back to the woman. 'What I'd most like to do is go to the Barry Manilow concert.'

'That's very good,' said the woman.

Sarah left home a year ago. It took Prudence as long to lock herself in the house. She did it gradually, sliding away from neighbours' questions and glances and morning coffee, making excuses to herself for not going out today, then not tomorrow, then not the day after. She pared away the things she would have thought necessary, had she thought about it before, to keep the house and Terry going. Her life became simpler and simpler. No dry cleaners, chemist, library, video shop, dentist, hairdresser, post office, watch mender, gents' underwear department, garden centre, DIY shop, no bitter chat. After six months, she went out only once a week, to buy food, but not to the supermarket. Then she knew she couldn't go out at all. She couldn't bear all those eyes. She was unnecessary.

Before Terry opened the front door to go to work the next morning, he gripped her shoulders.

'Remember what I said last night,' he said.

'What you said last night? What did you say last night?'

His grip tightened. She tried to free her shoulders.

'That you have to learn to depend on yourself again.' He pushed her. She stumbled back. Her dressing gown caught between her legs. 'You see,' he said, 'You're not even dressed yet.' Her shoulders hurt.

'You're going to be late for work,' she said.

He let go, opened the door and walked out. His shape in the frosted glass looked unwieldy. She turned away. She didn't want to see him for a second longer. She particularly didn't want to see the finger marks he'd left on the brass door handle.

That Joyce. Lucky bitch. All she needs is someone to hold her hand. That's two a penny. But me? I've got to stop them out there seeing me.

All right, Joyce, if you think you're so clever, I'll tell you. It's a question of disguise. If no one sees me, I won't see them. If I don't see them, I'm safe. Going out in disguise, I'm not really going out, am I? I can start looking for the right way out. She laughed. Her palms sweated. She left the porridge Terry hadn't eaten to go hard in the saucepan, the egg yolk to go orange on his plate.

Last year's coat wasn't any good. It was too small for her now and it was dark blue, a colour she hated. In any case, someone might recognise it. She put on her old grey gardening coat and looked at herself in the mirror. Nothing much of her showed.

She opened the front door. The cold slapped her face and she jerked her head back. Her face felt pulpy, the wrong colour. The cold wouldn't dry her sweat, nothing could do that. She peered out of the door, looked up and down the street. No one she knew. With slippery hands, she closed the door behind her. She could walk easily without looking up. She knew this street so well, she could tell by the paving stones which house she was passing, which kerb was approaching, how far she was from the corner round which the shop, and the shoppers, lurked.

Outside the shop, between the stacks of fruit and vegetables, ran an alley. At the end of the alley was a step. At the top of the step was the shop. Once inside the shop, she'd have to look up. She waited by the fruit and vegetables. Her hand went up to one of the stacks to steady herself. She held on to an orange. It rolled away. She'd been so glad to see out of the corner of her eye the bright oranges and reds and greens.

She snatched up a pint of milk and some biscuits and hurried to the end of the queue. A woman was unloading item after item onto the counter. She should do that kind of shopping in a cheaper place, a proper big supermarket. Why's she wasting her money here? Hurry up, you stupid cow, hurry, someone may come in, someone I know. By the time Prudence put her milk and biscuits on the counter she was sweating so much she was sure it was soaking through her coat. The man behind the counter smiled when he took her money. He'd seen her. She opened her mouth to speak but only a rattle came out. She looked at him, terrified.

He smiled without seeing her. The saliva came back into her mouth. 'Thanks,' she said.

He nodded and turned his smile to the next customer.

She was still two blocks from her house when she noticed the manhole cover. Its wrought-iron sides fitted comfortably over the hole there must be underneath. Prudence stopped. How square and squat and solid it was. She bent down to touch it. A cover over a manhole. Over a hole large enough for anyone to fall down or crawl down. Anyone, anything, at all. There was a groove and lip on one side, so you could lever it open. Funny, it must be new. She straightened up. She was pleased with herself, raised her eyes, glanced down the street. Three metres away a figure walked towards her. It was a woman she'd been friendly with when Sarah was in the juniors. Not even the manhole could save her now.

She walked quickly towards the woman, her eyes down, in a hurry, that's right, she didn't have time to stop. The woman was staring, she could feel.

'Hello, Prue,' she said, 'How are you? It's been a long time.'

Prudence didn't look at the woman's eyes. She knew they were scouring her puffy face, rubbing through the old coat, raking a hole right into the life underneath.

She said, 'Hello ...' All she could remember was the woman's eyes. 'Yes, I'm fine and Terry's fine and Sarah's fine, we're all fine in fact. To be honest I'm in a bit of a rush so I really must be going but it's been really nice seeing you. Bye, er ...'

Prudence stepped sideways, walked on, and as soon as she heard the woman's footsteps behind her continue and then recede, began to run. Not fast enough, not with her thighs rubbing and sliding and the blood pounding in her ears. Not nearly fast enough.

The front door closed behind her. She stumbled along the passage to the kitchen. Her legs shook, her face throbbed. She climbed onto one of the stools, leaned forward and laid her head on her arms.

*

Whatever made you think the coat'd be enough? You know they're waiting to find you out so they can say to themselves, oh my god, look at Prue, poor thing, thank heavens I haven't let myself sink that low, and then they glance at themselves in a shop window and smile and remember how they flirted with the butcher. She shivered. Only a pound of scrag end? The old man not getting the exercise he used to? I'd give him a bit extra if I was you. Keep him coming back for more. And before she could stop herself, she'd say, prim and red in the face, my daughter's left home, that's only two left to cook for now, you know. Suit yourself, he'd say, and slap the squashy pink-filled plastic bag onto the counter.

She opened the biscuits and began to eat, slowly at first and then, after the sixth biscuit, greedily. If they think they're going to see me like this again, they've got another think coming.

She tasted the ninth biscuit. It was like pellets of newspaper smeared with scouring cream. Everyone's on the same diet. Effluent, their own and everyone else's. She put the biscuits away, made a cup of coffee and lit a cigarette. Especially Terry. That's why he's looked so spruce and firm since I've been like this.

The white sheets clicked cleanly when Terry put his empty cup of drinking chocolate on the table next to the bed.

'I told you,' he said. 'You want to take it step by step, that's what you want to do.'

He couldn't see her face. She was leaning against the dressing table, her back to him. He settled his bulk into the bed.

'I suppose the light's staying on all night,' he said.

She walked out of the bedroom.

She shut the bathroom behind her and locked it. What a lovely thing to do. How lovely to wipe all traces of Terry off the pale blue tiles, the dark blue bath, the pale blue toilet. Put all his things away in the cupboard over the sink and you wouldn't know anyone used this room at all. Everything shone then. She cleaned the toilet. Outside the manhole was there and down there flowed the stuff of life, the waste, which she fed on. And as she fed, so she would feed. She shall feed her flock, like a reptile. So she didn't sweat anymore.

She looked at her face in the mirror. Lately she'd avoided the bathroom mirror because it was too well lit, too revealing. But tonight she saw herself exactly. There was something about her skin. Something. Resilient. And flexible. It fitted her, that's it. She looked more closely. Like scales. Yes. The pattern of smooth overlapping half circles arranged and rearranged itself over the lower part of her jaw. She smiled. The pattern rippled.

'Prue.'

The bathroom door muffled Terry's peevish voice. Prudence giggled.

'Prue. Darling.'

She stayed perfectly still.

'Prue!' A bellow.

'Coming.' The two-note melody drifted out of the bathroom.

No sweat, a piece of cake, easy as pie. I have what I need down there, downstairs, in the kitchen cupboard.

She left going out again for a while. She didn't want to rush him. He showed signs of disturbance as it was. When he found she hadn't washed up a single tumbler, he threw one of them on the kitchen floor. Prudence looked at the broken glass. It didn't bother her. Not with her skin. Which Terry, of course, hadn't noticed.

'You'll find the dustpan and brush second cupboard from the left under the sink,' she said. 'Unfortunately the vacuum's on the blink.'

She locked herself in the bathroom a lot. He heard much splashing and singing. She kept the bathroom spotlessly clean. The rest of the house she ignored and naturally the kitchen suffered most. One night, Terry was compelled to fry an egg for his supper. He saw how crusted the oven was with grease and old food, and lost his head. He pounded up the stairs, rushed at the bathroom door and shook the handle so violently she thought, with a rippling smile, that he'd dislocate his wrists.

'Don't do that, darling,' she called out. 'You'll hurt yourself.'

'You fucking slut.' His face was next to the door, she could hear. 'You fucking worn out old slut. You come out of there this minute and I'll show you who does what in this house.'

'Why, Terry,' she giggled, 'that's the nicest invitation I've had for ages.'

She wasn't frightened of him. It confused him. Before, she used to cringe when he lifted his hand to strike her. Now it fell limply to his side.

He looked at her. 'What is it? What is it?' he muttered. 'Why won't you ... ?'

'What, darling?' she enquired.

'What darling, what darling, I'll tell you what, darling. I expect some decent behaviour out of you, darling, some respect for my house and my marriage and that means for me, d'you hear? For me. And another thing,' he paused for breath.

She was filing her nails. They were a little long, thicker than before.

'Another thing, Mrs Terry Prudence Watkins. I thought you wanted to get better. Well, let me tell you, you've got worse. Since you've been out again, you're ...' his voice sagged '... I don't know.' He put his face in his hands. Then he looked up at her. He spoke evenly. 'I'm not putting up with this stupid behaviour for very much longer. D'you understand?'

'Oh, certainly I do, darling,' she said. 'I'm going out again. The day after tomorrow. I've decided.'

He breathed slowly. 'Prue, why don't we come to some kind of agreement. Um? I can see your going out has been a bit, well, disturbing. D'you agree?'

'Yes, yes, I do.'

'Well then, next time'll be less disturbing, won't it.'

She smiled. She could feel her scales gracefully slide and settle.

He said, 'And just so you can see that I'm with you all the way, I'm going to buy you something really nice.'

'Oh.'

'Yes,' he said, 'but you must promise me something first.'

'Yes.'

'None of this silly bathroom business.'

'No.'

'Right then, I'll buy you a new coat. You need a new coat, don't you.'

'Oh, yes,' she said.

Next day, she rang Sarah.

'I'm fine,' she said.

Sarah said, 'You could do it, you know.'

'What?'

'Leave him,' Sarah laughed. 'You'd cause a sensation. In the neighbourhood.'

Prudence lit a cigarette. She drew in the smoke, then breathed out into the phone. She must be careful. Sarah couldn't see her. Perhaps she could hear her.

'Mum, are you there?' Sarah sounded frightened.

'You're a good girl, Sarah.'

'Oh, Mum,' Sarah sighed. 'Look,' her voice was brittle, 'you could come and stay with me for a bit. Couldn't you. Now you're better. It'd give you time to think things out. And I'd look after you. Cook and that. I'd love to have you. Really.'

Prudence was silent.

'Mum?'

'Yes?'

'What d'you think?'

Prudence smiled into the phone. 'I said I'm fine.'

She put the phone down carefully. Sometimes she found the clink of her skin alarmingly loud. She sat perfectly still in the chair by the phone, except that her head, which poked forward, swayed from side to side.

Clothes weren't necessary anymore, but Prudence felt she must protect Terry. You never knew, perhaps tonight he'd see. She put on a polo neck jumper and trousers an hour before he was due home. She longed to soothe him, quell his fear with her unwavering look, quieten him so utterly that he knew nothing but the minute advance of her love. She wound round the kitchen preparing his meal. From the cupboard on the wall she took the packet of glistening, maroon, dried beans. One by one she dropped them into the coffee grinder. She switched it on. It clattered.

Terry grunted when she greeted him with a smile and an embrace. His skin felt very hot. She liked that. It made her want to curl up next to him.

'God, can't you turn the heating down?' he said.

He put a large carrier bag on the passage table. She unwound the scarf from his neck, unbuttoned his coat, spread her arms to slip the coat from his shoulders, hung up the coat and scarf, led him to the living room and the fire.

He said, 'You can take a look if you like.'

She smiled.

'Go on then,' he said.

She fetched the bag and put it in his lap. He pulled out a navy blue coat.

'I thought you'd like the colour,' he said.

She put it on. She could no longer feel the weight and texture of clothes. But he was so sweet, so tender.

'It looks nice,' he said. 'Definitely your colour. Comes out bigger than I thought, though. Strange.' He frowned. 'Go and take a look at yourself.'

She came back into the room and stood in front of him.

'Well?' he said.

She looked at him.

'Well?' His voice rose, his eyes widened. 'What d'you say?'

She took off the coat and lit a cigarette. The patches of sweat under his arms spread nearly to his nipples.

'Oh jesus, Prue, let's eat for god's sake.'

It was a bright clear morning and the street was deserted. Prudence walked out of the front door. The cold made her clumsy and sluggish. She had on the navy blue coat. She shambled towards the manhole.

If Terry, bent over the toilet, had been able to crawl to the bathroom door, he would have failed to open it. He was locked in. As it was, he knew nothing but the crimson advance of his pain.

Despite the cold, Prudence levered the cover off the manhole. The coat lay on the pavement. She slid into the drain.

By the second day of his sojourn in the bathroom, Terry was so weak he could no longer cry out. He didn't scream when he saw, he did see, he did, the flat snout and the flat, yellow, freezing eyes on the forehead rise towards him from the filthy well of the toilet.

The post-mortem showed the lining of Terry's guts ulcerated and enflamed to a bright scarlet by large amounts of lectin, a toxic protein found in raw or partially cooked red kidney beans. The post-mortem report concluded that cause of death was exhaustion.

Widow's Peak

Sylvia Petter

Jean-Pierre tipped my head back in the basin and started the warm water running. 'I'm sorry to hear about your husband,' he said.

I didn't answer.

'So sudden,' he added. 'Was it his heart?'

'Yes,' I said quietly as he rubbed a cool thick liquid over my hair.

'You don't have to talk about it,' he said. 'How about a midnight-blue tint to cover the odd grey, add a little glamour?'

'For a widow? That wouldn't be right.'

'You have to look after yourself. Life goes on,' Jean-Pierre said, and massaged my head.

Yes, it does, Jean Pierre. If only you knew. Yes, it was his heart that killed him. He shouldn't have split it in two. A heart attack. He'd always had a weak heart, but I must have thought he was simulating. I wasn't, of course, so I had to attack and I killed him in bed.

I didn't kill them all in bed, of course. Then, not being married, it wouldn't have been right. Anyway, I was far too young the first time.

I was ten and Wayne Smuthers eleven. It was just when school was about to break up and he'd asked me to go down the bush.

'What for?' I said.

'Show you the gorge.'

'I've been there,' I said.

'Not the place I know. Scaredy cat!'

'I am not!'

'Come on then.'

The bush was thick there and huge rocks littered the creek, as if they'd been thrown down by some angry god who'd lost at a game of jacks. They'd made crevices I'd slip into and sometimes I'd worry I'd get stuck and die a slow, starving death. Higher up there were caves, but I was never allowed to climb up to them.

'You going to one of the caves?'

Wayne didn't answer and just held out his hand. No boy had ever held out his hand to me before, well not when he didn't have to, so I took it.

'I'm game,' I said, and felt a funny shivery feeling.

No one saw us go down the back of the school and then across to where the blue gums start getting thick. They look like tall skinny soldiers and you can hear birds and lizards scuttling, but you hardly see any.

When we got to the gorge, Wayne let go of my hand. 'It's up there,' he said, pointing past the last boulder to a high platform in the rock-face.

'We'll never make it,' I said.

'Yes we will. Follow me.'

Wayne easily slipped through the crevice in the rock-face, but I had to hold my breath so I wouldn't get stuck. There were some footholds, but they didn't look natural.

'You make those?' I asked.

'Took ages,' he said proudly. He was halfway up the rock-face on the inside of the crevice. 'Come on. You can't fall. Just lean on the rock as you go up.'

I was puffing by the time I hoisted myself onto the ledge in front of the cave. 'So?'

'In the cave,' he said.

'I don't want to. Looks creepy.'

'Scaredy cat,' he said again and went in. So I followed.

An earthy smell of yeast came from the dark cave. 'Let's go home,' I said.

'Not yet,' he said and put his arm out, barring my way at the entrance. 'Bet you've never been kissed.'

I wasn't going to let on.

'I have so!' I said.

'Bet you don't even know how,' he said.

I wanted to run, but that funny feeling kept coming back.

'I do so.'

'So prove it,' he said, and flattened me against the wall. And then his wet mouth clamped on mine like he was almost swallowing me.

'Get out!' I yelled, and pushed back as hard as I could, but he just squashed me against the rock.

'I'm going to show you. No one else will,' he said as his pinned back my arms.

I put my head up and tried to move my mouth away from his. 'What do you mean?'

'You're just a fat goggle-eyed catfish. It's your last chance,' he said, grinning.

The evening sky was bleeding red through the tree-tops as I shoved him back. I couldn't believe my own strength and he tumbled to the edge of the ledge and rolled off. I was still shaking as I spat out the mouldy taste of him and wiped my glasses on my skirt. He'd just disappeared. Flown away. Gone. And then I heard him screaming.

'I'm stuck. Help! Get me out!'

I crawled to the edge. Wayne was pinned down in the crevice and blood was all over his face and arms. I squinted at him. He looked like a snow gum with his white arms and legs and the sticky red glistening on him like resin. He looked almost beautiful. Just seeing him like that made me feel so calm, happy even. I scrambled down the crevice wall and when I was just out of touching distance I saw there was no way I could get him out.

'Get help!' he whimpered. 'Please.'

By the time the search-party found him three days later he was dead. When I heard all the grown-ups clucking about how Wayne could never keep out of the gorge, I just remember thinking he'd lost his bet. It was all his own fault, wasn't it?

*

'*Not too hot?*' *Jean-Pierre asked as he rinsed the shampoo.*

  I gave a slight shake of my head.

  '*Some nourishment,*' *he said as he spread another cool liquid over my*
scalp. 'I'll leave it five minutes.'

My puppy fat melted, I started wearing contact lenses and learnt how
to kiss. But it never seemed what my girlfriends made it out to be. At
least not until I met Enzo.

  Enzo was the purser on a cruise ship up north and one of his jobs was
to organise show time. He'd get all the girls up on deck and make us
practise the can-can. After practice, he'd take me for a drink in the bar
and then back to his cabin. He showed me how to kiss all right, and lots
of other things, but I always held back. He said he loved me, so I
thought he could wait. But I didn't know he'd said the same thing to all
the girls on that ten-day cruise.

  I remember the day we had the show almost pat and he decided we
had to finish the finale with a Catherine wheel. All the other girls
managed it first go, but I was scared I'd go over the edge and I balked
every time.

  'Your rhythm's all wrong,' Enzo said. 'Haven't you got any soul, any
passion?' And he pushed me aside and said to one of the girls, a tall
leggy brunette who'd always been giving him the hairy eyeball, 'You
show her!'

  The brunette sprang a perfect wheel.

  'Now you do it,' he said to me.

  'I can't,' I said. Tears welled in my eyes and I thought my contacts
would fall out. So I went over to lean on the railing.

  'Watch me, then,' he said to my back.

  I turned around. He seemed to pull himself in like elastic, then,
almost bouncing off one foot, he careered straight at me. I gripped the
railing and, just as he was in flight, even lifting his hands from the deck
floor, I felt the railing loosen behind me and I pulled myself to one side.

Enzo went over the edge. He'd done exactly what I'd been scared of doing and landed in the ocean. They tried to save him, but it was a long way down and as he was going head over heels he must have split his skull on the hull, and then there was the propeller ... A bloody mess. I was shattered of course, but he *had* come on strong, and he'd betrayed and humiliated me.

After that, all the screws on the boat were checked so that no more could become loose – not even through twiddling.

Jean-Pierre rinsed my head with cool water.

'The tint has to take. Just relax,' he said, as the smell of the colour piqued my nostrils.

I was about to give up on men when I met number three. He was a nice enough chap, but he had that spiel with all his problems. Of course he was married, but I only found that out later. So to show him how broad-minded I was, I cooked him a meal – filet mignon with mushroom sauce. It's really so hard to tell death-cap mushrooms from the real thing. It was when I saw all the attention his widow got – the way she was coddled and fêted, and then her life started – that I decided to find a husband all my own. Stability, that's what I wanted. And marriage did confer a certain respectability.

'Just a few minutes more,' Jean-Pierre said as I started to fidget in my chair.

But number four still wasn't Mr Right. He was single all right, but just as I had at last reached full flame he suddenly cooled off. Unrequited love and a woman's scorn can be such a deadly mixture. As we'd been close, I, of course, knew all about his allergy. But was it my fault that I'd forgotten to take the bowl of beer from under the balcony table? Was it my fault that the wasps got angry when he kicked the bowl over? Was it my fault that I couldn't find his injection pack of antidote soon enough after they'd attacked him?

Jean-Pierre rinsed my head quickly and then covered it in a soft fluffy towel. 'Move over in front of the mirror while I put in the rollers,' he said.

I watched him intently as he worked, parting and twirling my long jet hair until my head was covered in a crown of glistening black coils.

'The infra-red dryer for a few more minutes and then you'll see the new you,' he said, and smiled at my face in the mirror.

I blew him a kiss and settled back.

Number five was the one. He wined me and dined me and we soon tied the knot. He was very gentle and calm and disliked too much effort, pleading his heart. Nobody's perfect, I thought, and so far he'd come closest to my idea of what was right. Why, he loved seeing me trip round the house with my duster, flicking the russet feathers over each fragile figurine. I had to admit as the years came and went that I enjoyed married life.

I can't recall when I first got suspicious. It must have been when he kept talking about his heart, but the medical exams all seemed reassuring enough, normal for him and the state he'd been used to. But one day, it was at the end of February, the florist's bill arrived. The flowers for Valentine's had been delightful, but two bunches? That's when I started snooping around. The two-timing bastard! My husband, a bigamist. No wonder his heart had always been weak.

Jean-Pierre rolled away the dryer and began unravelling my hair from the foam-rubber coils. I loved the way he brushed it out, and he was right: it shone and glimmered in the spotlights.

When I decided to kill my husband, I saw it as a charitable gesture. Two for the price of one, with the twist that I'd be helping a sister. And the word 'widow' has such a respectable ring to it. But I had to be careful; the last thing I wanted in my nice tidy house was a mess. Of course, it needed a lot of preparation – let's call it a foreplay of sorts, at which I had become expert. The diagnosis was heart attack from overexertion. His widow, the other one, came to the funeral, and while she made her condolences, which I had to return, I'm sure I caught a slight nod of approval.

'The style is just wonderful. Out of this world!' I said.

'You really should get out more,' Jean-Pierre said. 'Do you know how to dance?'

I nodded, admiring the way he'd pulled back my hair, how it looked like black silk falling softly to my shoulders, framing my face in a perfect heart-shape.

'There's a night club at the Holiday Inn. Lonely men go there to talk and whirl ladies round the floor,' he said, spraying Gossamer in the air just above my head. 'Younger ones, too,' he added with a wink.

I stood and twirled in front of the mirror. Then I kissed Jean-Pierre on the cheek and gave him a generous tip. I knew he was right, there was so much to live for.

And besides, I'd never married a hairdresser.

Stitch and Bitch

Jane Barker Wright

We called ourselves the Thursday Night Needlework Club, a title which by its very gentility suggested innocuousness, while our private name hinted at real anger, possibly conspiracy. If we had known where it was leading, perhaps the coffee wouldn't have been as strong, the white wine as icy, the snacks as full of protein. Weak tea and sweets breed compliance, not murder.

Or maybe it was just us, a malignancy that sprang from our combined force. Tina Sherman is a big woman, tall and solid; 'the tank', my husband calls her, rightly: there's a crush-and-roll-on ruthlessness in her. Right and wrong are sharply divided in Tina's mind. There's no neutral zone.

Suzanne is beautiful, exquisitely dressed and too thin, with one jumpy child and a spotless house and a rigid timetable of meals, laundry, shopping and cleaning. Suzanne sits down with reluctance and, when she crosses her long legs, her suspended foot sets up a small, urgent vibration that pervades the room. It's hard for Suzanne to sit down.

Laurie Moxon has been pregnant or lactating for the past ten years and seems to have lost herself somewhere in the process of wiping noses and bums. She searches for words. Given half the chance she'll cut your meat for you.

Janet should be working at the mine; she's an engineer and a damned good one, I bet, but she has pre-schoolers and the nearest daycare is a hundred miles away. The town's designers didn't allow for working mothers.

The truth is, we're all oppressed by our iconic forebears, those pioneer women in their sod huts who melted snow on top of wood-stoves and died in childbirth. We're reproached by our modern appliances.

Margaret Falls is a coal-mining town, brand new, slapped down like something made from a kit, in the middle of nowhere in the far north of BC. Some people call it God's country, but to me this country can only belong to the God who gives cancer to little kids and floods to Bangladesh, not to the God of ripe tomatoes and young love. The wilderness that surrounds us is so vast and cold and serenely potent, so indifferent to humanity, that it could shrug off our little town like a speck of lint.

In response, we become noisy and active. We have parties; we form clubs and teams and committees. We huddle together for warmth, we have babies, we drink too much. We ignore as much as possible the hinterland at our back doors and concentrate instead on the suburban façade: the blandly harmonised company houses, the streetlights, the sidewalks, the sod so freshly laid the seams still show. If you only look out of your front windows, you can pretend there are no grizzlies at the back.

Men are incidental to this story. Even Stan Putnam has no more than the minor role of victim. The men work at the mine and are well paid for it and come home and scrub off the coal dust (which tends to linger around the eyelashes) and finish their basements and are usually kind to their children and wives. We wives are appendages; important ones like arms and legs, but none the less incomplete without the torso, the man. We have babies and look after them and watch the long winter pass through our picture windows.

You have to understand the cold. And the dark. The cold and the dark are central. In the winter, there are weeks and weeks when you can't take a small child outside. If you have to, if you really have to, you hold the baby close to your mouth and you blow into its face so the air it inhales will be warm enough for it to continue to breathe.

Getting out alone becomes a quest for us and we'll use any excuse to do so: baby showers, Tupperware parties, quilting bees, anything. Out is hard to find in Margaret Falls.

So our little club has no noble purpose. We don't intend to raise our consciousnesses or to lobby for a library or to collect for the Heart Fund. We have no reason to meet. We're troubled by that: it's hard not to be noble. The needlework is just an excuse, although Suzanne sometimes mends with tiny, precise stitches and Janet works sporadically on a huge and ugly tapestry that she hauls around in a hockey bag. We drink according to our habit. Suzanne never has more than one glass of wine. Laurie and I get drunk on occasion.

We've never been a closed group. Other women come and then go, uneasy with the bitter jokes, the compulsive smoking, the edgy quality of our endurance. They're happy women, briskly dismissive of complaint. They want us to pull up our socks. They know towns like this. They understand how to survive and they fear that whatever we have may be catching.

It was Laurie who dragged Marlene Putnam in. Laurie's the kind of person who rescues baby birds and fretfully keeps them warm while they die. She felt sorry for Marlene in the way a mildly injured Emergency Room patient will pity another who is spurting blood.

I don't know why she thought we could help. Marlene wasn't one of us. We didn't want her. We'd met her at the Safeway and had taken note of the marks on her face. We knew that Stan, her husband, had been reprimanded for being drunk on shift at the mine. You don't get involved with people like the Putnams, not in a place like this. Their children walked to school past our house and all three studied the sidewalk as if it were capable of sudden and unpredictable violence. We looked at poor, sad Marlene and couldn't see ourselves. We blamed Stan, of course, but we also blamed her, his victim. *We* would have walked out long ago. *We* would have called the police …

I found her presence stifling. It was impossible to complain about Bill forgetting to take out the garbage or throwing his clothes all over the floor in front of a woman whose husband might punch her in the stomach for running out of milk. But she kept coming to the meetings, sometimes even bringing the children, an exception she was allowed in the way that a blind man is allowed to take his dog on the bus.

At first, Laurie tried to draw her out by describing her own situation in the bleakest of terms: the frustrating, transient nature of housework, the sleep deprivation, the excrement and spit and spilled food, the pathetic search for one interesting anecdote to be related at the dinner table. But Marlene just sat quietly and nodded as if these were her troubles too.

It was February when she finally broke. February will do that. In February the days begin pale grey at eleven and end piss-yellow at two. Up here, it's not the end of winter but the middle of it: we can have snow in July. And that February was especially bad because there was a chinook and we had to toil through the filthy slush in the sure knowledge that there would be snow and slush many times again.

The meeting was at my house that night. Marlene arrived with the kids again, so I made up the fold-out couch in the basement. She said *sorry, sorry* and scampered around tucking in blankets. She was so sorry I felt like slapping her. *No problem*, I said, *don't worry about it*. It was only later that I recognised the new fierceness in her, the assumption that she was correct to impose, that she was not begging but demanding and that the language of apology was used only because it was her vernacular, the language of command being foreign to her.

We settled the kids down and went back upstairs where she perched on the least comfortable chair in the house and I drank three glasses of wine before I even noticed. Suzanne began with a grievance against her son, who was beginning to sully the perfection of his childhood. He had always been so good, loved vegetables, scorned candy, and now (she blamed his playgroup) he was asking for war toys. Her sharp little needle jabbed in and out of the sock she was mending as she spoke.

'All kids rebel. Relax with him for once,' Janet said. 'What I want to know is why they won't pick up their things, in spite of bribes and threats and everything else. It can't just be laziness. It's got to be a conspiracy. Some subliminal suggestion on *Sesame Street* or whatever.

Ultimately they'll drive us bananas and never have to eat broccoli again.'

And after all those months of sitting with her legs together and her mouth closed, Marlene began to cry, silently at first, then noisily snorting and sobbing. We stared at her. What did we feel? Relief? Satisfaction? Pity? I think we'd run out of pity, used it all up. And Marlene didn't need it. She was a stronger force in her weeping than the stiff, conventional stoic she had been before. We let her cry as long as she wanted to. She didn't once say she was sorry.

'You and your stupid, stupid problems! What difference does it make if your kid doesn't eat his peas? What about me? What can I do?' she shrieked. We didn't need an explanation. All the unexpressed confidences were taken for granted. There was no longer the pretence that everything was fine, that her life was like ours, that she was there for the coffee and the gossip.

'I don't know,' Laurie said, crying too. 'I don't know. I wish I knew.'

'Surely the Ministry of Human Resources—' Suzanne began.

'I can't go to them.' Marlene was angry now. 'You think I haven't thought of that? And have some social worker looking through my cupboards and asking if I spank my kids?'

'Turn him in to the Mounties,' Janet said. 'That's what I'd do. The scum.'

'He'd kill me,' she said without inflection.

We looked at each other. This was far too big for the likes of us.

'Don't you have family somewhere?'

'If I had family, I wouldn't be here. My mum's dead. And my father's like Stan. They're good buddies, Stan and Dad.'

She spoke levelly and slowly like an instructor. 'He hits me. He hits the kids and then he's sorry, he's so sorry later and then it starts again and every time I'm afraid if supper's late or I forget to buy beer or I dent the car, he'll kill me. And sometimes I think how easy it would be to stick the carving knife through his chest while he's sleeping. I've looked it up. I know the exact spot to stick it in. I've done it a hundred times in my mind. But then I think, what would happen to me, what would happen to the kids? That's what it's like, in case you wanted to know.'

'Do you love him?' Janet asked. Tina laughed aloud, but it seemed a reasonable question to me. Love and hate are so close you can drift into one from the other without even knowing it. There's barely a boundary between the two.

'No,' Marlene answered. 'I've got that figured out now. I never did. I married him to get out of my father's house and I had kids because I got pregnant and every year I stay, he gets worse and it's only harder to leave. I thought when we moved up here and he got a steady job and a free house and all, he'd be better. But he's just the same. No, I don't love him.'

None of us said what we might have said, perhaps what we should have said: *Come and stay with me, Marlene. Stay as long as you like. I'll protect you.* But what else could we say? The silence was huge.

'If you did kill him, wouldn't that be ... what's that called?' Janet asked.

'Justifiable homicide,' I said. 'Maybe manslaughter. Anyway, there would be extenuating circumstances.' I'm good on this kind of thing. I read thrillers.

'Don't be so gruesome. Really,' Suzanne said.

'Oh no, it's not the killing him that stops me,' Marlene said, and she must have hoped we'd be shocked. 'I've kind of had those edges knocked off me, you know? But they'd take the kids away. Those are my kids. They're all I've got.'

'Why don't you just leave? Get in the car and drive south. Sixteen hours and you'd be in the city.'

'And one day Stan would find me and that would be it. You don't get it. To him, we're a unit. We're all a part of him.'

'I'd cut off his balls and put them in the blender,' Janet said.

We laughed, of course. Wouldn't you?

'Or wait until he's really plastered one night and push him down the basement stairs,' I suggested. 'Of course, you'd have to get him to stand right at the top. That might be hard. And who's to say it'd kill him? You wouldn't want a cripple on your hands.'

What do you say on a winter's night in a bravely lit room with the furnace roaring against the wind that howls down from the Beaufort Sea? What do you talk of besides gingerbread and babies and thick wool sweaters?

We met at Suzanne's house the following Thursday because her husband was on shift that night. Marlene brought the kids and put them to bed. It had been decided that they would stay the night. Marlene's house was on the way to Tina's, so it was Tina who walked Marlene home.

Stan's body was in the kitchen. He'd been stabbed repeatedly and two knives (carving and boning) were lying on the linoleum beside him. There were three glasses and an empty bottle of rye on the table. There was blood everywhere: it was fortunate that he hadn't been killed on the living-room carpet where the stains might have reduced the selling price.

Tina called the Mounties. She remembered not to touch anything. She found a little cherry brandy in the bottom of a bottle and coaxed it into Marlene. She was calm and sensible when she talked to the police. She was a good person to find the body.

The Mounties came to my house the following morning. I told them I'd seen Stan the night before when I stopped by to pick up Marlene and the kids – it was bitterly cold and Stan didn't like her to drive. I said he'd seemed fine ... well, maybe he'd had a few drinks. He'd been alone then but he might have been expecting someone else. He knew Marlene would go out; she went out every Thursday from eight until eleven. It was our needlework club night. The whole thing was a terrible shock. Tragic. Did they think a killer was on the loose? You never knew with drifters. Perhaps I should get a dog?

They thanked me and finished their coffee, put on their dripping boots and trudged down the street to talk to Janet.

The file remains open, as they say. There's no real reason to solve the case. In Margaret Falls, Stan's death is regarded as a gain rather than a loss. An inconvenience, though: the town planners didn't expect us to die here and there's no cemetery. They had to scrape clear a patch of scrub on the dump road, chip through the rigid soil and bury Stan there, twelve feet down where the frost won't get him. The Chamber of Commerce put up a really nice stone. Stan is our first corpse, after all, and we're modern pioneers, a part of history just for being in this place. No doubt old Stan will be written up one of these days. Murder is so colourful.

Last month, Marlene sold the house and moved to the coast. There are no jobs for women here and she's not a wife anymore. No one thought it strange that she left. I like to think of her down there in all that green and misty blue, in that soft place.

Even after so short a time, the mystery is acquiring fictitious edges, being transmuted into legend. There are those who point to Stan's sinful life and the bloody manner of his death and suggest the intervention of God.

And what's it like to kill, you wonder. It isn't as hard as you think and, like all those acts you've never committed but have considered at one time or another, it doesn't quite live up to your expectations. I thought with all those stab holes in him he must have looked like a piece of unpicked sewing, someone's first attempt, maybe.

It's not discussed at the Thursday Night Needlework Club. We're uncomfortable with the memory of the deed, if not the deed itself. And, besides, sometimes a patrol car stops on its rounds in front of the house where we're meeting. They always know where we are.

I like that.

The Mole Trap

Norma Meacock

That morning when I woke, the light was white gold. It dissolved the wooden window bars to silver. The small misted panes veiled blazing, blue, winter-frost sky.

A fierce current of life surged through me, the way fast-flowing water when it comes up against an obstacle, a rock, a boulder, will dash itself onto it and overleap it.

A few months before, I'd taken up flower painting. Eva persuaded me. She wanted to go but she didn't want to go by herself. The classes were held in the town, ten miles away, at night.

'It'll do you good,' she'd said, 'to get out. Don't worry about him. It's only a few hours once a fortnight. He'll be all right. And I think you need a break, to be honest. I think it's getting you down.'

And it gave me great pleasure. I enjoyed opening my box and selecting the long, tapering brushes. I enjoyed the fat colours of the paints in their neat white squares and the names of the colours. It connected me to myself.

Bang. Bang. Bang. He was knocking, thumping on the floor with his stick. That stick was the pivot on which my days turned. He'd reach his hand out and bang with it. And I knew what he'd say before I entered the room. I'd given him his breakfast. I'd given him his morning drink.

'Have we got him at last? Have you checked? I didn't see you out there. You haven't checked him this morning' – anxiously. 'He's come to the end of his luck. We'll get him one day this week, I tell you.'

'There, there,' I said soothingly, as to a child. 'Don't agitate yourself.

You dozed off for a bit so you didn't see me. Let me shake your pillows; then you can sit up and watch while I go and check again.'

In fact, I'd deliberately put the trap where he couldn't see it, however much he craned his neck. But I had to pass within sight of his window to reach it. He had a fine view of the lawn. That's what had started the business off in the first place.

'There's a bloody mole,' he'd said one morning – it was a good few weeks ago. 'Get the trap out. Go on. You know where it is. Bring it up here so I can look it over.'

'Oh, it'll turn and go back again,' I'd said confidently. The moles had always kept to the field. I'd never known one come into the garden.

It had seemed like a bit of excitement in his life at first. Every morning he'd look out of his window through the bird glasses to check the lawn and every morning the mole would have burrowed a bit further into it, heaving the earth up into a green tunnel or throwing out a tump of scraped earth.

I tried all kinds of old tricks to make it turn tail and head back into the sheep field. I'd no intention of setting the trap, that was the problem. It was the hands that troubled me. The lines of dirt in the wrinkles on the palm made them seem like an old hand and a child's hand all in one. Local farmers still pulled the moles out of the traps and hung them in strings on the gates. I couldn't bear to look at them when I was a girl and see the little hands begging.

The Defiance Mole Trap was a simple grab-device on a spring. You set the iron ring in the middle and pushed the trap somewhere into the mole's corridors. Then, when it snuffled along looking for worms and beetles, it jolted the ring. The four metal arms snapped together, held it tight and crushed the life out of it.

You could tell when the trap was set properly because the handles stood upright in the ground. Of course he wouldn't have been able to see this from the bedroom window without the binoculars, but he'd asked for these to watch the birds – and who would deny him that pleasure? For this reason I'd placed the trap just out of sight.

Bang. Bang. Bang. He was knocking again. He wanted to know if I'd checked. It was my evening out and my flower painting hung in front of me like the mirage of a garden, seductive and shimmering. I had to keep him sweet.

With its sinews and roped veins, the long flesh-coloured stick he'd cut from the yew tree a long time ago was like an extension of his bony frame.

'Was he there? Did we get him? God help me, I'll see that day.'

His eyes shone again with the blue-grey shine of steel.

The eyes of moles don't shine. They are drab pin-heads hidden deep in its fur, intense black holes like openings into darker pits.

'By God! I'll get up from my bed and walk, that day.'

'It is a cunning creature,' I said, 'so we must have patience. But let me make you your hot drink now. I have to do some painting. I expect you've forgotten that it's my class tonight.'

My fortnightly evening out came second only to the mole in his list of monstrous things.

He let his stick fall, pettishly. 'I don't want you to go. Stay at home. Just for this time. I really don't feel so well today. And suppose ...'

I refused to join in. I smiled cheerfully, kissed him on the forehead, smelling his sick hair, a baby's smell.

'You'll be fine,' I said. 'I won't be gone long. You can have a little sleep.'

There was nothing he could do about it. But he didn't like it. And nothing would have kept me in. I was entitled to go out. I needed to go out. Nothing he said would have made any difference.

And once, my life was there with him. But I'd moved it, out into that little space of hours every fortnight.

Had he collapsed in my arms – you hear of it happening that way sometimes – I still would have gone. What can you do for another when death comes? Each of us has our own death as personal to us as our lives.

And for him death was that mole, creeping closer day by day in his dark earth kingdom. Oh, I knew why he hated the mole. I had a lot of time to think as my life stretched out, punctuated by the clout of his stick on the floor overhead.

And as I opened my paintbox and chose the colours of the flower petals, those dense fragments of purple, of crimson, of blue, were wells sunk deep in my life.

So when Eva came round I put my coat on and followed her to the car cheerfully as usual and left him to it. And as usual we were back again by ten-thirty and I made our regular nightcap before she went home.

I carried a cup upstairs but he was already asleep and I was surprised at this because as a rule he liked to make sure I was back in my box again before he dropped off.

That night he let me be and I slept soundly until clear sunlight streamed through my window next morning.

His eyes, when I took up his breakfast, had a lively vivacity in them. He even attempted a little humour and pushed at his pyjamas to expose himself.

'We have him by the short and curlies today, girl,' he said. 'By God, we do! Fetch the dead bastard up to me.'

I said nothing. I collected the tray things and carried them downstairs. I ignored his repeated knocking and waited until the usual time before I went outside to examine the mole trap.

As soon as I got near I could see at once that somebody had tampered with it. The turf was roughed and kicked up as if a man had dragged his body across it over and over and scored it with his nails.

I realised what had happened, why he'd slept so well. I grabbed at the handles and tugged the trap out. The mole was cold dead. A thin dribble of blood had dried on its mouth. Its body was hard under the fur.

I carried the mole upstairs to him in my hands. All the time I was walking upwards and yet I seemed to myself to be walking down, down, down. And so slowly.

He knew it was dead. And he hungered for it. He stretched his spotted hand out for it but I wouldn't touch him. I laid it carefully on the bed. Then he seized hold of his stick and hammered on the floor in a triumphant frenzy of drumming until a coughing fit forced him to stop.

'My tablets ... My tablets ...'

I gave him his diamorphine pills and held the glass steady while he swallowed them.

I plumped his pillows and he lay back, beckoning me to put the mole in his hands. Before I picked it up I saw a detail that I'd never noticed. The mole had no arms. I mean, its hands grew directly out of its shoulders like fleshy wings glued on.

I looked at him. He was nearly asleep. The doctor had increased the strength of his pills for the pain.

'You're no threat to me any longer,' I said. And I marvelled at myself because I was saying it out loud.

Then a very old deep loathing rose up in me. I picked up two of the heaviest pillows and pressed them into his face. He kicked out convulsively but he'd exhausted himself. He hadn't the strength and I didn't let go. I held them there for a long time.

When it was over I put the mole in his hands. It was soft now and its grainy palm lay like a miniature in his long fingers.

Later in my room I could feel the warm sun on my back. Its light made the white chair dazzle and turned the red knitted squares of the patchwork blanket into crimson peonies, scarlet roses, blood-red poppies; sunlight and warm blood light, light of life.

Sitting Pretty

Pauline Holdstock

She felt comfortable sitting there, content, gratified and supremely comfortable. It was release, a pain eased, a whine silenced, an itch scratched, a thirty-six-hour girdle peeled stickily away from its compressed contents. She was luxuriously at rest.

It was her weight.

For years she had hauled it up and down stairs, heaved it into supermarkets and then stuffed it into and dumped it out of buses, all in the course of her labours in that unlikely and unrewarding alliance, her marriage. But at last she was letting it do exactly as it wanted. It made her seem, for the time that she sat there, weightless. It was as if her whole being had dropped, plumb-like into the vast, cushiony depths of her buttocks, accommodating, commodious hassocks that they were, to swallow at one go her whole cumbersome, bothersome bulk.

As a result, her head floated detached and smiling serenely above the empty, porridge-blotted pinafore, while her feet, they too, almost smiled down below.

Harbingers of trouble her feet were – always had been. When they were bad, taut and shiny and itchy with old chilblains, it always meant she had been standing too long at the sink or the ironing board, and that in its turn meant that *he* had stayed too long at the pub and would return with cheeks veined and purpled to match her ankles.

Her feet being such sore points, as it were, it was heartening to see them happy. And she *could* see them nestled there side by side on his waistcoat, overflowing the edges of their worn slippers like jumbo pork sausages escaping from their skins.

She could see them for she had drawn them in, bending her knees and letting her legs fall wide. She couldn't remember having been in such a position since their camping holiday, when the Portaloo was blocked and she had had to find a place in the bushes.Only last week she had seen an article called 'Posture Points' in one of her weeklies. There were comic-strip figures in right and wrong poses showing how to 'look inches taller', 'diminish unsightly rolls' and 'minimise chubby knees.' She wondered how many posture points she would lose for this one.

There really were only three positions she used of late. There was lying, like a downed dirigible, there was standing – the whole trouble with her puffa-feet – and there was sitting, or, more accurately, seated, always on something and always with her body articulated in the likeness of an armchair.

This was different.

Of course if *he* was around (well, he *was* around but never mind) she would never have been able to let herself go like this. Cruel he was. She often used to wonder why he didn't go on the road and do the clubs with his fat lady jokes. *Got a modelling job, my wife has, posing for Save-the-Whale. No, lovely lady my wife. Got picked up by the coast guard. Took her for an inflatable life-raft.* Nasty little mind. That's what he should have done, she thought. Gone and made some money with it. She wouldn't have minded. Not if he'd sent her half. Gone to live in Florida she would have. Where Doris went. Worn bikinis, too. *(How many, dear?)* She'd have looked all right brown. At least she was all smooth. Not lumpy like some fat people. Carriage, too, she had. *(More like undercarriage.)* And a nice face when she had her hair done. People with money had their hair done every day if they wanted. Someone to do it for them. Little higher at the back, ducks. Lovely! Someone to do everything for them.

The thought of it.

Oh, she'd have been all right if they'd had money. If he hadn't drunk it all. The sponge. The weedy sponge. He never did tell her how much he made. Well, she'd soon find out.

What a fool she'd been. All these years working and never seeing anything, not a glimmer, of her own money, let alone his. Trotting round every Friday like a trained poodle straight from payroll to the supermarket. She might as well have been paid in tea and butter. *(How about lard, dear?)* Rump steak, she answered, and settled down savagely.

She was getting angry again. It was too much, hearing his smirky remarks, his wheezy old croak again even if it *was* all inside her head. She had put an end to it and that ought to be enough. The little squirt.

She shifted her weight and thought for a moment that she saw his foot twitch. It was obscenely exciting to think it might have.

She shifted again, just slightly, but there was nothing and she decided it must have been a reflex. Like ants' legs. They do that.

Yes, it was a good likeness. Definitely an ant, mouth like a set of beaky little pinching jaws, skin like armour plate. Or a flea. Press it under your thumb and it jumps away good as new.

The only time she had ever got to him had been once early on. She couldn't even remember what it was about now but by God he'd been mad. Came at her with a broom, he did. A broom! And she'd been so amazed she had just stood there like a dumb animal while he did it.

All that afternoon she had cried, but not for the bruises. She had cried the way she had as a child when she had seen the cow get its leg stuck in the ramp at the market, with everyone poking and shoving and yelling at it and she not knowing why. She didn't cry these days, not in front of him, but she couldn't help trying to get to him still, even if it was no use. 'Look what you're doing to me! Look at the state of me! Can't you see?'

Even after the last time, when she knew he'd been having a bit with that tight-lipped, tarty Simpson woman, even then he'd had nothing to say. 'Take it easy, dear. You're upset. Take the weight off your feet.' He was always saying that. It was the only thing his pea-brain could ever come up with. *Sit down, dear. Take the weight off your feet.*

Well, here I am. Dear.

No, she shouldn't feel guilty about it. He had it coming all right—

Coming as it did from beneath her, the sound made her jump in a paroxysm of embarrassment. But when she realised that she had just heard the last earthly sound he was ever to make, the rush of hot colour that washed over her body was one of pleasure rather than fright.

She waited.

Slowly, slowly, the wash of heat subsided and in an orgasm of relief she smiled.

No, there was no feeling guilty. Twenty years is enough of feeding a sneering face that has nothing but bad jokes and beery breath to offer. It had been about time it got what it deserved. And tonight, when he walked in grinning through the door, simpering *(You shouldn't have waited up, dear. Don't want to miss your beauty sleep.)*, when he went on through to the back and relieved himself on her nasturtiums *(Not on your what?)*, when he came back in, upsetting the cat box *(Put the damn broom down, will you. You can do it in the morning.)*, picked up the rhubarb crumble she had saved for his dinner and dropped it *(Tits!)*, then it did indeed begin to be time.

Whether he meant to clear up the mess was never quite clear to her, but when he spoke about the broom, the damn broom again, and started to reach for it, then it was more than time.

She had hurled herself at him as he came at her, knocking him backwards into the cat litter and sinking her knees and her two hundred and eighty pounds into his chest. Then, with the grace and speed of an all-in wrestler, she had switched her position, turning one hundred and eighty degrees and holding him all the while beneath her so that his startled, pop-eyed, gape-mouthed face could take in the fundamental ponderability of its imminent fate, the gravity of it, as her buttocks came floating down like twin, lead-weighted parachutes settling to earth.

So here she was, still in this ungainly (was it lewd?) position, too happy to move.

Heavy and weightless at the same time. Free. If he could see her ...

But of course he couldn't. Not unless he had his eyes open ... And even if he had ...

Her mind blushed at the thought, but she settled herself at the same time more comfortably – and it felt delicious.

The Father

Jean Pickering

The moment he stepped from the elevator, Lodge felt someone watching him. He hung against the wall, intending, as Anna would have said, to case the joint. A continuous sheet of water flowed over a vast stone block, and a tier of galleries receded into the arch of the roof. Dodging the couples foxtrotting round the fountain, he worked his way along the perimeter. On the charter to San Francisco, the row behind had played with the notion of terrorism. 'All it needs is one grad student to check a bomb in the baggage, and three hundred jobs open up on the east coast,' they'd said.

In the bar he found the eyes he knew were on him. They belonged to a blonde five tiers up. She lowered her binoculars and waved. Lodge waved tentatively back. She raised the binoculars again, training them on him so long he hardly dared move. He was disappointed when she turned into the shadow. He signed the bill and put his credit card away. Rising to leave, he saw her coming across the lobby towards him.

She was taller than one expected, slender but wide-shouldered, with a stride that was a bit too long. He pulled himself up as straight as he could and smiled.

'Professor Lodge?' She extended a hand. 'I'm Miranda Watkins. You're in Early American, aren't you?'

'The Puritans.'

'You're giving a paper. "The City on a Hill: A Phenomenological Analysis". I intend to go to your session.'

She signaled for the waitress, and Lodge sat down again. He couldn't believe his luck. When she suggested they take a cab into Chinatown for dinner, he agreed so quickly he was almost embarrassed.

'I need to go upstairs,' she said. 'Come with me. If we separate, we may never find each other again.'

He looked round while she was in the bathroom. The bed was queen-sized. A bottle of Rémy Martin stood on the dresser. He strolled to the window and looked out at the Ferry Building clock. Miranda came and leaned against him. He examined her profile, calm in the reflected light. She turned to look at him. Something in her expression made one uneasy.

'So California really exists,' he said.

After dinner they walked along Grant, the pair of them towering over the grandmothers looking for bargains in bok choy or tea-smoked duck. It was hard to remember that only that morning one had been in Louisville. He yawned.

'Perhaps we should go back to the hotel,' said Miranda.

He walked her along the gallery to her room. Suddenly she leaned over the parapet and waved to someone in the lobby. Incredibly, the woman saw her and waved back. Miranda waved again.

'You're very glad to see your friend.'

'We've known each other since third grade.'

She held the door open for him to enter. 'Pour yourself a drink.' She emerged from the bathroom in a kimono tied at the waist with a silk scarf. He handed her a glass and she sat down facing the window. She had the most elegant feet he'd ever seen. Finely turned ankle tapered to slender instep and long straight toes. He looked at her polished nails and thought that if one didn't soon get her into bed, the nerve might fail.

She reached over and felt his chin. 'There's a razor in the bathroom.'

When he returned, she was already in bed. He threw off his pants, for the first time that evening feeling in complete control.

He slipped in easily. She was moist and, as Anna would have said, hot to trot. And so was he, tired as he was. He could have sworn she came almost at once, her buttocks jerking in his hands as he held her tight against him, but before an hour had elapsed she was on top of him, and he was up again, good as ever.

Miranda was looking at him when he woke up. He had time only to notice that her eyes were a tawny grey before she reached out for him. This woman can't get enough of one, he thought. And why not? A great fuck is food for the soul as well as the body, not to mention the ego – as Anna would have said.

The sense of well-being took hold like a new graft. He had never met a more compliant woman. In bed, she wished only to please. As for the rest of the day, she had nothing to do apart from attending an occasional session. He was glad she wanted to hear his paper. One wanted her to know he could do other things beside screw.

When he took his place on the dais, there were almost fifty people in the room. He caught sight of her at the back. For a moment he wondered if it really was his Miranda. She was so animated, girlish even, in the way she talked to the woman beside her.

The chairman was already beginning the introductions and Lodge was the first speaker. By the time he could look at Miranda again, she had fallen silent, the chair beside her empty now. He watched her while the other panelists had their turn. To them she gave the reflective attention one hoped she had devoted to him. Her face was so different in the act of love, when she cried out and squirmed under him. He felt the blood surge from his belly to his neck and groin, leaving his brain so deprived as to make him feel for an instant a dizzy space within his skull.

'Professor Lodge, that's your question, I think.'

He had a bad moment then, but with relief saw that the questioner was still standing. 'I'm afraid I didn't hear you, sir. Would you be so good as to shout in my direction?'

When the session was over, he looked for Miranda. She was hovering at the edge of the group collected round the dais. He made her wait without so much as a smile as he spoke with two argumentative young men – graduate students hot on the trail of error in the Establishment. At last he dismissed them and joined Miranda.

'Not bad, eh?'

'You were wonderful, Lodge, quite wonderful.'

While she ran a tub, he ordered canapés from room-service and went to get some ice. He poured himself a drink while he waited for her to take her bath. Looking down at the monstrous sculpture in the court-yard below – surely that conglomerate of stones did not represent a man – he found in his mind the question he'd been looking for. How much would she take?

Sadist! said Anna, but he strode to the bathroom and went in without knocking. Miranda lay in a foam bath, the bubbles leaving only her head and shoulders exposed. As he stared, she slowly stood, her body shining through the foam like some mythic woman rising from the sea of time. Her rosy breasts appeared, then her gleaming belly, the blonde coronet, the elegant legs. She waited motionless before him. He ripped off his clothes and took her down in the tub.

He picked himself off her cautiously, aware of scraped knee and bruised skull. 'I'm moving into your room.' His voice was so brutal he was almost ashamed of himself.

The arrangement gave him further opportunities to humiliate her. As they were getting into bed, he called Anna and conversed at some length. He put down the phone and turned to Miranda, his erection appearing when summoned. Only an hour or so earlier, he'd felt as though everything he'd owned had gone down the drain with the bath-water, but here he was as good as ever, coming back like a bad penny (damn Anna!)

By morning he'd run through his entire arsenal. Short of physical violence, he could think of no new ways to test Miranda. He watched her get out of bed, her fine body unconscious of his estimating eye, and for a second wondered whether he could inflict some hurt upon her. Still, there was something about the set of her shoulders that made one think twice before pulling the hair or sinking the teeth into the buttocks.

'You never did tell me when you're giving your paper,' he said.

'Ten-thirty. The Regency Room.'

'I shall certainly be there.' One had never actually read *The*

Bostonians; the James man at his alma mater had judged it a minor novel, of interest only to those who expected to make James their life's work.

He strolled in to find at least a hundred people in the tiny room. One could hardly find a place to stand.

He turned to the program to find out what was attracting such an audience. He realised he had misunderstood her thesis: it was not situational ethics she was discussing but sexual ethics. He decided not to stay and went to stroll along the gallery and linger outside her room, now theirs. At last she appeared, smiling when she saw him.

'Lunch!' he said.

'Sorry.'

She unlocked the door and went in. She was in the bathroom a few minutes. When she came out, her hair was brushed, her face newly made-up. She picked up her purse and left.

Lodge was left staring at the door. Should one charge forth shouting, commanding her to wait? He snatched up the binoculars and rushed out into the gallery, from which, happily, he could watch the elevator. He put them to his eyes, prepared by waves of nausea he understood were jealousy to see her greet some handsome stranger. He was dismayed (one felt like a fool) to see she was meeting the woman she'd sat next to at his session.

Now they were both in his line of vision. Had their coloring been more alike, he would have thought them sisters. He suddenly felt like a visitor to an alien culture, to which, no matter how much he studied it, one would always be an outsider.

When Miranda reappeared later in the day, she did not seem curious as to how he had spent his afternoon, nor inclined to speak about hers. She didn't ask whether he had gone out, nor how he got back in without a key, nor even if he'd had lunch. She went into the bathroom to draw her tub. When the sound of running water stopped, he took off his clothes and went in. Stalking over to the stool he banged up the seat and, planting his feet wide, took a long hard piss, finishing with the most resounding fart he could muster. He took his foreskin between thumb and index finger and shook it back and forth, wishing he had her by a handful of tender flesh.

'Lodge, call room-service. Order me some coffee.'

He glowered into the clear eyes but went to the phone and placed the order. He wandered round the room for a moment, and then put his clothes back on again.

The waiter brought up the coffee. Miranda appeared, naked, and poured herself a cup. She took it to the bed, threw back the covers and climbed in. Drinking the coffee down in one guzzle, she settled into the pillow and went to sleep. Lodge could think of nothing better than to get in beside her.

The next morning he was awake before her. The shallow rise and fall of her dreaming breath followed its own rhythm, its own reasons. When she opened her eyes and turned to him, smiling, he forgot everything but the warmth of her flesh.

'Check out at eleven,' she said.

Perhaps it was the thought of imminent parting that made the last time so good. As they twitched together in a final spasm, he heard himself groan, and lay spent, his head cradled in the curve of her neck.

Somehow he managed to crawl off her. He showered and began to dress while she was still lying there, her buttocks elevated on a pillow. He wanted to disturb her calm, needle her into some kind of action. He grabbed the note-pad, wrote down the area code, the department number, his office extension.

'You can't call me at home, but—'

She took the piece of paper and tossed it on the nightstand.

'Well, can I have yours?'

'What for?'

She stood up and began to wriggle into her pantyhose. She smoothed the sheer knit over the long feet, the fine ankles, the rounded kneecaps. There was something odd about the way she adjusted the crotch and snapped the elastic at the waist. It was as though she were alone, as though he weren't there.

'You don't want me to call you?'

'What's the point?'

'You don't want to see me again?' He took the brassière out of her hands and fondled her nipples. 'I made you come.'

When she reached to retrieve her bra, he felt as though he'd been handed the wrong script. He dropped his hands and put them back in his pockets.

'Look, it was just a three-day blow. It's over.' She grinned. 'Buck up, laddie.'

Where did she get such dreadful turns of phrase?

'Surely that's how men like it. Cliff-hanging sex, no strings attached. Clean breaks. Good-byes without regrets.'

Of course one wanted a clean break. He couldn't have her desperately calling every other day, even at the office. Of course he wanted it to end now, in this room, but he wanted – what? He wanted her to have regrets, to miss him, to sigh over him for a month or two.

She hooked up the bra and reached for a shirt. It did not quite cover her crotch. The thin nylon of the pantyhose did nothing to conceal the blonde mound, which suddenly made one feel uneasy. It struck him with the full force of discovery that it didn't lack anything at all. In its own way it was perfectly complete.

At home Lodge often found himself thinking of Miranda. Once he even picked up the phone to call her. Obtaining the school number through information, he reached the department secretary, and then replaced the receiver. He looked for conferences where he might run into her, and discovered that in August there would be one on feminist theory in Denver. He sent for the program and was overjoyed to see her name.

When he arrived at the hotel, he enquired at the desk. Staring at the shiny head of the clerk bent over the file, he saw instead Miranda's glistening body rising from her bath. Yes, Professor Watkins was registered at the hotel. Would you like me to ring her room, Professor Lodge? The clerk passed over the receiver. The phone rang and rang. Lodge wrote a note and left it at the desk.

He went to his room to wait for her call. Staring out at the town, at the mountains, he realised his flesh was tormenting him. His nerves were open at his body boundaries, waiting for Miranda's touch. Even his mind would not obey his directive to wait in peace. It leaped and raced ahead, sending message after joyful message to his groin.

He could sit there no longer. Anticipation propelled him out of his seat, round the room, into the bathroom, round the bed, out the door. He took the elevator down, wandered through the lobby, at last inched into the bar. His heart jumped when he saw a blonde head. He pushed forward, her name on his lips. A closer look showed his mistake. The head was the same, but the body all wrong, much too fat for his Miranda. Then he realised he had made another mistake. It was Miranda all right, but she had put on weight – fifteen, twenty pounds perhaps. He shoved through to where he could see her torso. In only eight months the elegant Miranda had become dumpy, thick of waist and ankle.

Lodge fell back, undecided whether to demand an explanation or creep away and hide. He ordered a beer he did not want and hovered at the corner of the bar. At last Miranda got to her feet, drawing glances in spite of her fat. Lodge's eyes ran over the outline of her bulging belly. The tell-tale shape made the blood rush so quickly from his brain that his head reeled. He grabbed at the bar to steady himself while his heart pounded like a wild thing. Miranda, laughing, leaning on the arm of her friend, passed him only a few feet away and went out into the lobby.

Escape Artist

Vicky Grut

On the third day of the argument Corazón got tired of it. She'd forgotten why she was angry with Robert, if she had ever been angry at all. Surely it was time to celebrate by now? She had gone into that audition quite light-heartedly. It wasn't her fault that they'd offered her the job. They'd sent her the draft script with her character circled in red on the first page, and they were going to pay her *money* to do it. It was quite miraculous and amazing, and most amazing of all was that Robert couldn't seem to be pleased for her. He only said, 'I've spent half a year writing a play for you and now you're planning to go and work for someone else. That's about all I need to understand.' (Work *for*, he said, as if she was some hired thing – that really hurt.)

She found him standing on the balcony, staring out at the view. Their flat was on the seventh floor of a high-rise; you could see for miles in the gaps between the other blocks. It had been mild enough lately but now the sky was turning a heavy purple in the distance and the air was suddenly damp and cool. She went and leaned herself against him.

'Don't be cross,' she murmured. 'I hate it when you're cross.'

He said nothing.

Corazón moved her cheek against his shirt. She closed her eyes and imagined how they would look to someone watching. There might be someone looking across right now from the walkway of the next block. She knew that they made an attractive couple; both quite small and wiry and a little secretive-looking. Robert, with his olive skin that tanned so easily and held its colour deep into the winter, was almost as brown as she, though he was truly English. (Perhaps he had some Gypsy blood?) They were as different as two people could be, and yet on the outside, from a distance, they seemed to be alike and that pleased her quite irrationally.

'Let's go to bed,' she murmured.

For a while he was silent, perhaps considering the idea.

A pigeon shaved by in slow motion. Then Robert said, 'It's Wednesday.'

'So?'

'We can't just up and go to bed in the middle of a Wednesday afternoon.'

'Oh,' she said.

On the ground below everything seemed squat and drastically foreshortened. A swaggering youth crossed the pock-marked grass with a pit-bull straining on a short leash. Some younger children were pulling the bark off what might one day have become a tree.

'All right,' she said.

'Anyway, I don't want to.'

Corazón leaned in again and ran two fingers lightly along his spine. Robert had a very straight back, thin but strong. He didn't move. She brought her body closer, resting her chin on his shoulder, slipping her arms around his waist, lifting the shirt away from his skin. She could feel him breathing. He didn't move. She ran the flat of one hand across his stomach, just touching, brushing across the hair at his navel. A plastic bag drifted slowly down from the eighth floor, splayed open in the wind like a jelly-fish. Corazón slid her hand down more, dipping her fingers in under his belt. Suddenly Robert shook her off quite violently. He went back into the flat.

Down on the ground one of the children had another in an arm lock. The pit-bull lifted its leg against what was left of the sapling. Corazón spat over the edge of the balcony, and watched the droplet gather speed and weight, barrelling down onto the bald grass. In the distance the sky gathered itself more tightly.

In the evening Robert lay on the sofa talking to his friend Anna for hours, not bothering to lower his voice.

'Cora's been offered this supposedly fantastic job – a new theatre company – they're called TNT!'

He left a pause for Anna to fill with laughter. Corazón could hear them both – laughing and laughing.

'I'm serious. Tech-ni-cally Not The-atre: TNT.'

The laughter grew nearly breathless, then died away slowly.

'They've got a grant to do a reworking of *Shakespeare* with some arty-smarty young director, you know – video-cameras strapped to the armpits and microphone-implants in their teeth, that sort of thing.'

He laughed again, then waited while Anna said something; more laughing.

Corazón sat in the bedroom trying not to listen. It was sad, she thought, the way Robert said 'young' as if it were a tribe he could never join again. She lifted her head and looked at her reflection in the mirror on the other wall. She practised making it go dead, then come alive again: dead, alive, dead, alive. She blurred her lashes together till her face became a biscuit-coloured pool with two ink-slash eyes. She could still pass for early twenties. Just about.

She got out her small collection of press clippings and spread them on the bed. There were none for the first play; a handful for the second and the third:

A brave piece of writing, energetically performed by the young company, notably Corazón Macmillan as Linda, who acts her little heart out. The play itself begins to unravel after the first act ...

Corazón Macmillan as Linda, the wide-eyed stranger who unwittingly shatters a close-knit circle of friends, is a talent to watch ...

The combustible Ms Macmillan as Maria brings an oriental flavour to an otherwise very English piece ...

Corazón Macmillan's Maria is an entrancing combination of narcissism and tenderness ...

'No, no, that's all up the spout,' Robert was saying. 'I'll have to cancel ... Well she's accepted it already ... Yes.'

Corazón could almost hear Anna saying: 'Poor Rob. But can't you just get someone else?'

Most of Robert's friends were far too sophisticated to look down on her. There'd been one in the early days who'd gotten very drunk and asked Robert if she was a catalogue bride, but he was more of an acquaintance really and Robert stopped seeing him after that. The rest of his friends made special efforts to include her in conversations. They alluded lightly to the Pacific-Rim countries, talked on and off about identity and Diaspora, but she knew that they found her a bit light: her skirts too short, her laughter too loud, her education too sketchy. They were disappointed that she had never been to the Philippines, that her father was a white man, that her mother was an accountant and not a peasant or a reformed prostitute. Robert said she imagined these things, but she knew that she was neither enough like them to be good company nor different enough to interest them. And they never laughed at her jokes.

Corazón folded away her cuttings and went into the kitchen. There was washing-up from the day before waiting by the sink. She ran hot water and dish-washing liquid into the bowl and plunged her hands in, shivering at the loveliness of the heat. She thought about the two plays. Robert's was a sparse, four-handed piece about a mixed-race woman passing for white in London in the 1950s. He'd written it specially for her – a gift of a part. But she knew it would all take place in some tiny back-room of a pub in front of a handful of friends. It would be like singing in heavy traffic, running the wrong way up an escalator: it would get her nowhere.

The other play was described as 'a response to *The Tempest*: an experimental multi-media event combining actors, dancers and video clips'. The plan was for them to develop it in three months of rehearsals, then tour it round the country. Robert said it was bound to be terrible. Maybe so, but at least she would meet new people, she would learn things, build up contacts and be paid. It was easy to see what she should do. Anyone could see it except for Robert.

She heard the phone in the sitting room click back into its cradle.

After a while she sensed rather than heard Robert in the kitchen behind her, padding about in his socks. Corazón passed the sponge across a plate, scooped it round the innards of a mug, skimmed along the rim of a glass. She felt him watching her.

'Rob,' she said softly, without looking round, 'can't you just try and see it my way for a minute? I'm not doing this to spite you or get back at you or anything.'

'I'm not stopping you am I?'

Corazón said nothing. She watched the light rocking on the surface of the bowl of water.

'Am I trying to stop you? You're free to do whatever you want. Just don't expect me to join in the celebrations that's all.'

She glanced up at his reflection coming and going in the cracked mirror which hung above the sink. She felt a cramp of guilt. He was five years older than she was and she knew he was beginning to feel things turning sour. It wasn't fun being on the margins any more. He longed for a homecoming, attention, applause. He thought she could help him get that. Shouldn't she be touched? It would be so easy, she thought, to give in and have him take her in his arms right now. All he wanted was that she give up a smallish part in an experimental production. Was that so very hard for her to do?

Robert stopped at her shoulder.

'What?' she said, lifting her head. Their eyes met in the mirror. She imagined the acute angle of their look, like a broken bone.

'I said I washed that already. That glass you've just washed. It was already clean.'

She opened her hand so that the glass fell back into the water with a crash.

'What is it?' she whispered. 'What is eating you up so?'

'Loyalty is not something you can explain, Cora. Either you feel it or you don't.'

Five years ago she might have picked up the glass and thrown it at the wall. Now she gripped the sponge under the water instead, where he couldn't see.

'Don't worry,' he said. 'I'm going out.'

'Where?'

'Don't know yet. I'll see who's around.'

'I won't be bullied, Robert,' Corazón shouted after him. 'I won't!' She'd given him six years, she thought. He had no right to ask her for more.

When it got dark, Corazón heated a can of soup for herself. Then she went into the sitting room and rang her friend Emily, lying on the floor and talking for about an hour. Corazón weighed up the two playscripts as she talked. Robert's was considerably fatter. Maybe it was just the kind of paper he used. She felt wistful.

'He's changed,' said Corazón. 'He used to like the way I rushed into things and didn't hold back, even if half the things I rushed into were wrong-headed. He used to say I inspired people, you know, the people we worked with.'

'You do,' said Emily, 'You do.'

'He doesn't say it anymore. These days he just seems to be picking fault – the way I breathe when I'm sleeping, the way I do the washing-up. He says I'm noisy and untidy and I always burn at least one thing when I cook. What can I say? It's true.'

'Poor honey,' said Emily.

Corazón felt tears of self-pity start in her eyes. Emily was so much nicer than Robert. Why couldn't she fall in love with Emily instead?

'Sometimes I think it's his friends,' she said to Emily. 'That Anna. She and Michael have always had it in for me. They just want him all to themselves – especially her. They hate me.'

'Oh come on now!'

'She certainly does. I can't help it if I'm not ugly, can I? Or short. She might have been able to tolerate me if I was a dwarf.'

'Co-ra!'

'Well it's true, isn't it?'

'You're wicked,' Emily said, still laughing.

Corazón balanced both scripts on the soles of her feet. She lay there looking at them, poised above her head.

'Would you say I was very childish?' she said in a small voice.

Emily stopped laughing. There was a silence.

'Robert says it was understandable when I was twenty but I ought to have matured more by now.'

There was an irritable click at the other end of the line. 'Don't feel you have to apologise for yourself, Cora. Who'd want a world full of Robert clones, anyway?'

Corazón thought about the bit in Robert's play where the man shouted at the woman: 'Off to chew me over with that bunch of harpies again?'

'Ach! You two have been working together too long, that's all,' Emily said. 'You need a break and it'll blow over. You've been through worse.'

'I'm not sure,' said Corazón. 'Maybe this is different.'

There was another silence. Then Emily said quietly, 'It wouldn't be the end of the world, you know, Cora. There are things you could do on your own that you will never do as long as you're with Robert.'

What? Corazón wondered. She felt a wave of desolation. She remembered the beginning, before they were lovers, when she'd seen him and known at once that he was the one she wanted. In those days she had not yet learned to censor herself and words still had free passage from her brain to her mouth. She'd pursued him quite shamelessly, barging uninvited into parties and picnics and weekends away until at last, lying beside that slow-moving yellow stream at Anna's parents' house, she got him to kiss her. She remembered watching him roll across the grass towards her, sun skewered in the water like a jellied pin, poplar leaves tapping and clattering lightly overhead, and all the others asleep, as if they were the only people left in the world. She'd been so sure of everything then. And when he kissed her, everything fell into place. He'd become her only place of abode; her domicile, her country, her single state. How could Emily say that it wouldn't be the end of the world?

Corazón drew in her legs and let the scripts slide to the floor. 'I'd better get off the line, I suppose,' she said because she thought she was about to cry.

'You hang in there,' said Emily. 'And call me whenever you want.'

'OK,' said Corazón.

At ten o'clock Robert rang to say that he was over at a friend of Tim's, and there were a couple of people there who might go on to Anna's or they might just stay where they were, but either way he was too drunk and tired to make it home. He didn't sound particularly drunk but nor did he sound cold like before, just ordinary. Corazón could hear people laughing in the background.

'That's fine,' she said brightly. 'Thanks for letting me know.'

The laughing was probably nothing to do with her, but still it wasn't a nice sound.

'Love you,' she said.

Perhaps he hesitated for a moment. In the background came the sharp crack of a beer can. Then he said: 'Bye.'

What else could he say, she thought afterwards, in the middle of a crowd?

The next morning, she woke just after dawn with the bedside lamp still burning and a book crushed under her head. She couldn't go back to sleep. She got up and went into the kitchen to make herself a cup of coffee. There was no milk in the fridge, nor any bread.

She realised suddenly that, because Robert had fallen into the habit of doing the shopping, she had no idea of what they had and didn't have in the way of food. The fridge was empty except for a carton of yoghurt and some floppy carrots. She looked hopefully in the store cupboard. There were a couple of bags of dried beans, a tin of fish, two tins of tomatoes, and, right at the back, a dusty packet of table napkins. Corazón reached in and retrieved it. It looked as if it had been there for years, probably left behind by the previous tenants.

These beautiful and durable two-ply cocktail napkins, it said on the back of the packet, *can be used when serving hors d'oeuvres, as finger wipes or as drinks coasters. Choose from our range of eye-catching primary colours or our subtle pastel shades depending on the occasion or the mood you wish to create.* She stared at these words for a long time: *the mood you wish to create.* For some reason she thought of her mother.

The sky was quite bright by now. She shook herself and tossed the packet back into the cupboard behind the jars and tins. She would go out and get some bread and milk from the shop in the 24-hour taxi place, she thought. But when she got to the front door it wouldn't open. She fiddled with the catch, shoved it in, then twisted, then pulled and lifted, rattled, pushed and pulled it over and over.

'Christ!' she shouted, kicking the doorjamb, then turning on the door itself until her foot was numb. She stopped, and listened to the silence settle. The understanding broke slowly. Without thinking, Robert must have turned the key in the Chubb as he left the flat the night before. There was no keyhole on the inside; they had never bothered to drill it through. She couldn't get out. She slid down onto her haunches beside the door, head on her knees.

She must have dozed off like that because the post seemed to come out of nowhere, rattling through the letterbox in a rush of sharp, wet air.

'Wait!' she yelled, scrambling up and calling through the flap. 'Excuse me! Wait a minute please!'

The postman had already begun to walk away. She heard his foot-steps slow momentarily. She yelled again.

'Excuse me! Could you come back a minute!'

The steps faltered.

'I'm locked in,' she called, 'Could you help me, please. I can't get out of the flat.'

There was a silence now.

'I'm trapped!' she yelled.

The silence dragged on, full of doubt.

'Help!' she called. 'Please let me out!'

That seemed to decide the matter. The footsteps resumed at once, rapping off along the walkway at a great pace, growing steadily fainter and fainter until they were quite gone.

It was easier to attract the milkman's attention because he had to bend down and collect the empties before he left the fresh pints, and she had a nodding acquaintance with him. He'd been doing the round for years, not like the postmen and women who came and went. He was obliged, at least, to answer when she called.

'If I could just pass the keys out, you could unlock the Chubb for me,' she said when she'd got him to come up to the door. They were both squinting sideways through the narrow slit of the letterbox, each bent at the waist. She could see his eyes and nose and the shoulder of his white coat; his peaked cap. He considered her with grave caution. Somewhere in some respectable house he had a wife and you could be sure she'd never been in this situation.

'What is the problem exactly?' said the milkman with a carefulness bordering on distaste.

'My boyfriend went out last night and locked me in by mistake.'

How tacky and occasional 'boyfriend' sounded, Corazón thought. Perhaps she should have said 'husband', but she had trained herself not to use the word because Robert despised such petit bourgeois pretensions. 'Marry?' he always said. 'What for? Why sign a contract drawn up by the state?' For herself she wasn't really sure. Sometimes she thought it might be nice. You could have a party for all your friends and people gave you presents. But that wasn't a very good argument. It wasn't as if they had a child or anything.

'Last night?' said the milkman.

'Yes.'

'You've been locked in all night?'

'Well, I must have been though I didn't know it until a minute ago ...'

'I never like to get involved in trouble between a man and a woman,' said the milkman through thin lips.

'You don't understand. There's no trouble. It was just a mistake.' Corazón could hear herself getting panicky. 'He's usually the last one out. He's used to locking the door. It's his habit, that's all.'

'You never know the right or wrong of it when it comes to couples,' said the milkman, straightening up a little. She could no longer see his cap, just his mouth and nose. 'You get mixed up and try to help one and next thing they both turn on you.'

'It's nothing like that!'

'But I can't agree with locking women up,' the milkman muttered. 'Can't agree with that. Not in this country.'

'Come on, I just want to get to the shops and get some breakfast. I'm hungry.' She tried to laugh but she knew there was a pathetic whining note creeping into her voice. For no reason at all the phrase from the napkin packet came into her head: *the mood you wish to create.*

'Go on,' said the milkman, sighing irritably, 'give me the keys. Just don't tell him it was me. I'm retiring in six months. I don't want any trouble.'

When he'd gone, Corazón leaned in the doorway, listening to the ever-fainter clink of milk-bottles disappearing down the walkway. She looked at the packet of cocktail napkins lying at her feet. What a disappointment she must be to her parents. A girl who never gave cocktail parties or served hors d'oeuvres, who gave no thought to creating moods through colour. What was it that she had in place of all the things her parents had wanted for her once? Robert?

She put one foot then the other across the threshold, but somehow with the way it had happened she no longer felt like going out any more. She would have the air of someone fresh out of prison, she thought; someone who had to be very careful not to have their privileges rescinded. Why couldn't she have been more imperious? More digni-fied?

She ran out into the middle of the walkway and yelled at the milkman's white departing back: 'I'm not a mail-order bride by the way, if that's what you were thinking!'

He didn't turn around.

'Men!' she hissed furiously through her teeth. 'Bastards!'

She shifted back and forth from one foot to the other, crossing and re-crossing the threshold. There was an elastic fury bouncing inside her. She ducked down and grabbed one of the fresh pints by the door, turning to go inside. Then she changed her mind. She came out of the flat running. She flew right up against the balcony rail before she let the bottle go. There was crash from below; but already she was swinging back for the second bottle. She flung this one high and far, and the milk came out of its shell, making a beautiful ragged arc against the sky before it sagged and fell.

There was a brief moment of elation. She felt as if she had struck a blow for the meek and the pretty; a blow for all those who lost arguments and couldn't think of the right words at the right time; a blow for all who were struggling to escape from bonds of their own making; for those who had nothing and no one but themselves to blame for it. Then she went to the edge and looked down at what she'd done. In the back of her head she heard her mother's quick hurrying voice: 'You have a very unfeminine temper, Corazón Macmillan. Men don't like that. If you are going to get on – even in this country– you'll have to learn to control yourself.'

When Robert came back he found her lying with her eyes half closed on the sofa, the two playscripts balanced on her stomach.

He threw his keys on the table with an easy swing, then went into the kitchen and put the kettle on. Corazón watched him through the service hatch. She could see that his mood had changed. He had a boyish tilt to his movements. His face was open and unrumpled.

'Some idiot's been smashing milk bottles out there,' he said. 'Could have killed someone.'

Corazón turned her head away. 'Nice time at Tim's friend's place?' she said.

'It was OK,' he said.

She heard him getting out the cups, measuring the coffee into them. The spoon rang out clearly against the china.

'Met some interesting people, another bloody war correspondent and a couple of actors; well, an actor and an *actress* to be absolutely precise.'

He came back into view through the glass hatch, smiling a little. Something had been resolved last night, she thought. She wondered when he would decide to tell her about it. She saw him open the fridge and look in. Then he frowned. She felt an inexplicable wave of loneliness.

'What's happened to the milk? Did he forget to deliver today?'

'You just passed it. Down on the path.'

He stared at her in disbelief. 'Both pints?'

'Yes.'

'Why?'

She shrugged.

He shook his head, laughing to himself. When he'd made the coffee he came back into the sitting room and perched at the end of the sofa by her feet, still smiling.

'What is it?' He shook his head. 'Not because I didn't come home last night?'

He peered down at her with something like tenderness, rubbing at the ends of her toes.

'You've nothing to worry about there, you know that.'

'I know,' she said wearily.

She used to be ridiculously jealous in the early days, but that was a long way off now; someone else's emotion. He didn't seem to have noticed that she'd changed.

'What then? I'll never figure you out. You're not premenstrual, are you?' He ducked like a man avoiding shrapnel. 'No?' He carried on laughing for a bit before he quietened down. 'Sorry,' he said. 'You OK?'

'I'm fine,' she said. She felt him watching her. He put out a hand and caressed her knee.

'You look pretty today,' he said, 'almost pink-cheeked.'

He ran his hand higher on her thigh and let it rest. Corazón didn't move. It was amazing, she thought, that he could not see how jagged and full of temper she was. She wondered what the actress looked like, whether he'd found her attractive.

They sat in silence for a while. He shifted his hand gently on her leg. She didn't move.

'Want to go to bed?'

Corazón considered the question. She wanted to be smoothed and stroked and calmed but not particularly by him. She wanted to stop being angry but not like this. Robert put his coffee cup down on the floor and let himself fall across her legs, his arm curled around her knees, his head resting in her lap. She felt a disconnected shudder of desire. Her eyes closed; she put out her hand to touch his hair. Some people liked to be tied up.

She thought about the time she'd locked him in the same way. She couldn't imagine him feeling confined. He'd have been briefly annoyed, the way he was annoyed when she forgot to put the top back on the jam or when she left the milk to go off on top of the fridge. Then he'd have set his irritation aside, gone and switched on his beloved computer and got on with his work. Work. Suddenly Corazón's eyes flew open. She knew now what had changed his mood, why he'd said: 'Well, an actor and an *actress* to be absolutely precise'. He'd found someone to replace her in the play.

She dragged her knees out from under him, struggling to her feet.

'Hey! What's the matter?'

Now there would be no more talk of loyalty or principle or conscience. He would encourage her to take the job with TNT. He would be pleased she was bringing in some money. It was all so neatly solved, so incredibly tidy.

'Get a grip, Robert. It's Thursday,' she hissed, swinging her hair behind her like a rope. 'We can't just go to bed in the middle of a Thursday.'

For a moment he stared. Then he rolled into the space she'd left on the sofa, covering his head and pretending shame. 'Ah, Cora. My merciless Cora!' He kept laughing, waiting for her to join him. She half wanted to, but she was angry. It was all very well for him to be sweet now – now that he didn't need her any more.

She looked at him, lying there, his handsome face turned towards her, amused and unguarded. Today he wanted her to forget, but in future he would come back to this job as an example of her fickleness and vanity, he would hold it up to her as a test of integrity failed. He could talk you mad. He could prove up was down. And how could she complain? It was what she had loved about him once.

Corazón walked over to the window and looked out at the concrete view. The clouds raced like dogs across the big sky. There was a Londis bag blowing among the pigeons; a smaller scrap of paper whirling away – someone's bus ticket perhaps. What did they have to show for all these years, she thought. No house, no car, no child, just some scrappy little cuttings in a folder and a packet of someone else's table napkins in a rented kitchen. Not a tie in the world. They were absolutely free and unfettered, both of them. This was how he'd arranged it.

He lay on the sofa still, watching her lazily.

'The original escape artist, that's what you are, Robert,' she said softly under her breath, 'The original bloody escape artist.'

'Eh?' He sat up and looked at her, still laughing. 'What did you say?'

But now she was silent, thinking of all the things that lay out there beyond the edges of this view: other people, other places, other ways of living. Right now I could just about die of sadness at what we've lost, she thought. I could sink. On the other hand ... She thought of the improvisation they'd done in the afternoon of the audition, the new director yelling, 'Good. Good. Keep going! Don't get scared now. Reach right in and tap that rage, Ms Macmillan. *Use* the emotion! Use the whole of the stage. Travel!' And suddenly, far off in the distance, she saw a bigger, more untidy and exciting life where no one would mind if she left the top off the jam and couldn't cook. I could be good, she thought. I could be so bloody brilliantly good it's almost frightening. I have it in me – everything I need. I don't have to live through him any more.

'Eh? What?' Robert said again. 'What's so funny? Why are you laughing?' He held out one arm. 'Come over here you crazy bird ...'

But she stayed where she was at the window, smiling out at the speeding, tumbling sky. And in the room behind her a puzzled silence grew, active as a storm of bees.

Beware the Gentle Wife

Deborah Bosley

'But we've spent our entire married lives saving for this trip. It was only the thought of our tenth anniversary on the *QE2* that kept us married to one another,' said Angela with unnecessary candour. Usually biddable and compliant, she had taken the news that her husband planned to divert their savings into property with uncharacteristic anger. She threw down her handbag and keys in temper; they made quite a sound. Next, she kicked her shoes across the room where they buffeted the skirting board before coming to rest beneath the television. Adam stared at them, afraid to meet his wife's eye.

'Well?' she asked.

'But I thought you wanted to live in the country, I thought you'd be pleased.' He ran an exasperated hand through his shiny, floppy locks – where, Angela noted with some satisfaction, the first signs of grey were beginning to appear. Hers had needed monthly colouring for as long as she could remember.

'Well, I might have been pleased had we done it ten years ago, but it was you who wanted to stay in London. Besides, you can't suddenly announce six months before we're supposed to sail that you want to cancel, we'll lose our deposit.'

'It's only a thousand pounds, Angie, we're quite able to absorb temporary losses.'

Not for the first time, Angela wished her husband wouldn't talk to her as if she were a business associate. Adam was fond of jargon and she was appalled at how often 'proactive' and 'downsizing' crept into the most banal conversations.

'But the point is, Adam, I don't want to move. I like our house, and you haven't even bothered to discuss it with me. What about my job? What about your job?'

'Angie, look, I'm as disappointed as you are about the cruise, but this is an investment in the rest of our lives. Properties like this come along once in a lifetime and you don't find them in the estate agent's window. It's a private sale, Rupert's old family homestead, no estate agents, no commission. It'll be our family home.'

'We don't have a family.'

'Yes, but we will. Soon we will.' How many times had she heard that? She rolled her eyes heavenwards and padded over to the drinks trolley where she fingered the bottles, wondering which one would best calm her.

'I thought you'd be pleased to give up work, I thought this would make you happy. All I want is to make you happy, Angie.'

She doubted that very much.

When they were first married, in their early twenties, Angela was very keen to start a family. To 'get cracking', as her mother put it. She had never been very good at school and didn't see the point in hanging around for some mythical career to establish itself. But with her husband's urging she took a job in an advertising agency as a secretary and had surprised herself at her competence and popularity. Nine years later she was an account-manager for some very big clients in the financial-services industry. Her earnings were not far short of her husband's. Adam, on the other hand, had always been ambitious. Adam wanted to get on. Adam didn't want a family. Not yet, he would tell her, not yet, darling. Adam was in his office most nights until ten p.m., where he was, apparently, doing something unfathomable with stocks and shares.

In reality he had been doing something unmentionable with his colleague Sarah Barker for about three years. So close had he become with Miss Barker that he wanted to spend every night of the week with her in the Barbican flat she called her home. The strident, rude,

Cheltenham-educated Miss Barker was someone with whom he could share forever. After three years of deliberation – Adam knew the importance of 'thinking things through properly' – he offered to leave the devoted Angela. But much to his surprise, Sarah was adamant that she didn't want to marry. 'I'd rather not be cited in your divorce if you don't mind, darling,' she told him after the lovemaking which had spurred his declaration. 'You've got a perfectly nice wife, you don't need another one. And I, my darling, do not need you.' God, he adored her. Weekday nights had become not nearly enough for him. He had offered to make excuses to spend the weekends with her too but mysteriously Sarah always declined.

Adam was thirty-five and felt that time, something he hitherto seemed to have buckets of, was marching on. His colleagues all had families and they recommended two or three or four children close in age to help keep their wives occupied during the long hours their husbands were away in the square mile. With Sarah, that would not be an issue. She worked at least as hard as Adam. But children or not, he still he needed a wife who was comfortable in the financial world. Somebody to take to dinner parties with pride and confidence. He had long since given up taking Angela, who made no effort to disguise her boredom – yawning during the pudding course, looking at her watch, tapping her fingers on the table with irritation and other assorted acts of deliberate sabotage. Didn't she want him to succeed? He had no such worries with Sarah. Sarah was electrifying; aggressive and maddeningly sexy. She had a way of engaging her superiors in heated debate to the mutual relish of all. She was widely lusted after in the city and the announcement of their engagement would be sure to stir up envy and admiration. He could see it all – the nudges in the washroom, 'you're a sly old dog, Boon, we had no idea,' etc.

It was with happy and optimistic heart that he made his final proposal of marriage to her during a working lunch alone in the boardroom. The poised Miss Barker had eyed him wearily, sighed, put down her Mont Blanc pen on the table and responded.

'You are sweet darling, but you see I've already made arrangements.

I'm going to marry Robert Hyde-Smith in June. He's the son of an old friend of Daddy's, known him for yonks and we get on terribly well. It seems like the right thing to do. Just a small ceremony up in Northumberland with the family. You don't mind do you, darling? Don't look so sad, Adam, you've still got Angela.'

She gathered together her papers and stood up.

'I've a two-thirty meet at Barings, I must get going. Probably for the best if we don't meet after work anymore, darling. Robert's a sweetie, but the wedding's getting close and I'd rather not rock the boat if it's all the same to you.'

So ended the dreams of Adam Boon. The best three years of his life dismissed so nonchalantly over a prosciutto sandwich. Anger followed disbelief with great speed and was chased by the desire to show her that what he had really valued all along had been his marriage to Angela. Robert Hyde-Smith indeed. That evening as Adam travelled on the Northern Line from Bank to Clapham Common he luxuriated in an unaccustomed sensation of warmth and relaxation at the thought of returning home to Angela. He had occupied himself all afternoon figuring it out, idling over a sheaf of meaningless papers and refusing all calls. He'd been a bloody fool wasting all that time on Sarah in that cold, meticulous flat of hers. Think of all the energy he could have put into his career! Was the sex even that good with Sarah? What a strain it had put on him! How difficult it had made life! The lies and excuses – the blank incomprehension on Angie's face and the sniggering beneath the covers of Sarah's bed. 'So, I'm the debentures project that's keeping you late tonight, am I?' Sarah would rasp throatily, her voice hoarse from love. 'My FTSE Index appears to be up again, darling, let me fuck you just one more time before I go.' Adam blanched at the appalling bad taste that had passed for humour.

An advancing tide of relief neatly filled the space Sarah left behind. Adam reflected that she'd done him a favour, really, marrying another man – God knows, he didn't want her advancing shelf-life on his conscience. She was thirty-four. Pushing it a bit. And such a cold woman, too. Not like Angie. His Angie, waiting for him in their dishevelled home, probably on the sofa nursing a glass of wine surrounded by newsprint and old books. Lovely, warm Angie with her wide hips and sweet, scrubbed face. How dear she would look with a baby in her arms. How happy she would be when he told her that she could now have the longed-for children and a lovely home in the country to put them in. Rupert's old place was still up for sale, they could simply scotch the cruise and pour all the money into remodelling the elegantly decaying Georgian house. He foresaw it all – the commute from Dorchester to Waterloo in the mornings, exchanging good-natured jokes about the hell of school fees and muddy boots in the hall. It would be so easy to make Angie happy – a delightfully simple soul really, the kind of wife a man really needs. All great men eventually returned to their wives he reflected with satisfaction. He studied his fellow passengers on the tube – adulterers all, no doubt – and pitied them. The Sarahs of this world were fine for thrills, but could they ever make good wives? Adam thought not. As the tube disgorged its passengers onto the platform at Clapham Common, Adam eschewed the lift and took the steps up to street-level two at a time.

Placing himself gingerly next to his wife where she had settled on the sofa, Adam took a deep breath.

'We can drive down to Dorset next weekend and look at it. You'll love it, darling. It's an old forge; needs some doing up, but the money we'll save not going on the cruise will pay for a brand new kitchen and bathroom. You can even have an Aga if you like.'

'Oh goody' said Angela.

'Just look at it, darling. If you don't like it we won't buy it.'

'And in the meantime I'm to speak to Cunard and try and worm our deposit back out of them.'

'If you wouldn't mind, my love, you're so good at that kind of thing.' Adam reached for his wallet in the jacket he had draped over the back of the sofa. He took out his platinum American Express card and handed it to her. 'Why don't you get yourself something nice while you're at it; my way of saying sorry.'

Angela looked at the card thoughtfully then smiled up at her husband. 'You're sweet'.

'Good girl, darling, good girl.'

At 9.02 a.m. the following morning, Angela dialled Cunard's sales office from her desk in fashionable Westbourne Grove. 'It's Mrs Boon here, reference number KT4315HQ.'

Angela drummed her fingers softly on her leather-topped desk while the Cunard representative brought up her details on the screen.

'Yes, Mr Adam and Mrs Angela Boon booked on the Panama Canal and Caribbean cruise sailing on 22 October for nineteen nights. How can I help you, madam?'

'Several things. I'd like to make some changes to my booking. I'd like to cancel my husband's reservation and upgrade my own but for a different date. Are there any earlier sailings?'

The clerk informed Angela that indeed there was an earlier sailing, 'but the only available date we have for that particular cruise is on 3 April, Friday week. I suppose that's too soon?'

'No, Friday week sounds fine.' Angela was beginning to enjoy herself. In ten years of marriage she had deferred to her husband's wishes. In the beginning it was out of love, but the same deference, over time, had simply become habit.

'And which upgrade were you looking for?'

'What's the best cabin you have?'

'The best is our Grand Suite, but that's already booked. The next best is our Luxury Suite.'

'How much?'

'£8,654 including port taxes and handling for that particular cruise, I'm afraid.'

'Don't be afraid, just book it. Will a platinum American Express do?'

'Certainly, madam.'

Angela had ten days to make her preparations; she would compile a 'to do' list that evening. Adam arrived home unusually early from the office for the second night in a row and found Angela in the study with a large drink and notepad.

'Hello, darling.'

'Hello, darling.'

'Good day? Did you buy yourself something nice?'

'Very nice, thank you.' Angela drained her glass and held it out to her husband for a refill. Adam Boon loosened his tie and exhaled. He hadn't imagined the transition would be so smooth. It was a good sign; a sign that he'd done the right thing. This was what really mattered, a good marriage. He felt rather pleased with himself and unusually tender towards his wife. He returned from the drinks trolley with a brimming glass, which he handed to her.

'So, are you going to show me what you bought?'

'No darling, it's going to be a surprise.'

'The dress or the Amex bill?'

Adam guffawed at his good-nature; his wife lowered her lids compliantly but said nothing.

'I expect I'll get a nasty shock when the bill comes in. Thank goodness it's not due for another three weeks, I've just paid the last one.'

'Well, you know how us girls are when we go shopping. Especially when we want to punish our husbands for letting us down.' Her tone was light.

'I expect I deserve everything I get.'

'Yes darling, I expect you do.' Angela continued her list.

'What are you doing?'

'Making a list.'

'Of what?'

'Oh, nothing much, just odds and ends I need to catch up on.'

'Darling, you are efficient; it's no surprise they love you at work.'

Angela smiled ruefully. They hadn't loved her very much when she'd told them that afternoon that she was going on a month's leave at the end of the following week. She hadn't quite found the heart to tell them that she wouldn't be returning at the end of her leave.

'I'll leave you to get on with it then. Should I make us some supper?'

'That would be lovely, darling, thank you. Hold on a second.'

She reached into her handbag and returned Adam's card to him.

'I think I've done enough damage for one day, you'd better have this back.'

The days flew by. Angela hadn't figured how much work there was in revolutionising one's life in secret. First there was the matter of finding a new home to return to after her cruise. She withdrew the totality of their savings from the building society – £22,000 – to pay the annual lease on a luxury flat in Twickenham. She'd always loved Twickenham – so green. Once paid, that left £6,000 to tide her over until she found another job, but she was forever being headhunted by rival agencies, so that wasn't much of a worry. She cancelled all her lunch appointments to move the little she really cared for from her marital home into storage. When Adam asked where all the paintings had gone, she told him it was high time they had a professional clean. ('Excellent idea, darling, where would I be without you?') She could always liquidate them for a few thousand pounds if things got really tight. Most of her clothes she didn't much care for and toiletries and kitchen equipment were easily replaced.

By the following Thursday there was just the matter of packing and composing her letter to Adam before she left for her mother's house in Andover. So handy for getting to Southampton the following morning.

'Mummy's a bit low – I said I'd go down tonight, take Friday off and make a weekend of it. You don't mind do you, darling?' she asked her husband on the Wednesday.

'No, darling, I expect the break from London will do you good. But I'll be there to collect you Saturday lunchtime so we can go and see the forge. You'll love it, darling, you really will.'

The letter was the hardest. Where to start? It took three hours on Thursday afternoon to compose. Between paragraphs, Angela roamed their small but expensive home in Clapham, shedding the odd tear.

Finally, at 6.30 p.m., she left the letter on the kitchen table where she also deposited her keys and walked out of their front door for the last time.

Adam,

I expect it will come as something as a shock to find that I have left you. That was always the move you expected to make. I discovered your relationship with Sarah about two years ago. It was quite by chance. I was driving past Bank tube station one afternoon on my way to your firm, in fact, for whom I have handled small amounts of advertising in the financial press. I saw you and a striking redhead embracing outside the Bank of England. Strangely, I wasn't surprised. During my meeting that afternoon with Rupert, I mentioned that I had seen the same woman outside your offices and that she seemed familiar to me. I was fishing on the off-chance and was surprised that Rupert should be so obliging. 'Oh yes, our Sarah,' he began. He then told me all about her. Brilliant mind, first-class education, ballbreaker on the trading floor, etc, etc. He must have had a good lunch, because he then swore me to secrecy, said he was about to tell me something nobody else in the firm knew about her. Apparently, she had an illegitimate son when she was sixteen who was raised by her family in Northumberland so that she could pursue a career. Jasper, I think he said his name was. Jasper attends Wellington College and his mummy – your Sarah – visits him at weekends. She plans to work in the City until she can find a suitable husband and return to Northumberland for good. Isn't that neat? I presume you know nothing about young Jasper, or your hatred of children would soon have put paid to that romance.

To begin with I was devastated. Do you remember that winter I had shingles? But as time wore on I came to see your affair as rather helpful. It has been many years since we have enjoyed one another and as time wore on I actually found myself feeling grateful to this woman for saving me the bother of having to care for you at all. And

Deborah Bosley

yet I continued to harbour my little fantasies about our cruise on the QE2. Some part of me hoped we would rediscover one another, find again the spark that led us up the aisle so early in our lives. When you said you wanted to use the money to buy a house, I knew beyond a shadow of a doubt that she'd dumped you. Even I, your sweet, grateful Angela, could not abide that. And so, my darling, I am taking to the high seas without you. To put your mind at rest, I did buy a dress with your card – a rather daring number in fuchsia by Jasper Conran, which I plan to wear at the Captain's Dinner (night four, I believe) – but I also paid for my passage with it. But like you say, darling, we're more than able to absorb any temporary losses. Bon Voyage, my darling, and good luck. My solicitor will be in touch.

Angela.

Leda and the Swan

Fay Weldon

When Gosling was two, his body was smooth, plump and bronzed. He ran in and out of the waves at the water's edge and was happy. 'He's a real water baby,' his mother would say fondly. But she carried his little brother in her arms, and her eyes were even softer and kinder for the baby than they were for the little boy, and Gosling noticed.

She called the older one Gosling in pure affection; and the younger one Duckling, which was even more affectionate. Gosling once pushed Duckling under the bath water, but fortunately help came in time; for Duckling, that is, not Gosling.

'Did your mother hope you'd grow up to be a swan?' asked Gosling's wife, interested.

'I don't know what she thought,' was all he said. He would volunteer information about his past, but did not like his wife to be too inquisitive. His past was a private planet, full of unscalable heights and hopeless depths where he alone was brave enough to wander. 'Anyway,' Gosling added, 'it's ugly ducklings, not goslings, who grow up to be swans. My little brother was the one she had hopes for.'

'Well, I think you grew up to be a swan,' she said. They had been married for a year when she said that. She was proud of him: his fine dark eyes, his smooth skin, his sexual confidence; the gregarious fits which interrupted his more sombre moods. She felt she was very ordinary, compared to him. Her name was Eileen, but he called her Leda, and this gratified her very much.

Eileen met Gosling in a London park at the edge of a swimming pool. He was a Sunday father; he took his little daughter Nadine swimming while, he complained, his ex-wife entertained her lover. Nadine did not share her father's enthusiasm for the water; no, but she endured it with patience and polite smiles. She was a good girl. Eileen, that Sunday afternoon, splashed about in the water happily enough, though she did complain of its coldness. But then her parents kept a hotel in Bermuda: Eileen had spent her youth in warm water, chasing sail boats. English water was hard and bitter with chlorine: why did so many people want to go in it? The pool was crowded.

Gosling and Eileen collided underwater: he had to help her to the surface. His hand, firm upon her arm, seemed to transmit some kind of magnetic current: at any rate his touch acted like an electric shock. She squealed aloud and snatched her arm away in alarm; nearly sank. They touched again, tentatively. Again she let out a little yelp. That made him laugh. 'We are seriously attracted to each other,' he said as they surfaced, and she had to agree. She was eighteen: he was thirty.

When she pulled herself out of the pool, she felt awkward and unattractive; she regretted her freckled, friendly face, her strong, muscular body: men liked her, but that was all. She worried at once about her epileptic brother: she would have to confess to it. Then who would want her? Her brother's existence spoiled everything. Her eyes were pink and smarting. She wished she were not a swimmer: she would like to be Diana the Huntress, chaste and fair; icy and cool like the moon, not goose-pimpled.

'I like swimming,' Gosling said.

'I love it,' she said, and forgot about Diana and thought his brown eyes grew troubled for a minute, and then he dived back into the water and swam lazily and confidently up and down the pool, knowing quite well she was waiting for him.

'You could be a champion if you tried,' said Eileen, as they drank hot chocolate from the drink-dispenser. Her mother had told her the way to win a man was to flatter him, and Eileen wanted to win Gosling as never before had she wanted to win a man.

'I don't want to be a champion,' he said. 'I just enjoy the water.'

'Oh, so do I!' And so she did: she loved the buoyancy of her body in this murderous liquid, which healed and soothed when it didn't kill. Water was both adversary and friend: it parted in front of her, closed behind her. How powerful she was when she cleaved the water. Eileen cleaved unto Gosling the day they met, and after that they never wanted to part. Not really. She didn't tell him all the things that swimming meant to her; partly because she didn't know she was unusual and thought most people felt the same, and partly because she did not want to love what he only liked. While Eileen had an intense relationship with water, Gosling just swam. He'd swum, he said, in the Atlantic, the Pacific, the Mediterranean, the Black Sea, the North Sea, the English Channel; even in the Dead Sea.

'But the Dead Sea isn't really water,' Gosling said. 'Its just a chemical soup.' The Dead Sea had brought tears to his eyes. He hadn't liked that. He was an engineer and travelled the world, bringing back to Eileen, who became Leda on their wedding day, all kinds of strange presents.

Leda stayed home and looked after her stepdaughter Nadine, and presently her own baby Europa, and joined a swimming club and won a race or two.

Leda told Gosling about her victories when he returned from abroad and he raised an eyebrow. 'Swimming is something to enjoy,' he said; 'it shouldn't be something competitive,' and she was obliged to agree. He told her about the ocean rollers of Florida and the surfing there, so they thought about these natural wonders instead of victories at the local swimming club.

The family went for an excursion to the seaside; Gosling and Leda and Nadine and Europa; they pottered about rock-pools and avoided the patches of oil on the sand, and Leda tried not to wonder how far was the coast of France and just how fast she could swim there.

Gosling swam and dived and ducked and lashed about. He was, oh yes he was, the real water baby his mother had defined; he was the gosling who was never quite the duckling who never quite became a swan. He was passed over for promotion. Perhaps he had spent too much time on foreign beaches, and not enough in foreign offices. But he was the man who liked swimming: he thought the world well lost for that. His mother had died of cancer, painfully, when he was a young man, at the time when it seemed important for him to renounce and defy her: at the wrong time.

He felt his mother had given him contrary instructions. She had named him Gosling, in the hope of his becoming a swan: she had called him water baby, and water babies surely did not grow up.

When he was on foreign trips he was unfaithful to Leda. He stayed in hotels where there were swimming pools, and always some girl, who did not swim but splashed about, who would admire Gosling's prowess, his lazy confidence in the water, his wet, rippling muscles which gave promise of excitement to come.

'It doesn't mean anything,' Gosling would say to Leda. 'I like them, I don't love them.' Gosling did not believe in lying. We must be honest with each other,' he'd say.

Leda started training in earnest. Her times startled the trainer at the local swimming club.

'You're four seconds off the Olympic crawl record,' he said.

'Four seconds is a long time,' said Leda.

But she talked about it to Gosling when he returned from New Zealand, where the beaches are long, white and clean, and the girls likewise.

'Crawl is not a swimmer's stroke,' he said. 'It's the competitor's stroke. An antagonistic, angry sort of swimming. Nothing to do with water, just with doing down your fellow human beings. At best see crawl as the getting-somewhere stroke, not the being-someone stroke.'

Leda thereafter swam breast-stroke instead of crawl, to her trainer's annoyance, but soon excelled in that as well. She swam for the county team and won a cup or two. And then rather a lot of cups. They began to line the walls.

'Of course back-stroke is the one that requires real swimming talent,' said Gosling. It was his own best stroke, and Leda's weakest. They swam a jokey sort of race, one day, back-stroke, and he won, and after that they were happy for a time. But she knew she had not really tried to win; just been polite; won time and his favour, just for a little.

Gosling was good company, liked good food, good drink and bad women; he could tell a good story. For some reason, friends who liked sport faded away, or perhaps they were gently mocked out of the house. Presently there was no one to ask exactly what the silver cups on the sideboard were, or to care, or admire. The task of polishing them became oppressive; there was so much else to do. Gosling referred to them in any case as 'Leda's ego-trip' and she began to be embarrassed for them, and of them. The cups went into the spare-room cupboard in the end; the surfboard came out of it, and they went on family week-ends to Cornwall, where they all surfed.

Surfing made Leda impatient: she did not like waiting about for the waves, or the messy rough and tumble of the water in their wake. She wanted to conquer the water, cleave it, and enlist its help to do so: as a man about to be shot might be induced to dig his own grave. It was a horrible simile, but one which came to mind, and made her ashamed.

Gosling loved the surf and the thrashing water. 'You have to abandon yourself to the sea,' he said. 'And then you reap its benefits. How anyone can waste their time in swimming pools, I can't imagine. You know why your eyes hurt when you've been in them? It's other people's piss does the damage – not chlorine, as is commonly supposed.'

When Leda came home from the swimming pool her eyes would be pink and swollen. When Gosling admired other women – not unkindly or over-frequently – he would always refer to their bright, wide, young eyes.

Sometimes Leda's heart ached so much she thought she was having some kind of seizure. She could not distinguish physical from mental pain. Still she swam.

One evening, when Leda was eight years married, and within a year or two of being past her swimming prime – which Gosling would mention in passing from time to time – and actually in the running for the English Olympic team – a fact which Leda did not mention to Gosling at all – Leda made her usual excuses and left for the pool. This was the evening when the final Olympic selection was to be made. Evenings were family time and it was Leda's practice to stay home if she possibly could, but tonight she had to go.

As Leda walked out of the house, a young woman walked up to it. 'Someone called Gosling live round here?' asked the bright, clear-eyed young girl. 'He wrote the number on a cigarette paper, but I lost it. You know what parties are.'

'Not really,' said Leda. 'I'm usually looking after the children.'

'God save me from children,' observed the girl, 'and, after children, from husbands. This one's mother should have called him Jack Rabbit.'

And the girl walked one way and Leda walked the other, and that night Leda knocked two seconds off her best and was selected for the England team. Pain in the muscles alleviated pain in the heart: concentration on the matter in hand lessened the bite of jealousy. There was no pleasure in the victory, the record, the selection, the smiles of those who'd trained her, believed in her, and now saw their faith justified. All Leda felt after the race, as she smiled and chatted, and accepted adulation modestly and graciously, was the return of pain.

When Leda got home that night, the bedroom smelt of someone else's scent, but Gosling made love to her sweetly and powerfully, and the electricity glanced from them and round them and seemed to embrace the universe and she knew he loved her, in spite of everything; in spite of her annoying habit of winning, coming first, competing. 'She was only here,' he said when Leda commented on the smell of scent, 'because you weren't. You were swimming.'

The word had become bad; somewhere between sinning and shamming. Gosling hardly ever swam himself, these days. It was as if she had stolen his birthright. He, who should have been a water baby, should have gambolled for ever on the water's edge, was now forced by Leda on to dry, arid land. She was his mother's enemy.

Photographers took pictures of Leda. Her body, once so unluminous, prosaic, now seemed something remarkable and beautiful. With it went the nation's hopes.

'I can't have Europa exposed to this kind of thing,' said Gosling. 'It's one step up from skin-flicks. Surely the least you could do is allow them to photograph you *clothed*.'

'But I'm a swimmer,' said Leda. 'They have to take me in a swimsuit.'

'You hardly have the figure for it,' he said.

He looked at her body without affection, without admiration, and raised his eyebrows at the folly of the nation.

But always, when the time came and the flag dropped and the water embraced her in its deathly, lovely clasp, Leda would fight it back with its own weapons; she would make it her servant. She would say, vaguely, when people asked her if she was tired or cold or nervous, that she was used to hardship. No one quite understood what she meant by this, for a friendly engineer-husband and a little daughter significantly named Europa could hardly count as hardship.

Oh faster, faster: concentrate the will. In the last resort it is not the muscles, not the training, that counts; not up there at the extremity of physical achievement: no, it is the will; it is the pulling down from the sky of a strength that belongs to someone else; in some other world where fish fly and birds swim and human beings are happy.

Swimming, sinning, shamming. Water blinding eyes, deafening ears, to sights that should not be seen and sounds that should not be heard.

On the night of the European Championships, Leda's mother rang from Bermuda: her brother was dying.

'You must fly out at once,' said Gosling. 'Not even you, surely, can put a competition above life itself.'

But Leda did. At seven forty-five she was not on a Boeing 747 on her way to Bermuda, but at the pool's edge at Wembley. She took half a second off her best time, came in first, and only then did she fly out, and her brother was dead when she arrived.

'But you're glad he's dead,' observed Gosling when she cried. 'Don't be so hypocritical,' and he was right, she was, because the epileptic fits had frightened her when she was a child. The writhing, the jerking, the foaming; somewhere in her mind between sex and swimming; something to be ashamed of; something to be admitted to boyfriends, and be ashamed of being ashamed.

Swimming, sinning, shamming. Something held between the teeth to stop the tongue being bitten off. Or was that boxing?

Leda had loved her brother, all the same, as she loved Gosling. Part of her, part of life.

'And you thought winning a race more important than seeing him alive for the last time!' he marvelled.

'I don't want to win,' she said. 'I can't help winning. You make me win.'

He didn't understand her. Leda cried. The more she cried by night, the faster she swam by day, eyes tightly closed against water out, or water in.

'It must be difficult for Gosling,' people began to say, 'being married to someone as famous as you.'

Famous? Did that count as fame? Her picture on the back page, the sports' page, not even the front? The Olympics were coming up. Gosling certainly found that difficult.

'Europa needs a natural life,' he'd say. 'You should never have had a child.'

Leda cried. Naiad, child of tears, creature of mythology. If you wandered round Mount Olympus, you could always find a Naiad weeping in the corner of some pool; half-tree, half-water, all female; creating the tears that filled the pool, that gave you enough to swim in.

Europa went off to boarding school to be out of the glare of publicity.

Gosling insisted. Poor little girl, her mother an Olympic swimmer! How could a child develop normally, in such a home?

Tears gave Leda an ethereal look; added eroticism to her body. Her freckles faded, as if the kisses of the sun were of no avail against the embraces of the night. And how they embraced! Leda and her Gosling; Gosling and his Leda: the music of the spheres sang around their bed. By night, in the forgetful dark, all was well. By day Leda remembered Europa, whom she should never have conceived, and missed her.

'In a way,' said Gosling, 'I suppose you could see something epileptic about winning swimming races, swimming faster than anyone else. It has to be done in a kind of fit. It certainly lacks grace. A matter of frothing and jerks. I can see it runs in the family.' And he laughed. It was a joke. 'I hope Europa is spared.'

Europa, aged six, home for the holidays, ran a very high temperature on the eve of the next Olympic trials; she had convulsions.

'Of course she doesn't have epilepsy,' said the doctor, surprised.

'Of course she has epilepsy,' said Gosling. 'He's only trying to comfort you. But drugs control it very well, don't worry.'

'Next time her temperature gets as high as that,' said the doctor, leaving, 'sponge her down, don't wrap her up.'

Leda was chosen for the final team. Flashbulbs clicked. Gosling shut the door in the face of newspaper people.

'This is unendurable,' he said, and slept on his side of the bed, not touching. When she put down an ashtray or a vase of flowers he would move it at once to a different place, as if to signify she did not exist. He would sprinkle condiments lavishly upon the food she cooked, as if to change its nature; or would push away the plate entirely, and say he was not hungry, and go out and come back with fish and chips, and eat them silently. Gosling was increasingly silent. When she went out training, he did not raise his head: nor did he when she returned.

Europa's illness returned. The doctor remained puzzled.

Europa's fever rose. Now it was one hundred and six degrees. Gosling wrapped her in blankets.

'Don't, don't,' cried Leda. 'We must cool her down, not heat her up.

'That's nonsense,' cried Gosling. 'When I was ill as a child my mother always wrapped me up well. Don't fuss. It's your fussing makes her ill.'

Leda seized Europa up, hailed a taxi, and ran with her into the hospital. Here staff put the burning scrap in ice-packs and her fever fell at once. In the morning she was perfectly well, nor did the fever return. Leda missed an eve-of-tour practice, but that was all. She did not go back to Gosling. She stayed at the hospital that night and the next morning her mother flew in from Bermuda to take care of Europa, and said of course Europa should go to Moscow to watch her mother win a gold medal: anything else was not just absurd but nasty.

The next night they all stayed in an hotel; grandmother, mother and daughter; and laughed and talked and cracked jokes and ate chips while photographers clicked and reporters asked questions which she did not answer. Finally she drove them out, and had her family to herself.

Gosling rang Leda just before she left for Moscow to say he could not face life without Europa; he had taken an overdose of sleeping pills.

'Die then', said Leda, and went on to win the gold.

The French Boy

Amanda Craig

Everyone I knew envied the Stevens sisters because of the French Boys. Why, we asked our mothers, couldn't we have a similar arrangement? It would earn them money and (we would add cunningly) improve our French. But our mothers would always look at us and say, 'Are you mad? Of course not.'

Mrs Stevens herself was an object of pity, if not outright contempt. She seemed to be permanently stirring mince glop in the kitchen of her tall, thin house – the type that is now worth hundreds of thousands, but was in the seventies part of a crumbling terrace, each with a sort of surprised look, not unlike that on Mrs Stevens' own face at having sunk so low. You wouldn't believe it, to see her long lank pigtails and long faded skirts, but Mrs Stevens had once lived in Paris. The French Boys were from that time. The young Mrs Stevens had kept in touch with the families she had known as a child, despite the fact that she was poor, whereas they, we gathered, lived the kind of lives we saw in French films: effortlessly chic and wealthy. Mrs Stevens had made the big mistake of coming back to England, getting pregnant at eighteen by a lecturer at college and immediately having two more babies. Now her life as a divorcee was spent trying to do fifty different things with mince.

Anyway, once a year, a French Boy, always on a business course, would arrive at the Stevens' house. Inevitably, he was short-haired, absurdly dressed in a navy blazer and loafers with tassels, but still that acme of desirability – French. The Stevens girls would shriek with laughter and immediately begin a furious competition to seduce him.

Millie's technique with a French Boy was to mooch over to him after supper and say, in her languid croak, 'Want to listen to my records?' Then, once the French Boy was in her room, she'd lock the door and drawl, 'Want to sleep with me?' (Their English, she explained, was never quite up to the Anglo-Saxon, at least not in the beginning.)

Needless to say, this approach, although somewhat lacking in refinement, was always successful, possibly because Millie, like all the Stevens sisters, was extremely beautiful.

Tasha's technique was different. Cass and I always suspected this was because she was blonde and looked a bit like Joanna Lumley in *The New Avengers*. Her stratagem was to get her victim drunk and then play a variant of Strip Poker, the catch being that she often disappeared just when the climax seemed inevitable. One would often meet poor Philippe, Antoine or Guillaume bent double by the agonies of sexual frustration on the stairs, carrying floral tributes to lay at her feet in the hope of getting lucky. Indeed, by the time she left home, Tasha had acquired a small fortune in jewellery, including two engagement rings, which I'm afraid to say she felt not the slightest compunction to return.

It made Cass hopping mad. The French Boys went around with the dazed look of bullocks who had just encountered the knacker's bolt; nevertheless, they were all nice Catholic boys at heart and sufficiently consumed by guilt as it was, without adding the seduction of minors to their sins.

'The instant I'm sixteen, I'm going to have it printed on my T-shirt,' said Cass, who did not so much hold a torch for the latest French Boy as about 1,000 joss-sticks.

'You could have it put on your T-shirt now,' I pointed out.

'Yes, but they'd tell on me.'

'They' being her sisters, of course. Mrs Stevens just shut her eyes and went on with the ironing. However, Cass and I knew it was an immutable rule that, in all stories about three sisters, the youngest always came out on top. (We had not then heard of Chekhov.)

'Let's face it,' said Cass, 'I'm Cinderella. Here I am, the downtrodden virgin of the house, but someday my prince will take me away from this grotty existence and then those two bitches will have their noses massively put out of joint.

Meanwhile, Cass kept on trying with the French Boys; it was a secret consolation to me that she failed. In most friendships, as in love affairs, there is one who is ascendant. It was quite clear to both of us that Cass led and I followed. We listened to Joni Mitchell, read *Honey*, painted our nails Biba-black and had made up our minds to run away the moment that we could.

We dreamed of far-off horizons and exotic places. It was bad enough being the only girls in school who didn't have flared jeans and platform clogs, but being stuck in England was far worse. The French Boys offered the only possibility of escape; it was rather strange, the sisters thought, that they were never invited for a reciprocal visit.

'At least they could ask me,' said Cass, plaintively. 'It's not as if I've done anything to anyone. Yet.'

Her sisters had taught her the basic philosophy, of course: men are like dogs: you have to get the upper hand, otherwise they'll use you like a lamp-post. The other part of this was: men are like cats: they'll only come on to you if you aren't interested. All three sisters had watched their mother weep salt tears into the pot of glop from an early age. There she was, trudging around with one basket of laundry after another, or heaving the ancient Hoover up and down the stairs, and frankly, we agreed, she deserved all she got in penance for not having a bit more spirit.

Then, one cold spring day, there was a flamey roar, like that of a dragon, and a Porsche appeared in front of the terrace. Out of it stepped a young man in a black leather jacket. His hair flowed to the nape of his neck. He wore a yellow cashmere scarf and crimson boots with cuffs. He was even handsomer than Doyle in *The Professionals*. He was quite simply divine.

'Wow!' we all said, and even Mrs Stevens came out of her customary torpor and shot to the door, all fluttering rags and smiles. Maximilian was the son of her French godmother, she explained, the one with a castle.

Cass did her best to make me leave as soon as possible, but I dug my heels in. All three sisters came downstairs for supper and leaned against the Aga, smoking heavily and drooling with anticipation while the table was laid. Mrs Stevens stirred her pot of glop with special vigour and sent Millie out to the off-licence to buy a bottle of red plonk.

Maximilian came in. He sat down. He eyed the plate of mince doubtfully and took a mouthful. He swallowed and turned pale.

'You call zis food?' Then he looked at the wine and demanded, 'You call zis drink?'

To this day, I don't know why we didn't brain him with the bottle and reply, 'Yes, you stuck up git, like it or lump it,' but we were all under his spell. Mrs Stevens was mortified and so were the three sisters. I was mortified – and I was just an observer.

And so it went on. Every morning, the girls would emerge for breakfast pale and lovesick, and Maximilian would disdainfully brew a small pot of real coffee and then shoot off to the business course in his Porsche. Every evening, the sisters would assemble round the Aga like three miserable, moulting birds. They lost their looks as well as their hearts. Their beauty had been dependent on an air of ruthless detachment; now it was gone.

Stripped, Millie, Tash and Cass became, well, just three north London girls with fraying nerves and split ends. They did not give up, of course. Each was convinced he was hers, as soon as she'd got her breath back.

But when Millie asked this French Boy if he'd like to listen to her records, he demanded, ''Ave you Piaf?'

'No, I'm afraid not,' said Millie, humbly. Maximilian shrugged, and that was the end of it. Tasha had only slightly more success. She got him plastered. But Tasha, unfortunately, became more so, and at the point where she usually suggested the game of Strip Poker, she burst into tears and ripped open her dress. Maximilian wouldn't so much as glance at her from then on. But Cass was undaunted.

'Perhaps he has got a girlfriend already,' I suggested.

'No.'

'How d'you know?'

'We steam open his letters,' she said.

'Then he must be gay.'

'He's got a copy of *Playboy* under his bed.'

'Well, then, perhaps he thinks all women have staples through their belly buttons.'

It soon became clear that, far from being uninterested in the opposite sex, Maximilian was an enthusiastic admirer. Every other night a different girl would stagger up the stairs to his room. The three sisters would listen, grim-faced, until the intruder staggered back down the stairs with a look like the cat that had got the cream. Except that these girls never came back.

'It's obvious,' said Tash eventually. 'It's because we're the landlady's daughters.'

'What?'

'Well, there can't be any other reason. I mean, just look at some of them.'

'They are older than you,' said Cass.

'In that case,' said Millie, 'we've got to get him to stay with someone else. But who?' Their eyes swivelled towards me ...

Millie did something, involving a disgusting brown stain, to the ceiling of his room and told her mother he'd done it. Luckily, my mother and Mrs Stevens seemed to spend half their lives drinking instant coffee in each other's kitchens, discussing whether they should take a lover or try smoking pot. Mrs Stevens obviously didn't mention the stain, and I think my mother had second thoughts after she actually saw Maximilian, but my air of indifference must have fooled her.

The three sisters revived at once and decided to throw a party. It was a perfect evening. In fact, it was a revelation to see how even Mrs Stevens could look, divested of her wooden spoon. She wasn't so ancient – indeed, she must have been only a year or so older than I am now. Not that Cass, Tash or Millie noticed. They were having too good a time, smoking dope and ensuring none of the others managed to corner the French Boy.

'What's the plan?' I asked Cass.

'Wait until he's had a few, then do a Millie.'

'Hasn't Millie done a Millie already?'

'She patently isn't his type.'

'So what is his type?'

'Me,' said Cass, with total self-assurance. 'I'm a nymphomaniac virgin; isn't that every man's dream?'

'What if you don't like it? Sex, I mean.'

Cass gave me a pitying look; but it was my turn to pity her. For around midnight, it transpired that nobody could find Maximilian. He had disappeared into his old room with a woman, nobody knew who. The three sisters got rid of their guests and waited on the stairs, white with rage. Overcome with curiosity, I waited too. We were awake all night.

'I'll kill whoever it is, absolutely kill her,' said Tasha. 'That dope cost me a fortune.'

At 8 a.m., Maximilian's door was still locked. About noon, out came ... Mrs Stevens, radiant with happiness and looking about eighteen. We, on the other hand, were absolutely wrecked.

'Who would think he'd prefer an old crone of thirty-five to us? D'you think she realises it's only a one-night stand?' Tasha whispered as we listened to her singing.

But it wasn't. To the astonishment of everyone, and the infinite chagrin of her daughters (who went to live with their father), Helen Stevens became Maximilian's wife.

Did she want revenge on her daughters for taking her youth? I don't know. It certainly never occurred to us that Cinderella could be over thirty, and divorced. She's still beautiful, for the marriage was a success, producing a son. He's eighteen, and coming to stay. For, just like his mother, I am a great believer in French Boys.

The Sound of the Horn

Clare Colvin

The water, ruffled by the wind, laps at the banks in an insistent under-tone. The rushes nod their feathery heads. The *étangs* are full with the winter's rain. They glint in the spring sun like curved pools of mercury.

At intervals, cars with horse trailers drive along the narrow road that runs between the two largest *étangs*. The tall trailers are harnessed to lowslung Peugeots or Citroëns, a combination that seems designed to part company at any moment. In the woods near the château fifteen trailers are already parked off the road. The horses clatter onto the tarmac. The hunt followers watch amid a buzz of conversation. The watchers wear green wellingtons with sage sweaters and corduroys, *comme il faut* for the occasion.

A huntsman in dark green opens the door to the hounds' trailer. The road is deluged with seething brown and white and waving sterns. The hounds are so eager for the chase that they are falling over each other. Now the stragglers of the hunt are arriving, a few riders who have hacked over and a late trailer or two. The Master of Hounds shoulders his hunting horn and waves at the new arrivals, then nods to his leading huntsman. It is time to begin the first draw.

The procession of horsemen follows the hounds, presenting to the eye-level of the onlookers leather saddles, booted legs and the glossy rumps and swishing tails of the horses. Look up at the riders' faces and you see a conscious pride, an awareness of the rightness of things. It is Easter Sunday and what better day to go hunting? There is pride in their horses, pride in the exercise, pride in the wildness of this perfect hunting country on the edge of the Touraine. For a few hours the present day is forgotten as they follow ardent tradition. The baying hounds, the call of the horn, the boar crashing through undergrowth deeper into the woods, taking them along the paths of their forebears. Through the wood they ride, breathing in the subtle yet heady scent of may blossom that swathes the blackthorn like *crème de chantilly*.

Now the last huntsman is passing by, riding a spirited chestnut horse that contains its energy by playing with the bit, dropping and catching it between its teeth. The rider is wearing a forest-green jacket and a leather belt at his waist to which is strapped a dagger in silver-chased scabbard. Round his shoulder, held in place by his upper arm, is a ring of shining brass – the coiled hunting horn. Beneath the velvet riding hat his face bears the conscious pride of the hunters, and a pride, too, in himself. He is in his mid-forties yet exudes an awareness of his attraction. The aquiline nose, the olive complexion, the unusually thick dark lashes and the hazel eyes are imbued with well-being verging on arrogance. In the shaped green jacket his body, though not slim, looks muscular. In a few years' time he will be overweight but at this moment, as he rides by, he is in his prime.

There is such energy in his physique, such confidence, that it is a shock to see his companion, who rides a few paces behind. She is young, about fifteen, and dressed in a black jacket that is loose on her frame. Her face is pale, her hair dark and straight, and she sits round-shouldered, holding the reins slack so that her horse's neck extends inelegantly. No marks for posture, for either horse or rider.

Just as your eyes were caught by the energy of the man so you are now struck by its negation. You can only wonder as you look at the girl, at the face without expression. You can only look and wonder, so young and so lifeless? How can that be? The man rides on and even in his green-clad back you read an overweening confidence.

You would find it even more curious were you to see Céline in other circumstances. At school, for instance, the expressionless face is full of life. She laughs, she gossips with her friends, she answers the teachers' questions brightly. It is only when she returns home that she assumes the blank mask.

It has to do with her father, naturally, the man in the hunting green with the complacent air. Céline, the watchful daughter, knows things that escape her mother. She found him out when she was ten. It was after the birth of her brother, little Jean-Luc, when Maman had been convalescing in hospital. A neighbour, Madame Cuvier, had been helping out at home. Céline can still see the scene that afternoon in early summer. She has returned from school and is sitting, as she sometimes does, against the banisters on the landing at the top of the stairs. It is a good place to hear where everyone is. There is a late afternoon hush and the sunlight slanting through the window has induced a warm somnolence. She hears the click-click of Madame Cuvier's high-heeled sandals on the polished floor of the drawing room. She sees her from her perch above, as Madame Cuvier crosses the hall. Madame Cuvier's light brown hair spills over her shoulders and halfway down her back. She is wearing a red vest and blue jeans. Her father is with her, but neither is talking, as if something has stopped their conversation. Madame Cuvier pauses by the staircase and turns towards him. For a moment their bodies are so close that Céline expects her father to be irritated, for he dislikes being crowded. Madame Cuvier says, and her voice has a husky catch to it, 'I must go home. I am expecting Charles back very soon.'

Her father's face is only a few inches from Madame Cuvier and Céline thinks, with the hot and cold embarrassment of an eavesdropper who is getting more than was bargained for, that they are about to kiss. But instead he says, and his voice has the same huskiness, 'Tomorrow, then?'

'Tomorrow will be easier,' she says. She puts her hand to his face and touches his mouth with one finger. He sways towards her but she has slid away from him and Céline hears the click-click of her heels as she walks to the front door.

'Don't forget,' he says in that low voice and the click-click pauses for a moment as she is lost to Céline's view. She hears the front door open and close and then she can only hear her father breathing. He sighs, with a forceful expulsion of air from the lungs, and walks up the stairs, his steps heavy on the polished wood. It is too late for Céline to escape. But he only glances at her absent-mindedly and says, 'How long have you been there?' – then, without waiting for an answer, goes into the bedroom and shuts the door.

After the Cuviers left the area there must have been someone else, for her father seemed to develop an interest in antique furniture and began to frequent auctions at Châtellerault. Céline would have known nothing for sure had not one of the school gossips told her that she had seen a woman getting out of their maroon Citroën by the main square. Céline's father had been at the wheel, she said, and watched for her reaction. The woman had red hair and was wearing a black leather mini-skirt. Céline said the first thing that came into her head: 'That would be our cousin Mathilde from Normandy. She is staying with us.' The gossip looked unconvinced, but said no more.

Céline wondered as she helped her mother in the kitchen whether it might be a kindness to tell her. Would she frown so anxiously over the cooking if she knew of her husband's monumental ingratitude? Olivier was not only unfaithful but a mealtime martinet. Céline remembered the incredulity of her schoolfriend Lucie at the pains her mother took.

'Maman just slaps it on the table and if Papa says, "What's this then?" she says, "If you don't like it, go and eat at the Vieux Logis."'

'My mother would never dare do that,' gasped Céline.

Lucie shrugged. 'Maman hasn't cooked anything for a year. She buys from the *traiteur* or else they go out to eat. She caught him cheating, you see, and now she hasn't the stomach to cook for him.'

Céline's resolution to tell her mother faltered at the thought of the ensuing breakdown in the cuisine. The unspoken knowledge about her father festered inside her. She became closer to her mother, providing comfort with her constant help, and was cool towards her father, as if to say, You may have fooled her but I know what you're about. Anna's wistfulness, as she went gently into middle age, touched her heart. Olivier, on the other hand, was resolutely youthful, maintaining that the forty lengths he swam daily was for the joy of exercise rather than the beginning of a losing battle against the years.

As her father's appetite for life increased, so Céline's diminished. At table, she insisted on small portions and picked at her food. Her mother would say, 'Are you not well, *ma petite*? Your little brother eats more than you do.'

Céline could hardly say, Your gross husband puts me off my food. But it was something about Olivier's expansive way of eating, his habit of scraping up the last glimmer of sauce, that made her pick ever more daintily, as if to show up his greed. She tried not to look at him while he was eating, but inevitably her eyes would be drawn to see if he was still as repellent. He would be sitting at the head of the table, an amused expression on his face as he looked at her plate.

'Céline is on the ultimate diet,' he would say. 'You must eat or you will fade away, and the boys won't look at you.'

Céline knew open hostility was impolitic. He was, after all, the provider. It was through him that they lived in a substantial house with shuttered windows on the edge of Neuilly-St-Martin. It was through him that they were able to keep two horses at the riding stables a few miles away, and it was he who often saved her the trouble of bicycling there, by taking her in his car, though his willingness to give her a lift had something to do with the fact that Madame Dubois was often, coincidentally, at the stables at the same time.

Her eyes were drawn to her father's hand loosely encircling the stem of his glass. A short, strong hand with a diamond pattern of lines on the olive skin. The hand that had touched Madame Dubois. Quite innocently, it might have seemed to a more detached observer. Madame Dubois had been leaning against the fence overlooking the training paddock, her right hand resting on her left forearm. She was wearing a short-sleeved shirt and jodhpurs. Olivier was standing beside her as they watched a horse being schooled. His hand had covered hers for a moment, and she had remained perfectly still. Their eyes met, and only then did she move away with a studied casualness. Céline had seen it all as she rode back from the far side of the paddock.

If she was asked what she particularly despised about Madame Dubois, she would have said, Wearing cosmetics with riding clothes. Hacking jackets *à l'anglais* did not go with lipstick and eyeshadow but no one had told Madame Dubois. She had moved to the area the previous summer with her husband, a banker from Paris, and, removed from her Parisian friends, had taken up riding again for occupation.

The first time Madame Dubois had joined the hunt, she had been kitted out as if competing in a dressage event in a made-to-measure black jacket that gave her an hourglass figure, white breeches, polished leather boots and a silk stock fastened with a gold pin. Other riders wore peaked hard hats, but Madame Dubois had a bowler with a curly brim. It provided a flattering frame for her *maquillage*. The huntsmen welcomed Madame Dubois, for she had the qualifications for instant entrée. She was rich, she was attractive, she rode well. Céline thought the huntsmen easily fooled, for she could see that underneath the *maquillage* the skin had lost its bloom, and there were lines, like brackets, around her mouth. Madame Dubois could not be a day under thirty-five yet she carried on as if she were Helen of Troy.

Nowadays, Céline judged the success of the hunt not by the speed of the chase but by the presence or absence of Madame Dubois. When she had been away for a few weeks on a trip with her husband, Céline felt the atmosphere of the hunt relax into the way it used to be. It was not just her father who was affected by Madame Dubois. She had the whole lot of them straightening their ties and drawing in their stomachs. Even the Master of Hounds, Monsieur de Laclos, softened to the dubious charm of Madame Dubois. She was one of those women, thought Céline, who demanded homage.

On this Easter Sunday she had hoped that Madame Dubois would have other commitments, but she could tell from her father's behaviour that this was not the case. They had left the house late after he had made a last-minute change of clothes. He had put on too much aftershave and it permeated the car. Céline wound down her window and remarked, 'I hope the hounds won't be put off the scent.'

'Why should they be?' he asked, but she simply said, 'What a beautiful day!' and lapsed into silence, feeling the breeze on her face. They were among the last arrivals. Céline watched Papa as he centred his hat carefully, using the car's extended wing-mirror. He peered at his face in the mirror, touched his well-shaved cheeks and drew his lip up to glance at his teeth. Céline suddenly felt what it must be like to be over forty, to need constant reassurance that everything was still in the right place. What will it be like when his teeth go? She felt a moment's protectiveness, then he straightened up, his well-pleased expression in place, and said, 'What are you waiting around for? We're already late.'

The last of the riders, they passed by the gathering, their boots on a level with the spectators' eyes. Dauphin champed at his bit and Olivier, one hand on the reins, lightly checked him. Céline let the reins lie on the neck of her bay pony, Alouette. Through the trees she glimpsed the large grey roan and the unmistakable hourglass figure of its rider. Céline's shoulders hunched. It was another day over which Madame Dubois would cast her well-maquillaged shadow.

Madame Dubois reined in her horse so that Olivier and Céline could catch up, and they rode on together to the draw. Olivier left them to take up his position as huntsman on the edge of the woods. As Madame Dubois turned, Céline noticed the mascara on her lashes was the sort which had thickening filaments. A particle had settled on her smoothly powdered cheek.

Really, Madame, thought Céline, you are going to look a mess by the end of the day.

As if she had read her thoughts, Madame Dubois took a compact from her pocket, looked at the mirror, then flicked off the speck. She smiled at Céline and said, 'We are all going to get very warm today. The sun is really beating down.'

A waft of expensive perfume drifted towards Céline. Jasmine with an undertone of musk. She said, looking straight ahead of her, 'I hope the hounds won't be put off the scent.'

'Why should they be?' asked Madame Dubois.

'It's such a warm day, isn't it?' Céline replied, and thought to herself, They are both exuding odours like a pair of skunks.

Madame Dubois edged closer to Maître Roland, the *notaire*, and began to chat to him, heedless of the rule of silence while the coverts were being drawn. Céline, relieved of her presence, breathed in the air. Now that the source of heavy perfume had removed herself, she could smell the indefinable yet unmistakable scent of may blossom. The hounds whined in the undergrowth, and there was a crashing of branches and a deep baying from the leader which was taken up by the entire pack. Monsieur de Laclos sounded the hunting call. Olivier raised his horn and blew the chords of 'quarry away'. The horses surged forward in anticipation, regardless of their riders.

The boar was mature, but fast as well. He took them through the woods where some of the riders crashed against the trees and bruised their knees or lost their hats. He went over the roughest terrain in the open, doubled back along water and ran across the scent of some hunt followers who had got ahead of the hounds. Monsieur de Laclos blew on his horn and gesticulated furiously at them.

'There are always a few *enmerdeurs* who get in the way,' Monsieur Charonnat said to Céline. They had been riding together since Alouette had stumbled and Céline had nearly ended up on the ground. Monsieur Charonnat had blocked off Alouette's escape route while Céline struggled back into the saddle. Georges Charonnat, who farmed in the next commune to Neuilly-St-Martin, had been a huntsman for twenty years and had supplied the hunt with ten couples of the best Haut Poitou hounds. He muttered, 'Those sort of people would be better off playing tennis. Weekend riders are not worth the trouble.'

They watched as the hounds cast around trying to pick up the scent. Monsieur Charonnat took an apple from his pocket, saying, 'A fine lunch for Easter, isn't it?'

'His dinner will be better,' said Monsieur Brosset, who had ridden alongside. Monsieur Brosset had a humorous face and spectacles that were dislodged frequently by the brim of his hat. He owned a building firm and was prosperous since the arrival of *les anglais*, with their curious idea that derelict barns could be turned into gracious country mansions.

'We're having gigot for dinner,' said Monsieur Charonnat. 'Gigot aux flageolets and moules to begin with. I got a bucket of them at the market yesterday. My wife nearly had a fit. She makes a wonderful moules marinière.

'With all this chasing of the boar, we should be having *sanglier* for dinner,' said Monsieur Brosset. 'What's the point of chasing something you don't eat?'

Monsieur de Laclos was gesticulating in their direction. Monsieur Charonnat gesticulated back, pointing at the ground.

'I'm dammed if he's going to get me crashing around in the woods looking for the boar. I need a breathing space,' said Monsieur Charonnat.

'The tired huntsman,' said Monsieur Brosset. 'You're all dropping like flies. I passed Olivier a while ago and he said he thought his horse was going lame.'

'The horse was going lame?' echoed Monsieur Charonnat. There was a reflective silence. Céline gazed around at the riders near the woods.

'He's not there,' she said. 'When did you see him?'

'Half an hour ago, I don't know,' shrugged Monsieur Brosset. 'Perhaps he will catch up now that we've stopped.'

'Not if the horse is lame,' said Monsieur Charonnat. The silence continued as they surveyed the followers of the field. Céline knew that they were, like herself, trying to ascertain the whereabouts of Madame Dubois.

Monsieur Brosset and Monsieur Charonnat exchanged glances. Unless she was lost in the depths of the wood along with the boar, she appeared to have left the hunt. The thoughts running through the men's minds were almost audible to Céline. Finally Monsieur Charonnat ended the silence.

'I've eaten boar that I've chased,' he said.

Monsieur Brosset gave a laugh, which he ostentatiously stifled.

'After it was hung,' Monsieur Charonnat went on, 'we marinated it for two days. With juniper berries. We cooked it for four hours in a slow oven in its juices and we had fresh chanterelles. It was delicious. Sanglier à la Rabelaisienne.'

Monseiur Brosset was struggling to control his mirth. He gasped, 'You must give me the recipe.'

The sound of the horn floated through the air together with the baying of the hounds.

'They've picked up the scent,' said Monsieur Charonnat. The call rang out again, and he sighed, 'Ah, what a sound! The mournful notes ... "*Dieu, que le son du cor est triste au fond des bois ...*"'

'Dubois', corrected Monsieur Brosset with a smirk.

'Des bois', insisted Monsieur Charonnat. 'It's the only line I remember, but I know each word.'

Monsieur Brosset was about to explain his little pun, but Monsieur Charonnat looked at him coldly, and he fell silent.

'Perhaps I should try and find Papa,' said Céline.

'Let Papa look after himself,' said Monsieur Brosset. 'I'm sure he's perfectly capable. Come along with us and enjoy the rest of the hunt.'

But her father's absence had filled her mind with a nagging distraction and at the next check she said, 'Alouette and I have had enough for the day. I'm going back now.'

As she turned away, she saw Monsieur Brosset edging over to no doubt to give his opinion on the whereabouts of Olivier. She took off her jacket and slung it in front of the saddle, feeling the warmth of the sun on her back. Away from the commotion, she could absorb the atmosphere of the surrounding country, the reed-lined ponds glinting in the sun, the tussocky grass emphasised by shadow. In winter the area was desolate and wreathed in mist, and you could believe the folk tales of ghostly hunters and hounds, of spirits that led you to lose your way in the marshes. Its character changed with the spring and summer because of the outsiders who came to fish and hunt. At weekends it was a sportsman's playground. She saw three men walking along the road, shouldering guns. Half the weekend people were galloping out of control and the other half were shooting at anything that moved. It was surprising there had not yet been an accident.

Céline retraced their earlier route. She felt at peace on her own, listening to the pigeons cooing, the whisper of a breeze through the aspens that turned the new leaves into sparkling points of light. The woodland thinned out into a large clearing that filled her with delight for it was hedged by banks of may blossom, swathe upon swathe spreading abundance in a sea of creamy foam. She rode round the side of the meadow close to the flowers. The air was filled with the humming of insects. Céline straightened her shoulders and breathed in the pervasive scent. It made her feel lightheaded.

As she rounded a curve in the thorn trees she saw more meadow and more banks of may blossom. At the edge of the woods, its reins knotted round the branch of a tree, was the grey roan of Madame Dubois. Its head drooped in a daze of boredom and it rested its hind leg. Nearby, with his head down, grazing, was Dauphin. He snorted at Alouette, then continued to nibble the grass. Strapped to the front of the saddle was Olivier's hunting horn.

Céline reined in Alouette. She was immobilised by an overwhelming curiosity. After a while she heard the sound of voices. Into the clearing emerged her father and Madame Dubois. Olivier was carrying on one arm his own green and Madame Dubois' black jacket. His other arm was round Madame Dubois. Céline could see her breasts under the carelessly buttoned shirt, free and mobile without the tailored constraint of the jacket. Her face looked younger and her arch expression had dissolved into dreaminess. Olivier was looking at her face with the indulgence Céline remembered from seeing him with Jean-Luc as a baby; the kind of look that is directed at the young and defenceless and loveable – that should not be directed at someone like Madame Dubois.

Olivier saw Dauphin grazing and said, '*Merde*. He's broken the reins.'

He handed the jackets to Madame Dubois and walked across to the straying horse. His shirt was tucked haphazardly into his breeches and, unlike Madame Dubois, he was wearing his boots. Did that mean, Céline wondered, that Papa had made love with his boots on? She could not imagine anything more gross.

Madame Dubois had turned away to pull on her boots, bracing her foot against the tree to which her horse was tethered. Olivier walked towards Dauphin and then stopped, for he had caught sight of Céline. He froze in midstride and stared at her with the baleful eyes of a cat, the affront at being intruded on far stronger than the guilt. His right hand strayed unconsciously towards his flies as if to check the fastening. As Céline felt his anger directed towards her, she looked away, and, giving Alouette a tug on the reins, rode back towards the road. She felt a constriction in her throat, the tension of having encountered something irrevocably unpleasant. Yet at the same time, why should she herself feel guilty? she wondered. It was Papa who had been caught out.

Not long after she had reached the trailer, the two of them emerged through the trees. Madame Dubois, not looking at Céline, rode towards her trailer. Olivier dismounted from Dauphin and handed the reins to Céline, saying, 'Hold him for me, will you, while I help Suzanne with her horse.'

His eyes were as neutral as if he was asking for a kilo of potatoes. She looked at him to see if he acknowledged their earlier meeting, but he was already walking over to the other trailer. She saw them leading the grey in and Olivier securing the door, and then the two of them in conversation. Madame Dubois looked towards Céline and they moved to the other side of the trailer where she lost sight of them. Then she heard a car door slam and an engine starting up. Olivier waited until Madame Dubois had driven off, then returned to Céline and said, 'Right, let's get these horses in.'

Without a word, Céline helped lead the horses into the trailer, her mind occupied with finding a way of opening the matter of his blatant infidelity. A statement that would shame him, would make him realise that the shabby way he behaved towards her mother was not to be tolerated. That if he had no morals, at least his daughter had and she would not be a party to his deception. She guessed what he had said to Madame Dubois when she had looked towards Céline. '*Oh, Céline ... that's all right, she won't say anything.*' He assumed that she would keep quiet, as she had before.

She hated sitting next to him in the car. He had thrown his jacket onto the back seat, and she could smell his sweat through his shirt, and a faint scent of may blossom in the air. She was repelled at being confined with him, her eyes drawn reluctantly to his hand on the gear stick, to the way his knee moved as his foot engaged the clutch. There was a mark of brushed-off earth on the breeches. She tried to put from her mind an image of him in the wood, an image that nevertheless recurred, of him kneeling on the ground, helping Madame Dubois off with her boots. She framed an opening question in her mind, 'How could you do this to Maman?' – but the question hovered unspoken, and the one which kept interceding, one that she would die rather than ask, was 'What do you think of Madame Dubois now?'

Olivier glanced at her closed face, as if inviting a discussion, but she stared in front of her. He changed to fourth gear, hummed a tune to himself, drove sedately on. Eventually he said conversationally, 'They are probably still chasing the boar. Where had they got to by the time you left?'

So that's his game, thought Céline. He is going to find out how the hunt went, so that he can tell it to Maman as if he had been there.

'We went round in circles,' she said. 'Up and down, round and round.'

'Sounds fascinating,' said Olivier.

She remained silent, refusing to say more, and stared out of the window at the passing countryside bathed in sun. She sensed a growing impatience from her father as her silence continued. Finally he said, 'You're as talkative as Marcel Marçeau, aren't you? And rather less amusing.' He switched the radio to France Musique. The rich sounds of an orchestral symphony filled the car.

As he listened to the music, his expression relaxed into a smile. The lush romantic strings diminished as the horn asserted its clear voice in a hauntingly sweet solo.

'If only I could play like that, I'd die happy,' remarked Olivier. Céline looked at him in disbelief and thought, You'd die happy with your boots on. Olivier turned the volume higher and asked, 'Guess the composer?'

Céline shook her head.

'It must be Tchaikovsky,' he said, 'but which symphony?'

'Could you please turn the volume down, I can hardly hear myself think.'

'Ah, you're thinking, are you?' asked Olivier in mock astonishment.

'I'm thinking,' said Céline, seizing her opportunity, 'and a lot of people are thinking. Monsieur Charonnat and Monsieur de Laclos are thinking about where you were when you were not at the hunt, and particularly Monsieur Brosset, to whom you told your story about a lame horse. Monsieur Brosset found it curious that you disappeared at the same time as her.'

'Monsieur Brosset has nothing better to occupy his mind with than speculating on what other people may be doing,' replied Olivier. 'I advise you not to fall into the same trap.'

He looked at her with a hard expression, and she turned her head away angrily and resumed her silence. As they turned into the yard of the riding stables, the music welled from the open windows of the car in a crescendo. A stable lad was walking Madame Dubois' horse to the water trough, but she had already departed. Olivier drew the car to a halt and continued to listen to the music. He frowned, as if about to say something, then paused as he thought again. Céline waited for him to speak.

'Tchaikovsky's Fifth,' he said. 'In E minor. I'm sure of it.'

For dinner that evening Anna had made her terrine de brochet. They sat round the dining table, a family of four, gathering after the day's distractions. Olivier had bathed and changed as soon as they had returned, and was now wearing a navy sweater and denims. His hair was newly washed and he exuded cleanliness. Céline sniffed as he poured her a glass of wine, and could detect no trace of the disgusting aftershave.

Olivier asked Anna, with an air of interest, 'How was Grand'mère today?'

'In very good health,' replied Anna. 'She had Tante Louise to lunch as well and she gave us her coq au vin. She said to let you know she missed you but I told her you were indispensable to the hunt. Did the hounds get the boar?'

'I shall find out tomorrow,' said Olivier. 'Dauphin strained a tendon so we had to leave before the end, but the boar was still giving them a chase, though inclined to go round in circles, wasn't he, Céline?'

'In any case, you both look very well from your day out,' said Anna. 'You have quite a colour from the sun.'

Olivier caught Céline's eye. He had a demure expression, and she realised she had been manoeuvred into colluding with him. As if it was not enough to cheat on Maman, he was now assuming her collaboration. Unless she spoke out, she would be an accessory to his infidelity, in complicity with him against her mother.

She stared coldly at him as she helped her mother clear away the plates. She must say a few words in the kitchen away from the ears of Olivier and of Jean-Luc. Yet her mother was now immersed in taking the pommes boulangère from the oven and arranging the gigot on a dish. Céline took the plates from the dresser and returned to the dining table, placing them heavily before her father. She directed a thought at the back of his head: Don't expect me to fall in with your game.

'Do try to put the plates down with more grace, Céline,' he said. 'You are dealing with Sèvres, not kitchenware from Prixunic.'

She kept her eyes turned from him during the rest of the meal. If he noticed her remoteness he gave no sign of it, and continued to talk to Anna and to exhort Jean-Luc to finish his food. After the cheese there was one of Anna's special tartes tatin. Olivier put his hand over hers.

'A wonderful dinner, *chérie*,' he said. 'You really are quite exceptional.'

Anna's face softened and glowed.

I must tell her, I must say something. The words were a refrain in Céline's mind. And now the right moment had come. Jean-Luc had been sent to bed and Olivier was in his armchair in the sitting room, waiting for coffee to be brought to him. Anna was, for a moment, sitting at the kitchen table as she waited for the water to boil. She looked tired.

'There is something I wish to say about Papa,' said Céline. Her mother looked vaguely at her as if her thoughts were elsewhere.

'I think he is rather too interested in someone,' Céline continued.

Her mother's gaze sharpened. She got to her feet.

'We need some sugar from the larder. There's none in the bowl.'

Following her to the larder, Céline went on, 'Maman, I realised at the hunt today that Papa is not as interested in chasing the boar as in chasing that woman who's always hanging around at the stables.'

Her mother turned and said angrily, 'I forbid you to repeat gossip about your father. I'm surprised at you, Céline, you should know better.'

She reached for the packet of sugar. Céline said to her back, 'I wouldn't have said anything if I hadn't been so worried. It's not gossip, Maman. You must listen, this is important.'

'What is important?' asked Olivier. He had arrived silently at the doorway of the kitchen. His eyes again brought to Céline's mind the baleful stare of the cat.

'What is important?' repeated Olivier. Céline returned his stare, refusing to be intimidated. She said, her voice shaking, but looking him straight in the eye, 'I was saying that your behaviour at the hunt today would justify gossip. Your liaison with Madame Dubois will be talked about for weeks. You may have thought the pair of you could disappear discreetly but everyone noticed.'

She waited for his anger to fall on her head. Instead, he laughed indulgently.

'*Ma pauvre pétite*, I'm sorry I neglected you at the hunt, but you had galloped off with Monsieur Charonnat and you weren't there when Dauphin went lame. Madame Dubois was, and she very kindly did not desert me.'

'That's not how it was,' said Céline. 'I saw you and Madame Dubois ...'

Her mother interrupted sharply. 'That's enough, Céline.'

And it was, for Céline realised that it was not in her to describe what she had seen – the unbuttoned blouse, the tails of Olivier's shirt carelessly tucked into his waistband. She knew that to say any more would turn her mother against her.

Olivier shook his head and smiled. 'Just because I was not able to look after you all the time … You really must learn to be more independent.'

Céline looked at her mother, who was watching her with an expression that was sad and understanding.

'It's easy to get the wrong idea,' said Anna. 'You're looking exhausted, *ma pétite*. I think you should go to bed.'

Céline continued to look at her, willing her mother to see her father as he really was. And it was while she was taking in Anna's face, the lines and grey hairs that were a veil to her prettiness, that it came to her that her mother was more aware than she knew.

'These things are no concern of yours,' said Anna softly. 'You may go to bed now. Olivier will help me with the washing-up.'

Averting her eyes from her father, Céline said, 'Goodnight, Maman.'

She walked from the kitchen and carefully closed the door behind her, hearing as she did her mother's voice murmur, 'Such a jealous little thing she is.'

Then, as the latch clicked shut and she stood alone outside, all she could hear was the sound of her father's laughter.

I Was in Love

Joyce Carol Oates

I was in love with a man I couldn't marry, so one of us had to die – I lay awake, my eyes twitching in the dark, trying to understand which one of us should die. He lived alone in a big drafty house and ruined himself with people, giving himself to people, letting them devour him in the anonymous disinterested manner of maggots, without passion. I lived with my husband and my son, and no one else came near me. He had no family. I had my parents and my husband's parents. Was I of more worth? I lay awake trying to understand which one of us should die, he or I. A future of love with him was a skeleton with quivering skin stretched on it, skin twitching in fear. The fear had to stop.

The months and years ahead were shaped as if by bones, in the shape of a skeleton. I felt this.

In the morning my eyes were dry. After my husband left, I sat at the table and I reached over to touch the dry crumbs on his plate. Toast crumbs. Someone came to the doorway behind me and stood there, watching. The silence was a shout. I needn't look around. After a few minutes I heard him saying something – my son Bobby saying something – so I looked around. The bones in my neck seemed to function oddly. There was a mechanical movement in them. Bobby was saying something in anger, pointing to his shirt. He is eight years old, my only child. Is it my fault that he is slight in the body, small, that he looks out of proportion? Or is it a trick of the eye? I worry about this. But the doctor says his development is normal. I accept this with relief, nodding, a grateful mother. 'Yes, he is a good eater, yes ...' I tell the doctor with gratitude, pulling the words out of another mother's mouth – a woman I heard chattering in the waiting room about her own small, slight, out-of-proportion son. As a child I stole things from drugstores and five-and-tens and the desks of friends, I stole things and became terrified and threw them all away; now I steal words from other people. There is a silence in me that needs filling up. 'Yes, a good eater. He even eats vegetables,' I always tell the doctor.

'This is ripped. This is rotten,' Bobby said angrily.

He flapped his arm to show that the shirt was ripped under his arm.

'How did you do that?'

'It's rotten!'

'It isn't rotten, what do you mean? Don't say that!'

I found some things in a closet rotten with damp once, children's clothes that didn't belong to us. It was in a place we rented in Maine. I lifted up the pajamas of a strange child, the pajama bottoms, and for some curious reason pulled at them, experimentally, drawing my hands apart. The material ripped.

Why had this made an impression on my son?

'Don't be silly, your shirt can't be rotten. Come here. Our things aren't rotten.' He came to me, staring down at the floor, pretending to be disgusted. His face shows disgust well. I put my arms around him. On Monday mornings he is never ready to go to school. I don't know why: our Sundays are tedious enough. Sometimes I drive out to 'get some things' and see my lover, a ten- or fifteen-minute visit, and rushed and desperate I drive home again, and for that period of time Sundays are not tedious for me. For normal people, Sundays are tedious. Bobby leaned heavily against me, then jerked away. This is a habit of his. When he jerks out of my arms – as if having just thought of something urgent – I feel the ghostly pain of a baby jerking in my body, wanting to get away. I feel also this child's small urgent strength.

'I put an orange in your lunch, honey.'

He said nothing.

'Are you eating them or throwing them away?'

He shrugged his shoulders.

His head seems large for his body. The back of it looks precarious. His fawnish brown hair is not enough to protect that delicate skull; I am terrified of his perpetual danger. At his school this past year, children have had strange accidents. A girl stuck her head through a small opening and couldn't get it back out – she butted her head through. Another girl was hit in the head by a swing seat, flying backward through the air and catching her right between the eyes. She must have been standing watching it. A boy was kidnapped, or abducted, but was found a few hours later walking around downtown – he couldn't remember much about the men who had picked him up. White men, he said. Unharmed and unworried.

I was in love with a man and could not think about these things. I had to think for hours each day of him, only of him. I was condemned to him. When the telephone rang I did not dare to answer it, for fear that it would be someone else. When the telephone rang I listened to it very carefully but did not answer. The ringing of a telephone is always louder in an empty house.

On that morning Bobby went to school as usual. A few complaints. No tears. I helped him on with a new shirt and the two of us threw the old shirt in a wastebasket, as if this were an important ceremony, a way of beginning the week. He seemed anxious to get rid of it and to make sure it was really thrown out. Yet it wasn't an old shirt – it was older than the shirt he consented to wear, but not an old shirt. Obviously he had ripped it on purpose. Why? I thought about asking him but decided against it; this was as good a way as any of beginning the week.

After he left, I drove out to get away from the house. I feared the telephone. I decided to have my hair cut – a first step. If I were to die, my hair should look right. I was not thinking of the open casket – a beautiful waxen face, peace, etc. – I was thinking of those shocking minutes when I would be found, in a motel room, in a fourth dimension. It was easy to imagine myself dead. I tried to park on the street but my rear-right tire kept hitting the curb, bouncing up and falling back down again. My body was jolted. As I hit the curb, slowly, again and again, I kept thinking of the distance between my lover and me; I thought of him out in his house, not eating enough. I thought of bringing him some raw vegetables and watching while he ate. It is not true that my son is a good eater, not as mothers understand good eaters. I sometimes can't remember if he has eaten at all. I take the plates from the table, scrape them off into the garbage dreamily, and without passion, having rid myself of passion earlier that day, I can't distinguish between my husband's plate and my son's plate and my own. The garbage disposal grinds everything up like a good stomach. The food disappears. After I had my hair cut I would go to a farmers' market and buy some raw vegetables.

I like to plan the future down to its most minute parts – fingernails and toenails.

I parked the car and locked it. I walked to a hairdresser's salon but they wouldn't take me; 'There's only one girl in today,' they said. I thought this must mean something. I walked down the street and looked into windows, looking for another sign. It was true that one of us had to die: which one? My heart pounded with the urgency of my hatred for our love, our condemnation of love; I was sick of it, I was fed up, I was looking for a sign ... In the looking-glass of a window I saw myself, a strangely eager woman. My face is a hateful face, too sharp. There is this perpetually alert, eager, intense look about it – overlarge eyes, a Semitic look, vaguely hunted. In my early twenties it seemed to me that men were hunting me down, several men, hounding and bullying me. One of them was later killed in a plane crash in the Atlantic, the plane dropping mysteriously out of the sky. His body was one of the few recovered, but it was only a body. Another was the man I did marry, finally.

In a drugstore I leafed through magazines, not buying anything. I have the look of a woman who always buys things; people trust me. My heart began to beat faster, as if I were approaching a revelation. To have our lives decided, his and mine, to have everything finished! I looked through a woman's magazine and was fascinated by several full-page, colored photographs of food. I would drive out to that old house and heap food upon my lover, make him eat. Why didn't he eat right? Was his indifference to food a kind of suicide, a way of eluding me? What did he think about when he was alone? He has a small, sweet, still smile ... he is an indefinite person, hardly defined. For years he has been on the move, packing up and driving across the country in his Volkswagen alone, leaving behind books, magazines, cracked plates, worn-out rotten clothing, worn-out friendships.... A photograph of broccoli amandine. Melted butter, almonds, lemon juice.... My stomach was an empty sack, useless, but I remembered the uses of other stomachs, grinding up food to provide life. It was my responsibility to feed several people and keep them living.

Walking along the street I saw how people, approaching me, did not remain in focus. My own skin is pale as potatoes cut swiftly with a knife, that surprised look of potatoes cut in half. My hair is dark with streaks of red and, lately, streaks of gray. My face is sharp and smoothly innocent, like the faces of drivers who run over animals but never know until they feel the impact that they have hit something; they may even see the animal on the road, watching them, but nothing is in focus until they feel with their thighs and buttocks the small shock of an animal being crushed by a heavy automobile. Once, at my in-laws', Bobby was playing in the driveway and my father-in-law nearly backed over him.

My car was parked strangely. The back-left tire was turned out, as if flirting with traffic on the street. I got in and drove slowly out toward the country. The house my lover is renting is drafty and ugly, not good for his health. There is no one to take care of him. My own husband weighs two hundred pounds, dresses well and warmly, eats well, is loved as a second self is always loved, without commotion. It is not necessary for me to look at him often. The two of us are permanently together, no worry. I feed him, give him warmth at night, pull up the blanket around his shoulders. He shudders and stumbles in his sleep, climbing small treacherous slopes. I keep him warm on these climbs. I don't have to think about it; it is like pulling a blanket up to keep myself warm. My thinking turns upon the other man. Each day I must think about him for a number of hours, and when I am not thinking about him, yet I am still thinking about him, aware of him, like an actor aware of someone approaching him onstage and yet not aware, communicating to the audience this double dimension. My head aches, the nerves in my eyes twitch with this doubleness. The relief of one of us dying will be felt everywhere.

Before falling in love, I was defined. Now I am undefined, weeds are growing between my ribs. The chore of thinking about a man for hours every day is worse than memorising Bible verses or dates in history. The calendar is always set in his favor: days in a new month already crossed out, blotted out, lost ... I stopped at a big modern supermarket, not the small grocery store I had wanted, and bought some vegetables – tomatoes, carrots, spinach. My heart was pounding with the sudden desire to make this man eat. He was too tall, too thin. His ribs showed. When he moved, they showed painfully, as if dancing beneath his skin, but to him it was only a joke, inconsequential bones. I lay on his bed and wept those effortless tears we weep in cold weather. He laughed gently, I wept gently, making the same sounds.

... He clutches his head, as if my tears are destroying him. 'You have either got to stay here or leave,' he says, clutching at his head.

He lived outside town but not in a suburb. Certain areas are zoned for suburban houses and neat colonial-style plazas with dry-cleaning stores and drugstores and small meat markets, all beneath the same white trim, in one long neat Williamsburg row. He lived in an unzoned country, in too much space and too little. There were vacant lots that would not remain vacant. WILL BUILD TO SUIT TENANT, signs said. The highway was cracked and pitted with mysterious holes, as if the land beneath it were surging at night, shrugging its shoulders. There was an airport nearby for small private planes, weedy and nearly deserted. There were hot-dog stands and bowling alleys and taverns out on the highway, all of them third-rate, marked for extinction. There were bungalows strung side by side, crowded strangely, though this was the 'country' and the factory-workers and mill-workers who lived in them were proud of living in the 'country' and not in the 'city'. Only a few farmhouses remained, big old homes on land that had retreated to one or two acres, their barns knocked down. My lover rented one of these houses. He thought it was attractive. There were cracks in the floor people might whisper through, blowing cold air up my legs. He spent most of his time in the kitchen. The house was not his, he rented it. He never owned anything. He only rented things.

My heart had been pounding dangerously and then it was relieved: yes, his car was in the driveway.

I began to hate him for my own fear of his not being home. I hated fearing him, fearing his absence. *Before I met you I must have been very happy*, I would tell him.

For instance, I worked on a committee to preserve standards in the city's public schools. We argued about the falling tax base and the rising tax assessments, we drank coffee and smoked and argued about the families (white) that were moving out and the families (Negro) that were moving in, the teachers who were leaving for better jobs, the 'unprepared' (Negro) students who were holding classes back, and my face would grow white, deadly white, as I denounced the white nervous families with money who were moving out, moving out! – constantly, steadily, daily moving out of our city! Bobby went to the neighborhood school where, every year, more little Negro children were showing up, prepared or unprepared, and it did not truly seem to me a matter of great importance whether he learned as much as he should have learned, or whether the school's best teachers were leaving. *I was very happy* on that committee, drinking coffee and smoking cigarettes and arguing violently, lengthily, happily, a mother and a wife and a citizen....

His car was home, he was home. I knocked at his back door. He came to open it, pushing his chair back from the kitchen table, blundering toward me, already smiling.

We embraced nervously. We kissed.

'How long can you stay?' he said, surprised.

He smelled of mildewy, damp, rotted mornings, a gentle odor. His face had a faint Slavic broadness and innocence to it, eyes without much color, hair dark brown and very thick. He was working on a book. He had been given a grant to write a book and to use the excellent library of an excellent university forty miles away. His book was going to explain the theory of space–time relativity in nineteenth-century poetry, with an emphasis on Shelley, I think ... I never listened when he explained it to me. Though the real future had no shape to him, though he never planned his life, each day to him had a shape tight and dry as the skeleton of a small animal, small enough to hold in the palm of one's hand.

I began to weep dry tears. He comforted me. I stood in his arms for a while and then jerked away, jerking out of his arms. 'Is he still here?' I whispered.

He tried to smile. I had sensed this guilt, that was why I had jerked out of his arms.

'Didn't you tell him to leave ...?'

'I did.'

'But he's still here? Where is he?'

'Upstairs, sleeping. He's sick, how can I kick him out if he's sick?'

A friend from the East, bumming his way to California, had been in this house for four days. Currents of electricity were jerking through me. My eyes twitched.

'Don't cry, please, you look so upset,' he said.

I pushed him away.

I had been thinking of his death, but now, to punish him, I saw that I was the one who would have to die. Then he could never look in the mirror at himself and say those words he said after we made love, *I am perfected.*

'Let's drive out somewhere,' he said. 'Can we go to your house?'

'No.'

'Can we go somewhere? For a drive?'

I went to the table where his books and papers were. He wrote in a small, neat hand, an accountant's handwriting. This always seemed to me his true self.

His 'true self' popped up at me from the dust jackets of his books, snapshots of a younger, more serious man, a promising young man. His 'true self' flashed to me one evening in New York when a cousin of his said to me, of him: 'We always loved each other. We're the same age. But there was this emptiness in him that was a sin – he got filled up with

anyone who came along. People filled him up. Then he left them, frightened, and then he met someone else and was filled up again, like gas.
He was always being inhabited by the spirit of someone else, so that
when I met him I could tell, in the first five minutes, what kind of
person it was now – hopeful or hopeless.' This man, the same age as my
lover, was Slavic in the face and his hair was thinner; therefore his skull
more vulnerable. A married man, separated. My lover had never
married and therefore could never be separated from other loves.

They wrote to him, they telephoned him, they showed up in his
rented rooms and flats and houses. They begged to stay with him and,
out of kindness and cowardice, he sometimes consented. 'She slept
beside me for the night,' he would tell me, tears in his eyes, 'she slept
on the outside of the covers, like a child ... in the morning we wept
together and she left.' He told me everything.

I had wanted him to die when he told me that. Now I'm not so sure.

I snatched up his schedule for the day; it embarrassed him when I
looked through his things. Every day he rose at six in the morning,
believe it or not, he rose and wound his watch, came downstairs, made
coffee, and wrote out his schedule for the day. Then he followed it,
every detail.

'*Turner* – what's that?' I said.

'A book I need. I'm going to drive to the library.'

'When?'

'I thought around noon.'

My heart pounded viciously.

'What if I had come to see you ... ?'

'I was going to call you first....'

'What if I hadn't been home, what if I had been on my way out here,
all the way out here?'

'I was going to wait ... you don't usually come after noon ...'

We stared at each other. It was plain that we were not in love.

'I'd better leave.'

'What?'

He had not shaved that morning, which meant that truly he had not expected me. On Friday we had spent several hours together, strolling around the art center. I delighted in wasting his time, wrenching his perfect schedule out of shape. I always waited for him to say, 'But I can't take the whole afternoon off ...' He never said it. Yet I felt that he wanted to say it. On Friday I had said I couldn't meet him for several days, he had had a headache, we went to a Cunningham's Drugstore and sat at the counter, he took several aspirin. A curiosity was stirred in me: I could make a man sick.

'Do you feel better? You didn't feel well on Friday.'

'On Friday?'

'Did the headache go away?'

'I guess it went away.'

He took my hands and stared at me. *This is nothing*, I wanted to say contemptuously, *my husband holds my hands also*! He was almost forty years old but looked twenty-five; there was a sham innocence about him. I wondered if he would age after my death. Would his fingernails and toenails continue to grow? Dead, I would be unavailable to him. Parting of the ways. My husband, my family, my in-laws, my friends would take care of me. Not him. On the morning of the funeral he would rise at six, wind his watch, make coffee, write out his schedule for the day....

'I'd like to get out of here. I need to talk to you,' he said.

'I should be leaving....'

'Why are you angry?'

'I'm not angry.'

'You look upset.'

We stood staring past each other. There was a kind of glow about us, not of love. I said finally, 'I want to die.'

He glanced down at his worktable, as if death might be a notation on a piece of paper, something I had read and stolen from him. His hands moved oddly, one of them rising as if to cover his face, the other tapping at his chest. Silence. I was always stealing jokes and small references from him; I played back to him his special loves, as if feeding him. (He had a complex jazzy vocabulary of slang and allusions based on popular music and left-wing corny slogans, farmers' and workers' movements certain liberals pretend to cherish, decades out of date. And there was a slightly gangsterish, adolescent flair to him, born of Saturday matinées when he was a skinny underfed kid in New York.) Alone, when I remembered these jokes, I could never remember that they were meant to be funny. It sickened me to think that I was playing a role with this man when he was not worth it.

'There is something empty in you – there's nothing in you,' I said bitterly. 'I can't fill it up. Let someone else fill it up. What's inside you ... what's empty inside you ... you yourself—' I stammered, out of breath. I could not look at him. He was wearing a familiar dark-green shirt buttoned all the way up to his neck, with the collar turned up, which meant that he imagined he was catching a sore throat. The shirt was not tucked in his pants. I hated that look, it reminded me of Bobby and his friends.

'Please, please ...' he said.

I closed my fist and hit the table.

'Why is he still upstairs?' I whispered.

He made a gesture that showed pain.

He sat shakily on the edge of the table and drew me to him. He stroked my hair. 'Don't cry, don't make both of us cry, don't be so evil ...' he said in a murmur. I suspect him of being a father: there is always a lullaby in his voice eager to show itself. His talent is for putting people to sleep. When we sleep together, really sleep, he draws the covers up over my bare shoulders lovingly, but with a father's love. I understand then that this is the way he has drawn up covers over other people's shoulders, just so, like this, with the same love.... He is not a defined human being.

I drew back to look at him. His face was not quite made up, like a mind not made up. Something was held back, guarded. He might have thought I would close my fist and strike him.

If, in love, your lover puts up with evil from you, then you are loved. You must always test him. 'If one of us died, really died ... ?' I whispered. He nodded. 'You've thought of it?' I said. He nodded again. His eyes were colorless. I felt the impact of my words sink in them, neutral-ising them, making them colorless. I wanted suddenly, thirstily, to drain the blood out of this man and be finished with him; then I could drive back home.

'Walk with me. Let me walk you out of it,' he said.

He put his arm around me and walked me into the other room, as if walking a sick woman. A woman who has taken too many pills, to call attention to her pettiness.

'I feel sick all the time. I can't work,' he said. 'You don't want to stay here with me and you don't want to go for a drive, you won't let me come to your house any longer.... On Friday you kept looking around as if you were expecting someone better to show up. Why did you do that?'

'Did I do that?' I said, alarmed.

'Why can't we go to your house?'

I hated him for one thing, mainly: his failure to admire my house. He must have noticed the good furniture, the curtains, the gold and silver and white, the heavy shaggy black rugs, but he said nothing.

'I'll go away,' I said.

'What will that solve?'

If he were dead, the telephone would ring with a different sound. I would always hurry to it, ready for an adventure. Walking in the park, I would answer the greeting of a strange man, I would take his extended hand, I would follow him into the bushes, into the trees! – I would be generous to everyone!

'I have to pick up Bobby from school this afternoon ... he has to go from school right to the doctor....'

This sentence began as a lie but ended as the truth. Bobby did have a doctor's appointment that day.

'But so what? That's this afternoon, that's hours from now.'

'I don't want to be upset when I get him.'

'Do I make you upset?'

'If one of us died, if we could decide something ...' I said with a smile.

'Do you want me to die?'

Holding my husband in my arms at night, I shed tears for the man I was not holding; I held the one man tighter, to imagine the other.

My mother had said wisely, 'After you're married, you'll discover that the best thing is to take care of your children and have parties. Do things for people, feed them and talk to them and keep them warm. Forget about the rest of it.' She meant love, forget about love, she was bullying me out of my anguish at the thought of marriage. It was time for me to marry; she had talked to me about what I should think about and what I should forget.

'I'll see you in a day or two,' I said wildly. I felt that I had to get away from him.

'But if you have until this afternoon ... ?'

'The appointment is for earlier. I have to pick him up earlier.'

'That's a lie.'

We walked back into the kitchen. The stove was large and blackened, ugly as a locomotive engine. It was nearly that size. The table was a workbench, littered with papers and books. For a few minutes we stood together, holding hands, in silence. We could think of nothing to say. Then my words slid uglily back onto something familiar: 'These people hanging on you ... I hate you for letting them ... you are so empty inside, there's nothing there.... They're ruining you!'

He walked me to the door. We looked out at the foundation of a barn, what was left of a barn. On the far side of 'his' pasture was a gas station, an unprospering place. I bought gas there sometimes, as if patronising local businesses would show my lover that I was interested in him, in the welfare of his community.

He leaned his forehead against the cracked glass of the door.

'They crawl in bed with you. They eat your food. They clip stories out of newspapers and mail them to you. All the spit that dribbles out of their ugly mouths! Don't you know they hate you? They want you to fail, like them, they want you to get burned up in a fire from them smoking in bed....' I began to cry again.

'Randolph doesn't smoke,' he muttered.

Love is testing. You prick him with a small needle. You reach behind his eyes with your fingernails and give a tug to the optic nerve. You accuse his friends of wanting him to die when you are the only friend he has and you are the only person who wants him to die: the others want to borrow money from him.

Suddenly everything changes and I think, *Why, I have brought myself to this man, why am I crying? I have brought my body and my love to him, why is he pressing his forehead against the door?*

'Look, please. I love you.' I touched his arm.

He seemed to be staring down from a dangerous summit. He did not trust me.

'I love you. Don't hate me.' I brought his hand to my lips and kissed it. Pleased, he stared at me. A dizziness rose in us like the sun. Evidently we were in love.

'I brought you something in the car. You don't eat right,' I said.

'Did you bring me something?' he said eagerly.

There was a dazed, futile look to him. We went out. He took the bag of vegetables out of the car, very pleased. It startled me to see how his face glowed.

'What is all this? Carrots? Spinach?'

'You don't eat right,' I said shyly.

'Thank you, it's so kind of you ... you are so wonderful....'

He stared into the bag.

We are exposed, being outside. Anyone could see us.

When we went back inside, he set the vegetables down carefully. 'You won't throw them away?' I said, teasing. 'You'll eat them?'

'Oh, yes. Yes. I'm hungry right now.'

We each ate a tomato. I fell in love with him, eating a tomato with him. My tongue prodded the flesh of the tomato; the seeds of tomatoes are very soft, a little slimy. They are more like human seeds than they are like the hard little pits of other fruits.

'I love you, I love you like this,' he said. His face glowed. He was not a handsome man, but his face glowed with innocence and excitement, behind his skin, warming it. If he died, what remained of him would be misleading: those photographs on his books, his cousin's remarks.

I loved him with a strength that rose in my blood, in silence. He was a man of beauty. I licked the tomato juice from my fingers.

Upstairs someone was walking around.

'These people are hell to me, yes,' my lover said, rolling his eyes skyward.

A confession.

'Why do you let them stay with you, then? Darling ... ?' He shrugged his shoulders.

'Too much love ... you love too much ... you're going to wear out and die,' I said, teasing. I loved him and I wanted to slide my hand inside his buttoned-up shirt, slide my hand between his ribs, take in my fingers his wonderful pulsating heart!

'I'll get rid of him today,' he said.

In his face was a glow for me, his love for me. I had wrenched him from his schedule. If I wanted, I could go to his table and turn it over, knock everything onto the floor. I had knocked some books down once, wounding him with my hatred. I had done it once, successfully, and had no interest in doing it again.

Randolph came downstairs noisily.

A short, rodent-like man, nervous, with a beard. A look of staleness and sweetness. Very helpless. He always looked as if someone had released him from a machine of torture just minutes before. Gratitude for being released, but memory of pain ... his face was pale and ravaged and curious, like a rat's face. In the distance there was the sound of jets. His eyelids fluttered, the sound must have frightened him.

He said, 'I'm going out for a walk.'

We did not reply. He buttoned his shirt all the way up to his chin and went out, as if to face danger.

'Tonight I'll tell him to leave. I will,' my lover said.

It was a vow.

We went upstairs. There were three bedrooms in this old house. The biggest one was my lover's, with a bed whose covers were neatly pulled back, and some suitcases that had not yet been totally unpacked, on the floor. The wallpaper was peeling. It looked as if it were weeping. We sank against each other as if trying to push past each other, speaking past each other. In the distance was the sound of jets, growing louder and fainter. I heard the voices of my family chattering at me, scolding me, *Why have you gone so far from us?* my mother said indifferently, *Is your need for love really so great?* I felt that she was relinquishing me, glad to be rid of me.

A woman spends time before mirrors, content to imagine herself always in a mirror, somewhere, her truest self, while her body walks around in the world. It is the mirror self that certain men love, and that loves them; the other self is busy scraping garbage off plates and emptying the drier of great hot coiled heaps of sheets and towels and underwear and socks. It is the mirror self that loves without exhaustion, loves with passion and violence, with tears; the other self puts the stained sheets in the washing machine and turns the dial.

I breathed from my stomach, from the muscles there. My breathing was painful. Pain shot up through my loins.

He cried out, 'Oh, did I hurt you ...?'

I said no.

He lay in my arms. His back was wet. His hair was wet. I could not move under his weight.

I closed my eyes and I was in my first bedroom again, sick or pretending to be sick. A heavy weight lay upon me. It was not a man but a quilt. I wanted to kick it off, sweating under it. I hate weights on me. You must always think about a weight when it is on you; you are not free to think about other things.

'Do you love me?' he said.

He raised his head to stare anxiously at me. His eyes were dim with small despairing veins. The irises were a very faint blue, a very faint gray.

I kissed him. His weight turned into panic.

'Then don't answer,' he said.

We were safe here, in his room. No one could spy on us. From the sky, this house was a weatherbeaten old wreck, not worth bombing.

I closed my eyes and saw small explosions of light. They reminded me of bees. I had seen bees in a line once, flying in a line. Like a whip. Since falling in love I had headaches, my eyes ached, my throat ached with the need to cry perpetually, my loins ached from the love of two men, I was the beloved of two healthy men. The bees were always present inside my eyes. I imagined them whipping across my body, stinging lightly and at random, giving off sparks.

When I was gone from him, my lover doodled pictures of me, heads and shoulders. He thinks I am beautiful and he loves me, therefore I lie with my arms aching beneath him, my belly slick with sweat. His pictures of me are not of me, but they show his love. I keep them in one of my bureau drawers where they will be found one day by my husband.

'Come see me tomorrow? Please?'

'You'll be alone here?'

'Yes. Oh, yes.'

When I left I was very happy. I drove down the highway and passed Randolph, rushing past, no time even to flash him a sign of victory.

Nothing has been decided, I thought. Why was I happy?

It was two-thirty already. I hadn't eaten. I felt sick.

I drove around until quarter to three, then I drove to Bobby's school. My happiness made me dizzy. I couldn't handle the car right. Felt shame in taking my son to the doctor: he was too slight in the chest! Why did the doctor lie and say that he was normal? Waiting at the curb, I tried to get my happiness out of my face, to keep my mouth still. My mouth kept wanting to smile a slick small smile, an evil smile. This is the smile of adultery. I pulled at my lips and my fingers came away stained with lipstick.

When Bobby and the other children piled out the door, I made a show of waving for him. He caught sight of me at once and hurried my way, as if to quiet me. He was carrying a book and a large piece of paper, taped to cardboard.

'Oh, what's that, honey?' I said. My voice was too loud. Its joviality must have startled my son. 'Did you draw that by yourself?'

A picture of a jet airplane.

'Are you hungry? Did you eat all of your lunch?'

He stared at me.

'What's wrong?' I said. 'You're not afraid of the doctor ... ?'

'No.'

'Are you all right? Honey?'

He looked away. There was something in my face that frightened him.

I drove. Bobby began to kick at the floorboard. I chattered toward him, reaching out with one hand to touch his hair. He glanced sideways at me.

'You been crying?' he said finally.

'What? Crying? Of course not.'

A strange tension rose in the car. The air between us grew hot. The men in my life are innocent and I am guilty, because they love me and I am loved by them. Beloved of too many men, I have given my body to too many men, my body is rebelling and wants to die. Bobby was leaning against the car door as if sickened by the odor of my body. *He can smell that other man*, a voice told me wisely.

'Sit up!' I said. 'Sit still! Stop that kicking!'

'You shut up!' he shouted.

Years ago he had tried, experimentally, to tell me to shut up. It had passed.

I said nothing.

'You shut up,' he whispered.

We looked at each other. In his face there was a glow of terror. He could not understand his words.

At forty miles an hour, driving this heavy car, I leaned and slapped his face. I felt his head strike the window.

He began to shout. He kicked. He writhed on the seat, throwing himself around. With my right hand I tried to keep him still, snatching at anything that was my property to snatch at – his hair, the collar of his jacket – I could see that his eyes were closed and his mouth opening and shutting tightly, opening into a high-pitched, furious wail, shutting tightly as if to bite the wail off.

'Stop it! You're crazy!' I cried.

He threw himself forward suddenly and banged his head against the windshield. He banged it again as if trying to butt through it. I pulled him back against the seat, yanking him back by his collar. We shouted toward each other. We were shouting past each other. He jerked away and snatched at the car door, which was locked, and turned to unlock it, pulling up the little safety knob – so fastidious in his desire to die! – and then he opened the car door while I screamed and tore at his jacket, but his strength was greater than mine. He threw himself out of the car.

My car skidded sideways. Something slammed into the front of it. It was like an amusement ride: I was thrown up, thrown sideways. I crawled across the seat, dripping blood, and thought of how heavy and still everything had become – the car itself, the dense air in the car, the sounding of someone's stuck horn right outside my head ... I had a few slow seconds before I would crawl out and stagger to my feet, dripping blood, and look back to see what had happened to my son.

Before the Change

Alice Munro

Dear R. My father and I watched Kennedy debate Nixon. He's got a television since you were here. A small screen and rabbit ears. It sits out in front of the sideboard in the dining room so that there's no easy way now to get at the good silver or the table linen even if anybody wanted to. Why in the dining room where there's not one really comfortable chair? Because it's a while since they've remembered they have a living room. Or because Mrs Barrie wants to watch it at suppertime.

Do you remember this room? Nothing new in it but the television. Heavy side curtains with wine-colored leaves on a beige ground and the net curtains in between. Picture of Sir Galahad leading his horse and picture of Glencoe, red deer instead of the massacre. The old filing cabinet moved in years ago from my father's office but still no place found for it so it just sits there not even pushed back against the wall. And my mother's closed sewing machine (the only time he ever mentions her, when he says 'your mother's sewing machine') with the same array of plants, or what looks like the same, in clay pots or tin cans, not flourishing and not dying.

So I'm home now. Nobody has broached the question as to how long for. I just stuffed the Mini with all my books and papers and clothes and drove here from Ottawa in one day. I had told my father on the phone that I was finished with my thesis (I've actually given it up but I didn't bother telling him that) and that I thought I needed a break.

'Break?' he said, as if he'd never heard of such a thing. 'Well. As long as it isn't a nervous break.'

I said, What?

'Nervous breakdown,' he said with a warning cackle. That's the way he still refers to panic attacks and acute anxiety and depression and personal collapse. He probably tells his patients to buck up.

Unfair. He probably sends them away with some numbing pills and a few dry kind words. He can tolerate other people's shortcomings more easily than mine.

There wasn't any big welcome when I got here, but no consternation either. He walked around the Mini and grunted at what he saw and nudged the tires.

'Surprised you made it,' he said.

I'd thought of kissing him – more bravado than an upsurge of affection, more this-is-the-way-I-do-things-now. But by the time my shoes hit gravel I knew I couldn't. There was Mrs B. standing halfway between the drive and the kitchen door. So I went and threw my arms around her instead and nuzzled the bizarre black hair cut in a Chinese sort of bob around her small withered face. I could smell her stuffy cardigan and bleach on her apron and feel her old toothpick bones. She hardly comes up to my collarbone.

Flustered, I said, 'It's a beautiful day, it's been the most beautiful drive.' So it was. So it had been. The trees not turned yet, just rusting at the edges and the stubble fields like gold. So why does this benevolence of landscape fade, in my father's presence and in his territory (and don't forget it's in Mrs Barrie's presence and in her territory)? Why does my mentioning it – or the fact that I mentioned it in a heartfelt not perfunctory way – seem almost in a class with my embracing Mrs B.? One thing seems to be a piece of insolence and the other pretentious gush.

When the debate was over my father got up and turned off the television. He won't watch a commercial unless Mrs B. is there and speaks up in favor, saying she wants to see the cute kid with his front teeth out or the chicken chasing the thingamajig (she won't try to say 'ostrich', or she can't remember). Then whatever she enjoys is permitted, even dancing cornflakes, and he may say, 'Well, in its own way it's clever.' This I think is a kind of warning to me.

What did he think about Kennedy and Nixon?

'Aw, they're just a couple of Americans.'

I tried to open the conversation up a bit.

'How do you mean?'

When you ask him to go into subjects that he thinks don't need to be talked about, or take up an argument that doesn't need proving, he has a way of lifting his upper lip at one side, showing a pair of big tobacco-stained teeth.

'Just a couple of Americans,' he said, as if the words might have got by me the first time.

So we sit there not talking but not in silence because as you may recall he is a noisy breather. His breath gets dragged down stony alleys and through creaky gates. Then takes off into a bit of tweeting and gurgling as if there was some inhuman apparatus shut up in his chest. Plastic pipes and colored bubbles. You're not supposed to take any notice, and I'll soon be used to it. But it takes up a lot of space in a room. As he would anyway with his high hard stomach and long legs and his expression. What is that expression? It's as if he's got a list of offenses both remembered and anticipated and he's letting it be known how his patience can be tried by what you know you do wrong but also by what you don't even suspect. I think a lot of fathers and grandfathers strive for that look – even some who unlike him don't have any authority outside of their own houses – but he's the one who's got it exactly permanently right.

R. Lots for me to do here and no time to – as they say – mope. The waiting-room walls are scuffed all round where generations of patients have leaned their chairs back against them. The *Reader's Digests* are in rags on the table. The patients' files are in cardboard boxes under the examining table, and the wastebaskets – they're wicker – are mangled all around the top as if eaten by rats. And in the house it's no better. Cracks like brown hairs in the downstairs washbasin and a disconcerting spot of rust in the toilet. Well you must have noticed. It's silly but the most disturbing thing I think is the coupons and advertising flyers. They're in drawers and stuck under saucers or lying around loose and the sales or discounts they're advertising are weeks or months or years past.

It isn't that they've abdicated or aren't trying. But everything is complicated. They send out the laundry, which is sensible, rather than having Mrs B. still do it, but then my father can't remember which day it's due back and there's this unholy fuss about will there be enough smocks, etc. And Mrs B. actually believes the laundry is cheating her and taking the time to rip off the name tapes and sew them onto inferior articles. So she argues with the deliveryman and says he comes here last on purpose and he probably does.

Then the eaves need to be cleaned and Mrs B.'s nephew is supposed to come and clean them, but he has put his back out so his son is coming. But his son has had to take over so many jobs that he's behind, etc., etc.

My father calls this nephew's son by the nephew's name. He does this with everybody. He refers to stores and businesses in town by the name of the previous owner or even the owner before that. This is more than a simple lapse of memory; it's something like arrogance. Putting himself beyond the need to keep such things straight. The need to notice changes. Or individuals.

I asked what color of paint he'd like on the waiting-room walls. Light green, I said, or light yellow? He said, Who's going to paint them?

'I am.'

'I never knew you were a painter.'

'I've painted places I've lived in.'

'Maybe so. But I haven't seen them. What are you going to do about my patients while you're painting?'

'I'll do it on a Sunday."

'Some of them wouldn't care for that when they heard about it.'

'Are you kidding? In this day and age?'

'It may not be quite the same day and age you think it is. Not around here.'

Then I said I could do it at night, but he said the smell the next day would upset too many stomachs. All I was allowed to do in the end was throw out the *Reader's Digests* and put out some copies of *Maclean's* and *Chatelaine* and *Time* and *Saturday Night*. And then he mentioned there'd been complaints. People missed looking up the jokes they remembered in the *Reader's Digests*. And some of them didn't like modern writers. Like Pierre Berton.

'Too bad,' I said, and I couldn't believe that my voice was shaking.

Then I tackled the filing cabinet in the dining room. I thought it was probably full of the files of patients who were long dead and if I could clear those files out I could fill it up with the files from the cardboard boxes, and move the whole thing back to the office where it belonged.

Mrs B. saw what I was doing and went and got my father. Not a word to me.

He said, 'Who told you you could go poking around in there? I didn't.'

R. The days you were here Mrs B. was off for Christmas with her family. (She has a husband who has been sick with emphysema it seems for half his life, and no children, but a horde of nieces and nephews and connections.) I don't think you saw her at all. But she saw you. She said to me yesterday, 'Where's that Mr So-and-so you were supposed to be engaged to?' She'd seen of course that I wasn't wearing my ring.

'I imagine in Toronto,' I said.

'I was up at my niece's last Christmas and we seen you and him walking up by the standpipe and my niece said, "I wonder where them two are off to?"' This is exactly how she talks and it already sounds quite normal to me except when I write it down. I guess the implication is that we were going somewhere to carry on, but there was a deep freeze on, if you remember, and we were just walking to get away from the house. No. We were getting outside so we could continue our fight, which could only be bottled up for so long.

Mrs B. started to work for my father about the same time I went away to school. Before that we had some young women I liked, but they left to get married, or to work in war plants. When I was nine or ten and had been to some of my school friends' houses, I said to my father, 'Why does our maid have to eat with us? Other people's maids don't eat with them.'

My father said, 'You call Mrs Barrie Mrs Barrie. And if you don't like to eat with her you can go and eat in the woodshed.'

Then I took to hanging around and getting her to talk. Often she wouldn't. But when she did, it could be rewarding. I had a fine time imitating her at school.

(Me) Your hair is really black, Mrs Barrie.

(Mrs B.) Everyone in my family is got black hair. They all got black hair and it never ever gets gray. That's on my mother's side. It stays black in their coffin. When my grandpa died they kept him in the place in the cemetery all winter while the ground was froze and come spring they was going to put him in the ground and one or other of us says, 'Let's take a look see how he made it through the winter.' So we got the fellow to lift the lid and there he was looking fine with his face not dark or caved in or anything and his hair was black. Black.

I could even do the little laughs she does, little laughs or barks, not to indicate that anything is funny but as a kind of punctuation.

By the time I met you I'd got sick of myself doing this.

After Mrs B. told me all that about her hair I met her one day coming out of the upstairs bathroom. She was hurrying to answer the phone, which I wasn't allowed to answer. Her hair was bundled up in a towel and a dark trickle was running down the side of her face. A dark purplish trickle, and my thought was that she was bleeding.

As if her blood could be eccentric and dark with malevolence as her nature sometimes seemed to be.

'Your head's bleeding,' I said, and she said, 'Oh, get out of my road,' and scrambled past to get the phone. I went on into the bathroom and saw purple streaks in the basin and the hair dye on the shelf. Not a word was said about this, and she continued to talk about how everybody on her mother's side of the family had black hair in their coffins and she would, too.

My father had an odd way of noticing me in those years. He might be passing through a room where I was, and he'd say as if he hadn't seen me there,

'The chief defect of Henry King,
Was chewing little bits of string—'

And sometimes he'd speak to me in a theatrically growly voice.

'Hello little girl. Would you like a piece of candy?'

I had learned to answer in a wheedling baby-girl voice. 'Oh yes sir.'

'Wahl.' Some fancy drawing out of the 'a'. 'Wahl. You cahn't have one.'

And:

' "Solomon Grundy, born on Monday—"' He'd jab a finger at me to take it up.

' "Christened on Tuesday—"'

' "Married on Wednesday—"'

' "Sick on Thursday—"'

' "Worse on Friday—"'

' "Died on Saturday—"'

' "Buried on Sunday—"'

Then both together, thunderously. ' "And that was the end of Solomon Grundy!"'

Never any introduction, no comment when these passages were over. For a joke I tried calling him Solomon Grundy. The fourth or fifth time he said, 'That's enough. That's not my name. I'm your father.'

After that we probably didn't do the rhyme anymore.

The first time I met you on the campus, and you were alone and I was alone, you looked as if you remembered me but weren't sure about acknowledging it. You had just taught that one class, filling in when our regular man was sick, and you had to do the lecture on logical positivism. You joked about its being a funny thing to bring somebody over from the Theological College to do.

You seemed to hesitate about saying hello, so I said, 'The former King of France is bald.'

That was the example you'd given us, of a statement that makes no sense because the subject doesn't exist. But you gave me a truly startled and cornered look that you then covered up with a professional smile. What did you think of me?

A smart aleck.

R. My stomach is still a little puffy. There are no marks on it, but I can bunch it up in my hands. Otherwise I'm okay, my weight is back to normal or a little below. I think I look older, though. I think I look older than twenty-four. My hair is still long and unfashionable, in fact a mess. Is this a memorial to you because you never liked me to cut it? I wouldn't know.

Anyway I've started going on long walks around town, for exercise. I used to go off in the summers, anywhere I liked. I hadn't any sense of what rules there might be, or different grades of people. That could have been because of never going to school in town or because of our house being out of town here where it is, down the long lane. Not properly belonging. I went to the horse barns by the racetrack where the men were horse owners or paid horse trainers and the other kids were boys. I didn't know any names, but they all knew mine. They had to put up with me, in other words, because of whose daughter I was. We were allowed to put down feed and muck out behind the horses. It seemed adventurous. I wore an old golf hat of my father's and a pair of baggy shorts. We'd get up on the roof and they'd grapple and try to push each other off but me they left alone. The men would periodically tell us to get lost. They'd say to me, 'Does your dad know you're here?' Then the boys started teasing each other and the one teased would make a puking noise and I knew it was about me. So I quit going. I gave up the idea of being a Girl of the Golden West. I went down to the dock and looked at the lake boats, but I don't think I went so far as dreaming of being taken on as a deckhand. Also I didn't fool them into thinking I was anything but a girl. A man leaned over and yelled down to me:

'Hey. You got any hair on it yet?'

I almost said, 'Pardon?' I wasn't frightened or humiliated so much as mystified. That a grown-up man with responsible work should be inter-

ested in the patchy itchy sprouting in between my legs. Should bother
to be disgusted by it, as his voice surely indicated that he was.

The horse barns have been torn down. The road down to the harbor
is not so steep. There is a new grain elevator. And new suburbs that
could be suburbs anywhere, which is what everybody likes about them.
Nobody walks now; everybody drives. The suburbs don't have sidewalks and the sidewalks along the old backstreets are unused and
cracked and uptilted by frost and disappearing under earth and grass.
The long dirt path under the pine trees along our lane is lost now
under drifts of pine needles and rogue saplings and wild raspberry
canes. People have walked up that path for decades to see the doctor.
Out from town on a special short extension of sidewalk along the
highway (the only other extension was to the cemetery) and then
between the double row of pines on that side of the lane. Because
there's been a doctor living in this house since the end of the last
century.

All sorts of noisy grubby patients, children and mothers and old
people, all afternoon, and quieter patients coming singly in the
evenings. I used to sit out where there was a pear tree trapped in a
clump of lilac bushes, and I'd spy on them, because young girls like to
spy. That whole clump is gone now, cleaned out to make things easier
for Mrs B.'s nephew's son on the power mower. I used to spy on ladies
who got dressed up, at that time, for a visit to the doctor. I remember
the clothes from soon after the war. Long full skirts and cinch belts and
puffed-up blouses and sometimes short white gloves, for gloves were
worn then in summer and not just to church. Hats not just to church
either. Pastel straw hats that framed the face. A dress with light summer
flounces, a ruffle on the shoulders like a little cape, a sash like a ribbon
round the waist. The cape-ruffle could lift in the breeze, and the lady
would raise her hand in a crocheted glove to brush it away from her
face. This gesture was like a symbol to me of unattainable feminine
loveliness. The wisp of cobweb cloth against the perfect velvet mouth.
Not having a mother may have had something to do with how I felt.
But I didn't know anybody who had a mother that looked the way they

did. I'd crouch under the bushes eating the spotty yellow pears and worshipping.

One of our teachers had got us reading old ballads like 'Patrick Spens' and 'The Twa Corbies', and there'd been a rash of ballad-making at school.

> *I'm going down the corridor*
> *My good friend for to see*
> *I'm going to the lav-a-to-ry*
> *To have myself a pee—*

Ballads really tumbled you along into rhymes before you had a chance to think what anything meant. So with my mouth full of mushy pear I made them up.

> *A lady walks on a long long path*
> *She's left the town behind.*
> *She's left her home and her father's wrath*
> *Her destiny for to find—*

When the wasps started bothering me too much I went into the house. Mrs Barrie would be in the kitchen, smoking a cigarette and listening to the radio, until my father called her. She stayed till the last patient had left and the place had been tidied up. If there was a yelp from the office she might give her own little yelping laugh and say, 'Go ahead and holler.' I never bothered describing to her the clothes or the looks of the women I'd seen because I knew she'd never admire anybody for being beautiful or well dressed. Any more than she'd admire them for knowing something nobody needed to know, like a foreign language. Good card players she admired, and fast knitters – that was about all. Many people she had no use for. My father said that too. He had no use. That made me want to ask, If they did have a use, what would the use be? But I knew neither one would tell me. Instead they'd tell me not to be so smart.

His Uncle came on Frederick Hyde
Carousing in the Dirt.
He shook him Hard from Side to Side
And Hit him where it Hurt—

If I decided to send all this to you, where would I send it? When I
think of writing the whole address on the envelope I am paralysed. It's
too painful to think of you in the same place with your life going on in
the same way, minus me. And to think of you not there, you somewhere
else but I don't know where, is worse.

Dear R., Dear Robin, How do you think I didn't know? It was right in
front of my eyes all the time. If I had gone to school here, I'd surely
have known. If I'd had friends. There's no way one of the high-school
girls, one of the older girls, wouldn't have made sure I knew.

Even so, I had plenty of time in the holidays. If I hadn't been so
bound up in myself, mooching around town and making up ballads, I
could have figured it out. Now that I think of it, I knew that some of
those evening patients, those ladies, came on the train. I associated them
and their beautiful clothes with the evening train. And there was a late-
night train they must have left on. Of course there could just as easily
have been a car that dropped them off at the end of the lane.

And I was told – by Mrs B., I think, not by him – that they came to
my father for vitamin shots. I know that, because I would think, Now
she's getting her shot, whenever we heard a woman make a noise, and
I would be a little surprised that women so sophisticated and self-
controlled were not more stoical about needles.

Even now, it has taken me weeks. Through all this time of getting
used to the ways of the house, to the point where I would never dream
of picking up a paintbrush and would hesitate to straighten a drawer or
throw out an old grocery receipt without consulting Mrs B. (who can
never make up her mind about it anyway). To the point where I've given
up trying to get them even to accept perked coffee. (They prefer instant
because it always tastes the same.)

My father laid a check beside my plate. At lunch today, Sunday. Mrs Barrie is never here on Sundays. We have a cold lunch which I fix, of sliced meat and bread and tomatoes and pickles and cheese, when my father gets back from church. He never asks me to go to church with him – probably thinking that would just give me a chance to air some views he doesn't care to hear.

The check was for five thousand dollars.

'That's for you,' he said. 'So you'll have something. You can put it in the bank or invest it how you like. See how the rates are. I don't keep up. Of course you'll get the house too. All in the fullness of time, as they say.'

A bribe? I thought. Money to start a little business with, go on a trip with? Money for the down-payment on a little house of my own, or to go back to university to get some more of what he has called my unnegotiable degrees.

Five thousand dollars to get rid of me.

I thanked him, and more or less for conversation's sake I asked him what he did with his money. He said that was neither here nor there.

'Ask Billy Snyder if you're looking for advice.' Then he remembered that Billy Snyder was no longer in the accounting business; he had retired.

'There's some new fellow there with a queer name,' he said. 'It's like Ypsilanti, but it's not Ypsilanti.'

'Ypsilanti is a town in Michigan,' I said.

'It's a town in Michigan, but it was a man's name before it was a town in Michigan,' my father said. It seems it was the name of a Greek leader who fought against the Turks early in the 1800s.

I said 'Oh. In Byron's war.'

'Byron's war?' said my father. 'What makes you call it that? Byron didn't fight in any war. He died of typhus. Then he's dead, he's the big hero, he died for the Greeks and so on.' He said this contentiously, as if I had been one of those responsible for this mistake, this big fuss over Byron. But then he calmed down and recounted for me or recalled for himself the progress of the war against the Ottoman Empire. He spoke of the Porte and I wanted to say that I've never been sure if that was an actual gate, or was it Constantinople, or the Sultan's court? But it's always best not to interrupt. When he starts to talk like this there's the sense of a truce, or a breathing spell, in an undeclared underground war. I was sitting facing the window, and I could see through the net curtains the heaps of yellow-brown leaves on the ground in the rich generous sunlight (maybe the last of those days we'll get for a long while by the sound of the wind tonight) and it brought to mind my relief as a child, my secret pleasure, whenever I could get him going, by a question or by accident, on a spiel like this.

Earthquakes, for instance. They happen in the volcanic ridges but one of the biggest was right in the middle of the continent in New Madrid (pronounced 'New Mad-rid,' mind you) in Missouri, in 1811. I know that from him. Rift valleys. Instability that there is no sign of on the surface. Caverns formed in limestone, water under the earth, mountains that given enough time wear away to rubble.

Also numbers. I asked him about numbers once and he said, Well, they're called the arabic numerals, aren't they, any fool knows that. But the Greeks could have managed a good system, he went on to say, the Greeks could have done it, only they didn't have the concept of zero.

Concept of zero. I put that away in my mind like a package on a shelf, to open someday.

If Mrs B. was with us there was of course no hope of getting anything like this out of him.

Never mind, he would say, eat your meal.

As if any question I asked had an ulterior motive, and I suppose it did. I was angling to direct the conversation. And it wasn't polite to leave Mrs B. out. So it was her attitude to what caused earthquakes or the history of numbers (an attitude not just of indifference but of contempt) that had to be deferred to, had to reign supreme.

So we come round to Mrs B. again. In the present, Mrs B.

I came in last night at about ten o'clock. I'd been out at a meeting of the Historical Society, or at least at a meeting to try and organise one.

Five people showed up and two of them walked with canes. When I opened the kitchen door I saw Mrs B. framed in the doorway to the back hall – the hall that leads from the office to the washroom and the front part of the house. She had a covered basin in her hands. She was on her way to the washroom and she could have gone on, passing the kitchen as I came in. I would hardly have noticed her. But she stopped in her tracks and stood there, partly turned towards me; she made a grimace of dismay.

Oh-oh. Caught out.

Then she scurried away towards the toilet.

This was an act. The surprise, the dismay, the hurrying away. Even the way she held the basin out so that I had to notice it. That was all deliberate.

I could hear the rumble of my father's voice in the office, talking to a patient. I had seen the office lights on anyway, I had seen the patient's car parked outside. Nobody has to walk anymore.

I took off my coat and went on upstairs. All I seemed to be concerned about was not letting Mrs B. have it her way. No questions, no shocked realisation. No *What is that you have in the basin, Mrs.B., oh what have you and my daddy been up to?* (Not that I ever called him my daddy.) I got busy at once rooting around in one of the boxes of books I still hadn't unpacked. I was looking for the journals of Anna Jameson. I had promised them to the other person under seventy who had been at the meeting. A man who is a photographer and knows something about the history of Upper Canada. He would like to have been a history teacher but has a stammer which prevented him. He told me this in the half hour we stood out on the sidewalk talking instead of taking the more decisive step of going for coffee. As we said good night he told me that he'd like to have asked me for coffee but he had to get home and spell his wife because the baby had colic.

I unpacked the whole box of books before I was through. It was like looking at relics from a bygone age. I looked through them till the patient was gone and my father had taken Mrs B. home and had come upstairs and used the bathroom and gone to bed. I read here and there till I was so groggy I almost fell asleep on the floor.

At lunch today, then, my father finally said, 'Who cares about the Turks anyway? Ancient history.'

And I had to say, ' I think I know what's going on here.'

His head reared up and he snorted. He really did, like an old horse. 'You do, do you? You think you know what?'

I said, 'I'm not accusing you. I don't disapprove.'

'Is that so?'

'I believe in abortion,' I said. 'I believe it should be legal.'

'I don't want you to use that word again in this house,' my father said.

'Why not?'

'Because I am the one who says what words are used in this house.'

'You don't understand what I'm saying.'

'I understand that you've got too loose a tongue. You've got too loose a tongue and not enough sense. Too much education and not enough ordinary brains.'

I still did not shut up. I said, 'People must know.'

'Must they? There's a difference between knowing and yapping. Get that through your head once and for all.'

We have not spoken for the rest of the day. I cooked the usual roast for dinner and we ate it and did not speak. I don't think he finds this difficult at all. Neither do I so far because everything seems so stupid and outrageous and I'm angry, but I won't stay in this mood forever and I could find myself apologising. (You may not be surprised to hear that.) It's so obviously time that I got out of here.

The young man last night told me that when he felt relaxed his stammer practically disappeared. Like when I'm talking to you, he said. I could probably make him fall in love with me, to a certain extent. I could do that just for recreation. That is the sort of life I could get into here.

*

Dear R. I haven't gone, the Mini wasn't fit for it. I took it in to be over-hauled. Also the weather has changed, the wind has got into an autumn rampage scooping up the lake and battering the beach. It caught Mrs Barrie on her own front steps – the wind did – and knocked her side-ways and shattered her elbow. It's her left elbow and she said she could work with her right arm, but my father told her it was a complicated fracture and he wanted her to rest for a month. He asked me if I would mind postponing my departure. Those were his words – 'postponing my departure'. He hasn't asked where I'm planning to go; he just knows about the car.

I don't know where I'm planning to go, either.

I said all right, I'd stay while I could be useful. So we're on decent speaking terms; in fact it's fairly comfortable. I try to do just about what Mrs B. would do, in the house. No tries now at reorganisation, no discussion of repairs. (The eaves have been done – when the Mrs B. relation came I was astonished and grateful.) I hold the oven door shut the way Mrs B. did with a couple of heavy medical textbooks set on a stool pushed up against it. I cook the meat and the vegetables in her way and never think about bringing home an avocado or bottle of arti-choke hearts or a garlic bulb, though I see all those things are now for sale in the supermarket. I make the coffee from the powder in the jar. I tried drinking that myself to see if I could get used to it and of course I could. I clean up the office at the end of every day and look after the laundry. The laundryman likes me because I don't accuse him of anything.

I'm allowed to answer the phone, but if it's a woman asking for my father and not volunteering details I'm supposed to take the number and say that the doctor will phone back. So I do, and sometimes the woman just hangs up. When I tell my father this he says, 'She'll likely call again.'

There aren't many of those patients – the ones he calls the specials. I don't know – maybe one a month. Mostly he's dealing with sore throats and cramped colons and bealing ears and so on. Jumpy hearts, kidney stones, sour digestions.

R. Tonight he knocked on my door. He knocked though it wasn't all the way closed. I was reading. He asked – not in a supplicating way of course, but I would say with a reasonable respect – if I could give him a hand in the office.

The first special since Mrs B. has been away.

I asked what he wanted me to do.

'Just more or less to keep her steady,' he said. 'She's young and she's not used to it yet. Give your hands a good scrub too, use the soap in the bottle in the toilet downstairs.'

The patient was lying flat on the examining table with a sheet over her from the waist down. The top part of her was fully dressed in a dark-blue buttoned-up cardigan and a white blouse with a lace-trimmed collar. These clothes lay loosely over her sharp collarbone and nearly flat chest. Her hair was black, pulled tightly back from her face and braided and pinned on top of her head. This prim and severe style made her neck look long and emphasised the regal bone structure of her white face, so that from a distance she could be taken for a woman of forty-five. Close up you could see that she was quite young, probably around twenty. Her pleated skirt was hung up on the back of the door. The rim of white panties showed, that she had thoughtfully hung underneath it.

She was shivering hard though the office wasn't cold.

'Now Madeleine,' my father said. 'The first thing is we've got to get your knees up.'

I wondered if he knew her. Or did he just ask for a name and use whatever the woman gave him?

'Easy,' he said. 'Easy. Easy.' He got the stirrups in place and her feet into them. Her legs were bare and looked as if they'd never known a suntan. She was still wearing her loafers.

Her knees shook so much in this new position that they clapped together.

'You'll have to hold steadier than that,' my father said. 'You know,

now, I can't do my job unless you do yours. Do you want a blanket over you?'

He said to me, 'Get her a blanket. Off the bottom shelf there.'

I arranged the blanket to cover the top part of Madeleine's body. She didn't look at me. Her teeth rattled against one another. She clenched her mouth shut.

'Now just slide down this way a bit,' my father said. And to me. 'Hold her knees. Get them apart. Just hold her easy.'

I put my hands on the knobs of the girl's knees and moved them apart as gently as I could. My father's breathing filled the room with its busy unintelligible comments. I had to hold Madeleine's knees quite firmly to keep them from jerking together.

'Where's that old woman?' she said.

I said, 'She's at home. She had a fall. I'm here instead.'

So she had been here before.

'She's rough,' she said.

Her voice was matter-of-fact, almost a growl, not so nervous as I would have expected from the agitation of her body.

'I hope I'm not that rough,' I said.

She didn't answer. My father had picked up a thin rod like a knitting needle.

'Now. This is the hard part,' he said. He spoke in a conversational tone, milder I think than any I have ever heard from him. 'And the more you tighten up the harder it will be. So just – easy. There. Easy. Good girl. Good girl.'

I was trying to think of something to say that would ease her or distract her. I could see now what my father was doing. Laid out on a white cloth on the table beside him, he had a series of rods, all of the same length but of a graduated thickness. These were what he would use, one after the other, to open and stretch the cervix. From my station behind the sheeted barrier beyond the girl's knees, I could not see the actual, intimate progress of these instruments. But I could feel it, from the arriving waves of pain in her body that beat down the spasms of apprehension and actually made her quieter.

Where are you from? Where did you go to school? Do you have a job? (I had noticed a wedding ring, but quite possibly they all wore wedding rings.) Do you like your job? Do you have any brothers or sisters?

Why should she want to answer any of that, even if she wasn't in pain?

She sucked her breath back through her teeth and widened her eyes at the ceiling.

'I know,' I said. 'I know.'

'Getting there,' my father said. 'You're a good girl. Good quiet girl. Won't be long now.'

I said, 'I was going to paint this room but I never got around to it. If you were going to paint it, what color would you choose?'

'Hoh,' said Madeleine. 'Hoh.' A sudden startled expulsion of breath. 'Hoh. Hoh.'

'Yellow,' I said. 'I thought a light yellow. Or a light green?'

By the time we got to the thickest rod Madeleine had thrust her head back into the flat cushion, stretching out her long neck and stretching her mouth too, lips wide and tight over her teeth.

'Think of your favorite movie. What is your favorite movie?'

A nurse said that to me, just as I reached the unbelievable interminable plateau of pain and was convinced that relief would not come, not this time. How could movies exist anymore in the world? Now I'd said the same thing to Madeleine, and Madeleine's eyes flicked over me with the coldly distracted expression of someone who sees that a human being can be about as much use as a stopped clock.

I risked taking one hand off her knee and touched her hand. I was surprised at how quickly and fiercely she grabbed it and mashed the fingers together. Some use after all.

'Say some—' she hissed through her teeth. 'Reese. Right.'

'Now then,' my father said. 'Now we're someplace.'

Recite.

What was I supposed to recite? Hickory dickery dock?

What came into my head was what you used to say, 'The Song of Wandering Aengus'.

'"I went into a hazel wood,/ Because a fire was in my head—"'

I didn't remember how it went on from there. I couldn't think. Then what should come into my head but the whole last verse.

> *'Though I am old from wandering*
> *Through hollow lands and hilly lands,*
> *I will find out where you have gone,*
> *And kiss your face and take your hands—'*

Imagine me saying a poem in front of my father.

What she thought of it I didn't know. She had closed her eyes.

I thought I was going to be afraid of dying because of my mother's dying that way, in childbirth. But once I got onto that plateau I found that dying and living were both irrelevant notions, like favorite movies. I was stretched to the limit and convinced that I couldn't do a thing to move what felt like a giant egg or a flaming planet not like a baby at all. It was stuck and I was stuck, in a space and time that could just go on forever – there was no reason why I should ever get out, and all my protests had already been annihilated.

'Now I need you,' my father said. 'I need you round here. Get the basin.'

I held in place the same basin that I had seen Mrs Barrie holding. I held it while he scraped out the girl's womb with a clever sort of kitchen instrument. (I don't mean that it was a kitchen instrument but that it had a slightly homely look to me.)

The lower parts of even a thin young girl can look large and meaty in this raw state. In the days after labor, in the maternity ward, women lay carelessly, even defiantly, with their fiery cuts or tears exposed, their black-stitch wounds and sorry flaps and big helpless haunches. It was a sight to see.

Out of the womb now came plops of wine jelly, and blood, and somewhere in there the fetus. Like the bauble in the cereal box or the prize in the popcorn. A tiny plastic doll as negligible as a fingernail. I didn't look for it. I held my head up, away from the smell of warm blood.

'Bathroom,' my father said. 'There's a cover.' He meant the folded cloth that lay beside the soiled rods. I did not like to say, 'Down the toilet?' and took it for granted that that was what he meant. I carried the basin along the hall to the downstairs toilet, dumped the contents, flushed twice, rinsed the basin, and brought it back. My father by this time was bandaging the girl and giving her some instructions. He's good at this – he does it well. But his face looked heavy, weary enough to drop off the bones. It occurred to me that he had wanted me here, all through the procedure, in case he should collapse. Mrs B., at least in the old days, apparently waited in the kitchen until the last moments. Maybe she stays with him all the way through now.

If he had collapsed I don't know what I'd have done.

He patted Madeleine's legs and told her she should lie flat.

'Don't try to get up for a few minutes,' he said. 'Have you got your ride arranged for?'

'He's supposed to've been out there all the time, she said in a weak but spiteful voice. 'He wasn't supposed to've gone anyplace.'

My father took off his smock and walked to the window of the waiting room.

'You bet,' he said. 'Right there.' He let out a complicated groan, said, 'Where's the laundry basket?' remembered that it was back in the bright room where he'd been working, came back and deposited the smock and said to me, 'I'd be very obliged if you could tidy this up.' Tidy up meaning doing the sterilising and mopping up in general.

I said I would.

'Good,' he said. 'I'll say good night now. My daughter will see you out when you're ready to go.' I was somewhat surprised to hear him say 'my daughter' instead of my name. Of course I'd heard him say that before. If he had to introduce me, for instance. Still, I was surprised.

Madeleine swung her legs off the table the minute he was out of he room. Then she staggered and I went to help her. She said, 'Okay, okay, just got off of the table too quick. Where'd I put my skirt? I don't want to stand around looking like this.'

I got her the skirt and panties off the back of the door and she put them on without help but very shakily.

I said, 'You could rest a minute. Your husband will wait.'

'My husband's working in the bush up near Kenora,' she said. 'I'm going up there next week. He's got a place I can stay.'

'Now. I laid my coat down somewheres,' she said.

My favorite movie – as you ought to know and if I could have thought of it when the nurse asked me – is *Wild Strawberries*. I remember the moldy little theater where we used to see all those Swedish and Japanese and Indian and Italian movies and I remember that it had recently switched over from showing *Carry On* movies, and Martin and Lewis, but the name of it I can't remember. Since you were teaching philosophy to future ministers your favorite movie should have been *The Seventh Seal*, but was it? I think it was Japanese and I forget what it was about. Anyway we used to walk home from the theater, it was a couple of miles, and we used to have fervent conversations about human love and self-ishness and God and faith and desperation. When we got to my rooming house we had to shut up. We had to go so softly up the stairs to my room.

Ahhh, you would say gratefully and wonderingly as you got in.

I would have been very nervous about bringing you here last Christmas if we hadn't already been deep into our fight. I would have felt too protective of you to expose you to my father.

'Robin? Is that a man's name?'

You said, Well yes, it was your name,

He pretended he'd never heard it before.

But in fact you got along pretty well together. You had a discussion about some great conflict between different orders of monks in the seventh century, wasn't that it? The row those monks had was about how they should shave their heads.

A curly-headed beanpole was what he called you. Coming from him that was almost complimentary.

When I told him on the phone that after all you and I would not be getting married, he said, 'Oh-oh. Do you think you'll ever manage to get another one?' If I'd objected to his saying that he would naturally have said it was a joke. And it was a joke. I have not managed to get another one but perhaps have not been in the best condition to try.

Mrs Barrie is back. She's back in less than three weeks though it was supposed to be a month. But she has to work shorter days than she did before. It takes her so long to get dressed and to do her own housework that she seldom gets here (delivered by her nephew or her nephew's wife) until around ten o'clock in the morning.

'Your father looks poorly' was the first thing she said to me. I think she's right.

'Maybe he should take a rest,' I said.

'Too many people bothering him,' she said.

The Mini is out of the garage and the money is in my bank account. What I should do is take off. But I think stupid things. I think, What if we get another special? How can Mrs B. help him? She can't use her left hand yet to hold any weight, and she could never hold on to the basin with just her right hand.

R. This day. This day was after the first big snowfall. It all happened overnight and in the morning the sky was clear, blue; there was no wind and the brightness was preposterous. I went for an early walk, under the pine trees. Snow was sifting through them, straight down, bright as the stuff on Christmas trees, or diamonds. The highway had already been plowed and so had our lane, so that my father could drive out to the hospital. Or I could drive out whenever I wanted to.

Some cars went by, in and out of town, as on any other morning.

Before I went back into the house I just wanted to see if the Mini would start and it did. On the passenger seat I saw a package. It was a two-pound box of chocolates, the kind you buy at the drugstore. I couldn't think how it had got there – I wondered if it could possibly be a present from the young man at the Historical Society. That was a stupid thought. But who else?

I stomped my boots free of snow outside the back door and reminded myself that I must put a broom out. The kitchen had filled up with the day's blast of light.

I thought I knew what my father would say.

'Out contemplating nature?'

He was sitting at the table with his hat and coat on. Usually by this time he had left to see his patients in the hospital.

He said, 'Have they got the road plowed yet? What about the lane?

I said that both were plowed and clear. He could have seen that the lane was plowed by looking out the window. I put the kettle on and asked if he would like another cup of coffee before he went out.

'All right,' he said. 'Just so long as it's plowed so I can get out.'

'What a day,' I said.

'All right if you don't have to shovel yourself out of it.'

I made the two cups of instant coffee and set them on the table. I sat down, facing the window and the incoming light. He sat at the end of the table, and had shifted his chair so that the light was at his back. I couldn't see what the expression on his face was, but his breathing kept me company as usual.

I started to tell my father about myself. I hadn't intended to do this at all. I had meant to say something about my going away. I opened my mouth and things began to come out of it that I heard with equal amounts of dismay and satisfaction, the way you hear the things you say when you are drunk.

'You never knew I had a baby,' I said. 'I had it on the seventeenth of July. In Ottawa. I've been thinking how ironic that was.'

I told him that the baby had been adopted right away and that I didn't know whether it had been a boy or a girl. That I had asked not to be told. And I had asked not to have to see it.

'I stayed with Josie,' I said. 'You remember me speaking about my friend Josie. She's in England now but she was all alone then in her parents' house. Her parents had been posted to South Africa. That was a godsend.'

I told him who the father of the baby was. I said it was you, in case he wondered. And that since you and I were already engaged, even officially engaged, I had thought that all we had to do was get married.

But you thought differently. You said that we had to find a doctor. A doctor who would give me an abortion.

He did not remind me that I was never supposed to speak that word in his house.

I told him that you said we could not just go ahead and get married, because anybody who could count would know that I had been pregnant before the wedding. We could not get married until I was definitely not pregnant anymore.

Otherwise you might lose your job at the Theological College.

They could bring you up before a committee that might judge you were morally unfit. Morally unfit for the job of teaching young ministers. You could be judged to have a bad character. And even supposing this did not happen, that you did not lose your job but were only reprimanded, or were not even reprimanded, you would never be promoted; there would be a stain on your record. Even if nobody said anything to you, they would *have something* on you, and you could not stand that. The new students coming in would hear about you from the older ones; there'd be jokes passed on, about you. Your colleagues would have a chance to look down on you. Or be understanding, which was just as bad. You would be a man quietly or not so quietly despised, and a failure.

Surely not, I said.

Oh yes. Never underestimate the meanness there is in people's souls. And for me too, it would be devastating. The wives controlled so much, the older professors' wives. They'd never let me forget. Even when they were being kind – *especially* when they were being kind.

But we could just pick up and go somewhere else, I said. Somewhere where nobody would know.

They'd know. There's always somebody who makes sure that people know.

Besides that would mean you'd have to start at the bottom again. You'd have to start at a lower salary, a pitiful salary, and how could we manage with a baby, in that case?

I was astonished at these arguments which did not seem to be consistent with the ideas of the person I had loved. The books we had read, the movies we had seen, the things we had talked about – I asked if that meant nothing to you. You said yes, but this was life. I asked if you were somebody who could not stand the thought of someone laughing at him, who would cave in before a bunch of professors' wives.

You said, That's not it, that's not it at all.

I threw my diamond ring away and it rolled under a parked car. As we argued we were walking along a street near my rooming house. It was winter, like now. January or February. But the battle dragged on after that. I was supposed to find out about an abortion from a friend who had a friend who was rumored to have had one. I gave in; I said I'd do it. You couldn't even risk making inquiries. But then I lied, I said the doctor had moved away. Then I admitted lying. I can't do it, I said.

But was that because of the baby? Never. It was because I believed I was right, in the argument.

I had contempt. I had contempt when I saw you scrambling to get under the parked car, and the tails of your overcoat were flapping around your buttocks. You were clawing in the snow to find the ring and you were so relieved when you found it. You were ready to hug me and laugh at me, thinking I'd be relieved too and we'd make up on the spot. I told you you would never do anything admirable in your whole life.

Hypocrite, I said. Sniveller. Philosophy teacher.

Not that that was the end. For we did make up. But we didn't forgive each other. And we didn't take steps. And it got to be too late and we saw that each of us had invested too much in being in the right and we walked away and it was a relief. Yes, at that time I'm sure it was a relief for us both and a kind of victory.

'So isn't that ironic?' I said to my father. 'Considering?'

I could hear Mrs Barrie outside stomping her boots, so I said this in a hurry. My father had sat all the time rigid with embarrassment as I thought, or with profound distaste.

Mrs Barrie opened the door saying, 'Ought to get a broom out there—' Then she cried out, 'What are you doing sitting there? What's the matter with you? Can't you see the man's dead?'

He wasn't dead. He was in fact breathing as noisily as ever and perhaps more so. What she had seen and what I would have seen, even against the light, if I had not been avoiding looking at him whilst I told my tale, was that he had suffered a blinding and paralysing stroke. He sat slightly tilted forward, the table pressing into the firm curve of his stomach. When we tried to move him from his chair, we managed only to jar him so that his head came down on the table, with a majestic reluctance. His hat stayed on. And his coffee cup stayed in place a couple of inches from his unseeing eye. It was still about half full.

I said we couldn't do anything with him; he was too heavy. I went to the phone and called the hospital, to get one of the other doctors to drive out. There's no ambulance yet in this town. Mrs B. paid no attention to what I said and kept pulling at my father's clothes, undoing buttons and yanking at the overcoat and grunting and whimpering with the exertion. I ran out to the lane, leaving the door open. I ran back, and got a broom, and set it outside by the door. I went and put a hand on Mrs B.'s arm and said, 'You can't' or something like that, and she gave me the look of a spitting cat.

A doctor came. He and I together were able to pull my father out to the car and get him into the back seat. I got in beside him to hold on to him and keep him from toppling over. The sound of breathing was more peremptory than ever and seemed to be criticising whatever we did. But the fact was that you could take hold of him now, and shove him around, and manage his body as you had to, and this seemed very odd.

Mrs B. had fallen back and quieted down as soon as she saw the other doctor. She didn't even follow us out of the house to see my father loaded into the car.

This afternoon he died. At about five o'clock. I was told it was very lucky for all concerned.

I was full of other things to say, just when Mrs Barrie came in. I was going to say to my father, What if the law should change? The law might change soon, I was going to say. Maybe not, but it might. He'd be out of business then. Or out of one part of his business. Would that make a great difference to him?

What could I expect him to answer?

Speaking of business, that is none of yours.

Or, I'd still make a living.

No, I would say. I didn't mean the money. I meant the risk. The secrecy. The power.

Change the law, change what a person does, change what a person is?

Or would he find some other risk, some other knot to make in his life, some other underground and problematic act of mercy?

And if that law can change, other things can change. I'm thinking about you now, how it could happen that you wouldn't be ashamed to marry a pregnant woman. There'd be no shame to it. Move ahead a few years, just a few years, and it could be a celebration. The pregnant bride is garlanded and led to the altar, even in the chapel of the Theological College.

If that happened, though, there'd likely be something else to be ashamed or afraid of, there'd be other errors to be avoided.

So what about me? Would I always have to find a high horse? The moral relish, the rising above, the being in the right, which can make me flaunt my losses.

Change the person. We all say we hope it can be done.

Change the law, change the person. Yet we don't want everything – not the whole story – to be dictated from outside. We don't want what we are, all we are, to be concocted that way.

Who is this 'we' I'm talking about?

R. My father's lawyer says, 'It's very unusual.' I realise that for him this is quite a strong, and sufficient, word.

There is enough money in my father's bank account to cover his funeral expenses. Enough to bury him, as they say. (Not the lawyer – he doesn't talk like that.) But there isn't much more. There are no stock certificates in his safety deposit box; there is no record of investments. Nothing. No bequest to the hospital, or to his church, or to the high school to establish a scholarship. Most shocking of all, there is no money left to Mrs Barrie. The house and its contents are mine. And that's all there is. I have my five thousand dollars.

The lawyer seems embarrassed, painfully embarrassed, and worried about this state of affairs. Perhaps he thinks I might suspect him of misconduct. Try to blacken his name. He wants to know if there's a safe in my (my father's) house, any hiding place at all for a large amount of cash. I say there isn't. He tries to suggest to me – in such a discreet and roundabout way that I don't know at first what he's talking about – that there might be reasons for my father's wanting to keep the amount of his earnings a secret. A large amount of cash holed away somewhere is therefore a possibility.

I tell him I'm not terribly concerned about the money.

What a thing to say. He can hardly look me in the eye.

'Perhaps you could go home and take a very good look,' he says. 'Don't neglect the obvious places. It could be in a cookie tin. Or in a box under the bed. Surprising the places people can pick. Even the most sensible and intelligent people.

'Or in a pillow slip,' he's saying as I go out the door.

A woman on the phone wants to speak to the doctor.

'I'm sorry. He's dead.'

'Dr Strachan. Have I got the right doctor?'

'Yes but I'm sorry, he's dead.'

'Is there anyone – does he by any chance have a partner I could talk to? Is there anybody else there?'

'No. No partner.'

'Could you give me any other number I could call? Isn't there some other doctor that can—'

'No. I haven't any number. There isn't anybody that I know of.'

'You must know what this is about. It's very crucial. There are very special circumstances—'

'I'm sorry.'

'There isn't any problem about money.'

'No.'

'Please try to think of somebody. If you do think of somebody later on, could you give me a call? I'll leave you my number.'

'You shouldn't do that.'

'I don't care. I trust you. Anyway it's not for myself. I know everybody must say that but really it's not. It's for my daughter who's in a very bad condition. Mentally she's in a very bad condition.'

'I'm sorry.'

'If you knew what I went through to get this number you would try to help me.'

'Sorry.'

'Please.'

'I'm sorry.'

Madeleine was the last one of his specials. I saw her at the funeral. She hadn't got to Kenora. Or else she'd come back. I didn't recognise her at first because she was wearing a wide-brimmed black hat with a horizontal feather. She must have borrowed it – she wasn't used to the feather which came drooping down over her eye. She spoke to me in the lineup at the reception in the church hall. I said to her just the same thing I said to everybody.

'So good of you to come.'

Then I realised what an odd thing she'd said to me.

'I was just counting on you to have a sweet tooth.'

'Perhaps he didn't always charge,' I say to the lawyer. 'Perhaps he worked for nothing sometimes. Some people do things out of charity.'

The lawyer is getting used to me now. He says, 'Perhaps.'

'Or possibly an actual charity,' I say. 'A charity he supported without keeping any record of it.'

The lawyer holds my eyes for a moment.

'A charity,' he says.

'Well I haven't dug up the cellar floor yet,' I say, and he smiles wincingly at this levity.

Mrs Barrie hasn't given her notice. She just hasn't shown up. There was nothing in particular for her to do, since the funeral was in the church and the reception was in the church hall. She didn't come to the funeral. None of her family came. So many people were there that I would not have noticed that if someone hadn't said to me, 'I didn't see any of the Barrie connection, did you?'

I phoned her several days afterwards and she said, 'I never went to the church because I had too bad a cold.'

I said that that wasn't why I'd called. I said I could manage quite well but wondered what she planned to do.

'Oh I don't see no need for me to come back there now.'

I said that she should come and get something from the house, a keepsake. By this time I knew about the money and I wanted to tell her I felt bad about it. But I didn't know how to say that.

She said, 'I got some stuff I left there. I'll be out when I can.'

She came out the next morning. The things she had to collect were mops and pails and scrub brushes and a clothes basket. It was hard to believe she would care about retrieving articles like these. And hard to believe she wanted them for sentimental reasons, but maybe she did. They were things she had used for years – during all her years in this house, where she had spent more waking hours than she had spent at home.

'Isn't there anything else?' I said. 'For a keepsake?'

She looked around the kitchen, chewing on her bottom lip. She might have been chewing back a smile.

'I don't think there's nothing here I'd have much use for,' she said.

I had a check ready for her. I just needed to write in the amount. I hadn't been able to decide how much of the five thousand dollars to share with her. A thousand? I had been thinking. Now that seemed shameful. I thought I'd better double it.

I got out the checks that I had hidden in a drawer. I found a pen. I made it out for four thousand dollars.

'This is for you,' I said. 'And thank you for everything.'

She took the check in her hand and glanced at it and stuffed it in her pocket. I thought maybe she hadn't been able to read how much it was for. Then I saw the darkening flush, the tide of embarrassment, the difficulty of being grateful.

She managed to pick up all the things she was taking, using her one good arm. I opened the door for her. I was so anxious for her to say something more that I almost said, Sorry that's all.

Instead I said, 'Your elbow's not better yet?'

'It'll never be better,' she said. She ducked her head as if she was afraid of another of my kisses. She said, 'Well-thanks-very-much-goodbye.'

I watched her making her way to the car. I had assumed her nephew's wife had driven her out here.

But it was not the usual car that the nephew's wife drove. The thought crossed my mind that she might have a new employer. Bad arm or not. A new and rich employer. That would account for her haste, her cranky embarrassment.

It was the nephew's wife, after all, who got out to help with the load. I waved, but she was too busy stowing the mops and pails.

'Gorgeous car,' I called out, because I thought that was a compliment both women would appreciate. I didn't know what make the car was, but it was shining new and large and glamorous. A silvery lilac color.

The nephew's wife called out, 'Oh yeah,' and Mrs Barrie ducked her head in acknowledgement.

Shivering in my indoor clothes, but compelled by my feelings of apology and bewilderment, I stood there and waved the car out of sight.

I couldn't settle down to do anything after that. I made myself coffee and sat in the kitchen. I got Madeleine's chocolates out of the drawer and ate a couple, though I really did not have enough of a sweet tooth for their chemically colored orange and yellow centers. I wished I had thanked her. I didn't see how I could now – I didn't even know her last name.

I decided to go out skiing. There are gravel pits that I believe I told you about at the back of our property. I put on the old wooden skis that my father used to wear in the days when the back roads were not plowed out in winter, and he might have to go across the fields to deliver a baby or take out an appendix. There were only cross-straps to hold your feet in place.

I skied back to the gravel pits whose slopes have been padded with grass over the years and are now additionally covered with snow. There were dog tracks, bird tracks, the faint circles that the skittering voles make, but no sign of humans. I went up and down, up and down, first choosing a cautious diagonal and then going on to steeper descents. I fell now and then, but easily on the fresh plentiful snow, and between one moment of falling and the next of getting to my feet I found out that I knew something.

I knew where the money had gone.

Perhaps a charity.

Gorgeous car.

And four thousand dollars out of five.

Since that moment I have been happy.

I've been given the feeling of seeing money thrown over a bridge or high up into the air. Money, hopes, love letters – all such things can be tossed off into the air and come down changed, come down all light and free of context.

The thing I can't imagine is my father caving in to blackmail. Particularly not to people who wouldn't be very credible or clever. Not when the whole town seems to be on his side or at least on the side of silence.

What I can imagine, though, is a grand perverse gesture. To forestall demand, maybe, or just to show he didn't care. Looking forward to the lawyer's shock, and to my trying even harder to figure him out, now that he's dead.

No. I don't think he'd be thinking of that. I don't think I'd have come into his thoughts so much. Never so much as I'd like to believe.

What I've been shying away from is that it could have been done for love.

For love, then. Never rule that out.

I climbed out of the gravel pit and as soon as I came out on the fields the wind hit me. Wind was blowing snow over the dog tracks and the fine chain traces of the vole and the trail that will likely be the last ever to be broken by my father's skis.

Dear R., Robin – what should be the last thing I say to you?

Goodbye and good luck.

I send you my love.

(What if people really did that – sent their love through the mail to get rid of it? What would it be that they sent? A box of chocolates with centers like the yolks of turkeys' eggs. A mud doll with hollow eye sockets. A heap of roses slightly more fragrant than rotten. A package wrapped in bloody newspaper that nobody would want to open.)

Take care of yourself.

Remember – the present King of France is bald.

Larry's Words, 1983
Carol Shields

The word *labyrinth* has only recently come into the vocabulary of Larry
Weller, aged thirty-two, a heterosexual male (married, one child) living
in Winnipeg, Manitoba, Canada. He doesn't bother himself with the
etymology of the word *labyrinth*; in fact, at this time in his life he has
zero interest in word derivations, but he can tell you plain and simple
what a labyrinth is. A labyrinth is a complex path. That's it. It's not
necessarily something complicated or classical, as you might think. The
overpass out on Highway 2 is a kind of labyrinth, as Larry will be happy
to tell you. So is the fox-and-geese tracery he stamped into the backyard
snow as a child in Winnipeg's West End. He sees that now. So's a
modern golf course. Take St George's Country Club out in the St James
area of the city, for instance, the way it nudges you along gently from
hole to hole, each step plotted in a forward direction so that you
wouldn't dream of attacking the whole thing backwards or bucking in
any way the ongoing, numerically predetermined scheme. And an
airport is a labyrinth too, or a commercial building or, say, a city subway
system. It seems those who live in the twentieth century have a liking
for putting ourselves on a predetermined conveyor track and letting it
carry us along.

A maze, though, is different from a labyrinth, at least in the opinion
of some. A maze is more likely to baffle and mislead those who tread its
paths. A maze is a puzzle. A maze is designed to deceive the travellers
who seek a promised goal. It's possible that a labyrinth can be a maze,
and that a maze can be a labyrinth, but strictly speaking the two words

call up different *ideas*. (Larry read these definitions, and their relationship to each other, three years ago, in a library book called *Mazes and Labyrinths: Their History and Development*.)

If he had not married Dorrie Shaw, if he had never visited Hampton Court, his life would have swerved on an alternate course, and the word *labyrinth* would have floated by him like one of those specks in the fluid of his eye.

He finds it paradoxical that while his life is shrinking before his very eyes, his vocabulary should be expanding. It's weird. It's far-out. It's *paradoxical* – that's the bouncy new word he's been saying out loud lately, not to show off, but because it 'pops' on his tongue. It's a word he's only recently taken into his brain, last week in fact. 'Isn't it paradoxical,' his sister Midge said to him over the phone, 'that I kicked my husband out because he was just plain queer, and now I've moved in with him because he's queer and he's sick and maybe dying?'

'It's what?' Larry asked her, ashamed of his begging tone, his needy need to know what words mean. 'What did you call it?'

'A paradox. You know, like ironic.'

'Oh, yeah. Right.'

He went the next day and bought himself a pocket dictionary and he keeps it down at Flowercity. It's on a shelf under the counter, handy. There are people, he's noticed, whose vocabularies stand a step or two higher on the evolutionary staircase, and he's had this idea lately that words can help him in the future or maybe even with his present difficulties. The empty white echo he sometimes hears can be calmed by words. It might be the solution: that all he needs are some new words, big or little it doesn't matter, as long as their compacted significance registers, in his head, on his tongue. He could increase his overall word power, add a new word every day. Who knows what's likely to happen if he sharpens up: the way he talks, the way he thinks. There are men and women who live by cunning and silence, but he doesn't want to be one of them, grunting, pointing, holding back. He wants to be ready when the time comes to open his mouth and let the words run out like streaming lava.

There are people out there who imagine they want to pass straight through language to clarity, but Larry Weller of Winnipeg, Canada, wants, all of a sudden, at age thirty-two, to hang on to words, even separate words that sit all on their own, each with a little brain and a wreath of steam around its breathed-out sound: cantankerous, irrepressible, magnanimous. And, yes, ironic. You can discuss this idea of words, but you'll need more words just to get started: hypothesis, axiomatic, closure.

He was a dreamy kid growing up, and after that a dreamy adolescent, just letting his life happen to him. It took him years to get himself wide awake, and lately he's been feeling that he's dozing off again, collapsing inward like the shrink-wrapped merchandise on the rack at the front of the store, the little plastic bottles of Vita-Grow and Root-Start and Mite-Bomb. The music that pours out of the radio all day at the store has flattened his brain with its wailing. He's reached a dead end in his job – branch manager of a so-so flower shop – where he's been for fourteen years. An impasse. (That's another of his new words; he got that one from TV.) Besides his job stalemate, he's got a wife who won't sleep in the same bed with him anymore, at least not until he promises to sell their house and move upmarket.

Upmarket. He doesn't need to look that one up. He hears it all the time these days, and little by little he's absorbed more or less the sense of what it means. Last year he and Dorrie traded in their old Toyota and 'moved upmarket' to a *brand-new* Toyota. Not a huge move, just a subtle shift upward. (The word subtle he can pronounce, but not spell, but then he doesn't need to spell it, does he?)

The florist chain he works for used to be called Flowerfolks, until *it* went upmarket, becoming Flowercity with a whole new clientele and a different product line: more exotics, more artificials and dried stuff. Ryan, his four-year-old son, has gone 'upmarket' too, toddling off to junior-kindergarten in co-ordinated outfits manufactured by OshKosh and Kids-Can-Grow.

It's ironic, Larry thinks, *ironic* that his wife Dorrie grew up in a pokey little lace-curtainy house over on Borden Road, her mom and dad and six kids packed into four rooms, no basement, a garage full of junk, so that when she and Larry first bought the Lipton Street house, a fixer-upper if there ever was one, she thought they'd arrived at a palace. Well, not now. She's got her eyes on the Linden Woods subdivision, but she can't get Larry motivated to move out that way. He's worked too hard on the hedge maze in the Lipton Street yard, which is just beginning to take shape.

So who's going to buy a house, Dorrie says, that's got a yard choked to the gills with bushes?

One of these days she's going to get a bulldozer in there and clear the whole thing out. This bush business is driving her straight up the wall. That's an expression she's picked up from Larry's English mother, and these days just about everything drives her up the wall.

Or else drives her bananas. Like, for instance, the way her husband, Larry, talks. Those big words he's spouting. She hadn't figured him for a show-off when they first met back in 1976, so how come he's exploding these days with fancy words?

Is this a fair accusation? Well, yes and no. A lot of Larry's recently acquired vocabulary is clustered around his *preoccupation* with mazes. He's lifted his collection of new words from a series of library books, and they've stuck to him like burrs. Dorrie says he's trying to put her down when he uses these words. She says he always has his nose in a book. He used to be fun, he used to make her laugh, but now all he can talk about are such things as: turf mazes, shepherd's race, Julian's bower, knot garden, Jerusalem, Minotaur, *jeu-de-lettres*, pigs-in-clover, frets and meanders, the Trémaux algorithm, *pavimentum tessellatum*, fylfot, wilderness, unicursal, topiary, nodes, the Mount of Venus, *maisons de Dëdalus*, Troy-town, cup-and-ring, ocular or spiral, serpent-through-waist, chevron.

On and on. He's astonished himself to think he's taken in so many words in the last few years, harpoons aimed straight at the brain, and that he actually remembers them.

One of Larry's steady customers down at the flower shop is Mrs Fordwich, who popped in the other morning, ordering flowers for the annual Chamber Music Fund Raiser, and, since it was getting close to Christmas, Larry suggested a basket of mixed poinsettias. 'I don't think so, Larry,' she said slowly. 'I mean, poinsettias at this time of the year! It's a little banal, don't you think?'

Banal. It seems to him he's heard that word before, and now, from Mrs Fordwich he detects, along with the word's lazy, offhand delivery, a shade of dismissal in her voice. He stares at her woundedly. But what exactly does banal mean?

Later, he reaches under the counter for his dictionary. The definition of banal is: meaningless from overuse; hackneyed; trivial. There are punctures in Larry's overall perception, he sees, that will exclude him, cripple him unless he smartens up – and what else? He'll be left all his life with that drifting, stupid, *banal* crinkle on his puss: *Hey, would you mind running that by me one more time. I didn't quite catch—*

This is no one's fault exactly; this is what you'd expect, given Larry Weller's history, his background, his *banal* take on the world.

Carnations are probably banal too, he reasons. Asparagus fern sure as hell is banal. Chrysanthemums? Definitely, those poofy pots from Safeway with the bow stuck on the side. And maybe, just probably, he's a little banal himself

A *spokeshave* is a cutting tool having a blade set between two handles, and it's used for rounding wood or other materials.

Larry had never seen or heard the word spokeshave until he and Dorrie and their little boy, Ryan, were invited, along with a few other neighbors, over to Lucy Warkenten's apartment for a Christmas drink.

Lucy lives next door to the Wellers on the second floor of an old house, and works as a bookbinder, using a screened-off corner of her living room for 'a studio'. Larry has always felt friendly toward Lucy, who is about forty years of age and lives alone. She wears long creased skirts and Mexican sweaters and lots of wooden jewellery. Artsy-fartsy, Dorrie calls her, one of your old-time cactus-cunt virgins.

The party was held late on a dark Sunday afternoon, and Lucy had candles burning all around the room. Under a white-painted, sparkle-strewn twig of a tree she had placed wrapped toys for the Lee children who lived downstairs and for four-year-old Ryan: tiny windmills to construct, intricate puzzles, Japanese pencils. There was a bowl of spiced wine punch on the coffee table and plates of fruitcake and cookies. After everyone was served, eating, drinking, and chattering away to each other, Lucy Warkenten drew Larry over to the window and showed him how his maze looked when viewed from above.

His heart jumped to see that, even under a layer of snow, the maze's pattern stood out clearly. Its looping paths, doubling back and forth on themselves, possessed a tidiness and precision he hadn't thought to imagine. 'Watching that maze take shape,' Lucy told Larry solemnly, touching his sweater cuff with the flat of her hand, 'has given me more pleasure than you can know.'

'I think I do know,' he said, and in saying so surrendered a secret he'd once thought necessary.

She showed him her own work corner with its range of tools. *Vellum tips*, marbled *endpapers*, *slips*, *cords*, a *lying press*, the stack of *millboard*, silky *headbands*. Tacked on the wall was a recipe for *glair*, an egg-white mixture that binds gold leaf to paper. A paged book was called a *codex*, she explained to Larry – the word comes from the Latin, meaning wood.

Larry had never heard any of these words before, at least not as they applied to the art of bookbinding, and it made him squint at Lucy through the late afternoon candlelight, seeing her suddenly as someone who lived every day inside the walls of a foreign language, only not really foreign at all. While the other people in the room chatted and snacked on cheese and swallowed glasses of wine, Lucy showed Larry her current project, which was putting between new 'boards' an old volume, and covering it with pale gray goatskin. 'The trick,' she said, 'is to make it look as though the leather has just grown there.' The book was titled *Deep Furrows*, written some sixty years ago by a Canadian socialist called Hopkins Moorhouse.

'Is it any good?' Larry asked.

'What?'

'The book.'

Lucy shrugged. 'Dead boring. But one of Moorhouse's descendants wants it rebound.' Then she said, 'A good binding can preserve a book for hundreds of years.'

Hundreds of years! Larry thought of his fragile floral arrangements, how he never holds out hope for more than a week.

'A work of art!' Lucy pronounced, and he thought at first she was talking about the half-bound book in her hand. In fact, she had put the book down and was looking out her window once again, gesturing toward the sight of his snowy maze, etched in shadow, a strange, many-jointed creature hunkering down beneath the cold moonlight, asking nothing of anybody, not even the favor of being noticed.

Larry's first word as a child was *pop*, and according to family legend he liked to say it over and over, a long sputter of happy pops with a punchy emphasis on the final *p*. Larry's folks, his mum, his dad, decided finally it was just a noise and not a real word, but Larry's mother, Dot, wrote it down anyway in Larry's baby book on the page titled 'Our Baby Learns To Talk.'

Larry's sister Midge, two years older than Larry, was credited with *dog* as her first word. According to family legend, she pronounced it clearly, cleanly, and then she barked a soft baby bow-wow to indicate that she connected language with content. Even at twelve months she was smart as a whip.

Once, years later, Midge said to Larry, 'Maybe you weren't really saying pop at all. Maybe you were saying poop.'

'Maybe you were saying God when you said dog,' Larry told her. 'Like those kids who get things backwards, what d'ya call that again?'

'Dyslexia,' she supplied, somewhat sternly.

'Right,' he said. 'Dyslexia, dyslexia, dyslexia.'

Sometimes Larry sees his future laid out with terrifying clarity. An endless struggle to remember what he already knows.

When Larry was a kid his mother was forever listening to the radio – while she cooked or ironed or did her housework – and sometimes, out of curiosity, she stopped the dial at a place where foreign languages came curling out of the radio's plastic grillwork: Italian or Portuguese or Polish, they were all the same to Larry, full of squawks and spit and kicking sounds.

'Jibber jabber,' Larry's father called this talk, shaking his head, apparently convinced, despite all reason, that these 'noises' meant nothing, that they were no more than a form of elaborate nonsense. Everything ran together; and there weren't any real words the way there were in English. These foreigners were just pretending to talk, trying to fool everyone.

Larry knows better. Everyone in the world walks around with a supply of meaningful words inside their heads, bundled there like kindling or like the long-fibered nerve bundles he remembers from his high school general science class. At the very least these words possess the transparent clarities that point to such objects as floor, window, chair, ball. The more dangerous and toxic words came later and with difficulty, but everyone eventually got themselves equipped with a few. Bus route. Property tax. Paycheck. Pedestrian. Words were everywhere; you couldn't escape them, and along with the shape of the words came comprehension, like a gulped capsule. The world itself seemed to hold a word in its mouth, a single-syllable hum, heavy and vowel-laden and ready as a storm warning to announce itself.

As for himself, he doesn't have enough words yet, he knows that. Not nearly enough.

Larry's mum and dad came to Canada from England back in 1950, but after all this time they still say railway, for example, instead railroad. Larry's mother calls her kitchen stove a cooker, and Larry's dad says petrol instead of gasoline. Larry wouldn't dream of saying railway or cooker or petrol himself, but the words coming out of his parents' mouths feel delicately edged and full, and give his heart every time he hears them, a twist of happiness, as though fumbling, stumbling mother and father have, if nothing else, improvised for themselves a crude shelter in an alien land. They can hide there. Be themselves, whatever that means.

'Mazel tov,' says Larry's friend Bill Herschel, at weddings, birthdays, football games, at any festive occasion.

Larry, growing up next door to the Herschel family, has learned to say it too. The phrase sits on his tongue like a wad of soft caramel. *Mazel tov*. It pushes right past what he's capable of thinking or feeling, so that he opens his mouth and becomes an eloquent maker of fine sounds and of brilliant music. A celebrant, a happy boy; later, a happy man.

The word *sex*? What did it mean? 'Well,' Larry's mother said, plainly embarrassed (this was a long time ago), 'it has to do with hugging and kissing and lying in bed.' Then she said, 'It's mostly for men.'

Years later, when he was a man himself, in his mid-forties, body softening, but his brain ticking along one more skeptical track, Larry Weller lay in a woman's warm embrace and heard himself instructed in what she termed the *tantric* mysteries. Tantric? Sex, she explained in her pebbly voice, could be deeper and more frightening than he knew. You could climb inside the word *sex* and grow yourself a new skin: rough, hairy, primal, unrecognisable. You could go right to the edge of that word and forget your own name, you could bury yourself in your body and find your way out to another existence.

What? Larry asked himself in his plodding, stubborn, and possibly imperious way, what does any of this *mean*?

Damn, hell, Jesus, God, piss, shit, screw, fart, fuck, prick, cunt, balls, asshole, motherfucker.

Larry Weller knows all these words. How could he live in the world if he didn't? They're like coins, for carrying around in your pocket and spending when you feel like it. No one's going to put you in jail for what you open up your mouth and say. (Well, not around here anyway.) Larry's wife, Dorrie, says fucking this, fucking that all the time. It helps to keep her from going bananas, she says. Larry sometimes refers to something or other as being fucked up, but he's careful not to say it around his young son. One fuck-talking parent is enough for a kid to handle.

Sometimes people don't even know what they're saying. Words can slip loose from their meanings. There's a young, slender and beautiful Vietnamese woman who comes into Larry's flower shop every Friday afternoon to take advantage of the weekly happy hour: all cut flowers at half-price between four and five p.m. She points shyly to what she wants, three tulips, say, some sprays of foliage or whatever – then she counts out her money carefully on the counter, picks up the wrapped flowers and says, bowing politely, sweetly, 'Okay, I bugger off now.'

There is in the English language a rollcall of noble words. Nation. Honour. Achievement. Majesty. Integrity. Righteousness. Learning. Glory.

Larry knows these words – who doesn't? – but almost never uses them. These are the words of those anointed beings who take the long view. Whereas he lives in the short view, his close-up, textured, parochial world, the little valley of intimacy he was born into, always thinking, without knowing he's thinking. Living next door to the great words, but not with them. His share of the truth – what truth? – is going to come (when it comes) modestly packaged and tied with string, he knows that.

In the future, though, he'll learn to bring his words to conclusion, but then, sliding into a shrugging second gear, arrive at an abrupt half-embarrassed stop, as if to say: these words aren't really me, they're just the clothes I wear.

Like almost all men, Larry will be called upon in his life for a moment or two of genuine eloquence, and these instances will coalesce around that ceremony known as the marriage proposal. 'Will you marry me?' he said to Dorrie Shaw back in 1978, his mouth full of sharp minerals. To a second wife, whom he has not yet met, he will say, simply, 'I want to live with you forever.'

He actually made these pronouncements, full of doubt and also hope. Full of amazement that he knows the words and that such simple words will suffice.

'I'm married to a maze nut,' Dorrie used to say in the old days when she and Larry were newly married. She said it fondly, as wives do, shaking their heads over their husbands' indulgences, the way Larry's mother exclaims over her husband's corkscrew and bottle-opener collection, which has now reached 2,000 specimens, and which she is obliged to dust and number and keep in reasonable order, a collection whose point she has never questioned, nor felt qualified to question.

Dorrie gave her husband, Larry, a paperback book called *Celtic Mazes and Labyrinths* on their first wedding anniversary, and inscribed it: 'Happy memories of Hampton Court', calling to mind their honeymoon in England where Larry saw his first maze.

It's maze madness, she says now, that's what he's got. It's a form of insanity. It drives her crazy, sitting in the middle of a writhing forest. Mazes remind her of a bunch of snakes, and she hates snakes.

It's a passion, an obsession.

The word *obsession* feels too boxy and broad for the round cavity of Larry's mouth, so he simply says to friends or family or anyone who asks, that he's 'into' mazes. A hobby kind of thing. He plays it down. He doesn't know why, but he'd rather not let people know how 'into it' he really is, that it's like a ripe crystal growing in his brain and taking up more and more space.

It's not only mazes themselves he thinks of, but the *idea* of mazes, and the idea is a soft steady incandescent light bulb at the edge of his vision; it's always there, it's always switched on. He can turn his gaze at will and watch it, casting its glow on the supple sleeping aisles of shrubbery around his house, their serpentine (ser-pen-tine) allure, their teasing treachery and promise of reward.

The hedge maze in Larry's yard employs three varieties of plants. The hearty cotoneaster *(Cotoneaster horizontalis)* – which turns red in the fall and which lends itself nicely to pruning tools – makes up the outer ring of the maze. Common caragana *(Caragana arborescens)*, feathery green and not quite so prunable – not at all, in fact – forms the walls of the middle ring. And alpine currant *(Ribes alpinum)* leads into the heart of the maze, where Larry plans to install a small stone fountain one day. (He's already sent off to a supply house in Florida for a design catalogue.)

He's put in his hedge stock bare root in the spring, which adds up to half the cost of waiting till summer and buying the individual plants in pots. Naturally he shops around and uses his florist's connections in order to get a good price. (After all, he's got a mortgage, he's got a little kid who's starting swimming and gymnastics lessons.)

There's a paradox – that useful word again – built into the shrubs he's chosen. He wants the plants to grow fast so that his overall design will be realised, but, at the same time, you can't have *really* fast-growing shrubs in a maze or you'll spend your whole life shaping and cutting back new growth. He's had to come to terms with that *dilemma*, he's had to *accommodate* that fact. (There's pain involved in these new words, the way they hint at so much time lost, time wasted all those years of unknowing.)

Why has Larry committed to memory the Latin names for his shrubs? Because he senses – vaguely – that they deserve the full dignity of his attention. They've survived a couple of tough Manitoba winters, and they're looking good. Really good. So far, not one has shrivelled and died. They seem, in fact, to love him. Shrubs, he feels, are shy exiles in the plant kingdom. They're not quite trees, not quite anything, really, but they have, nevertheless, been awarded by the experts out there, your professors, your writers of gardening books, full botanical classification. (He sees them even in the wintertime with a kind of love, their elegance and sprigged look of surprise.)

He loves the Latin roll of the words in his mouth – *Leguminosae* – and he loves himself for being a man capable of remembering these rare words, for being alert, for paying attention, particularly since he has not always in his life paid sufficient attention. This is something entirely new. His jittery spirits are soothed by the little Latinate sighs and bumps. He hopes, optimistically, that the words that live in his head will eventually find their way to his mouth. Perhaps he'll even learn to flip them off his tongue unselfconsciously, to secrete them through his pores. What else, really, does he need in his life but more words? When you add up the world and its words you get a kind of cosmic sandwich, two thick slices of meaning with nothing required in between. Sometimes, though, he wishes he wouldn't: wouldn't try so hard. What did he used to think about before he tried? What was it that stood behind his eyes – before he figured out how to find the right words?

There are a few words that are missing even from Larry's new under-the-counter dictionary. His sister, Midge, for instance, is divorced from her husband, but she's living with him again. What's the word for her status now? And for her husband? And for what passes between them?

What can he call the feeling he has for his son, Ryan? That mixture of guilt and longing, that ballooning ever-protective, multi-limbed force that's too big to cram into the category of love.

When he hits a traffic light on his way home from work, sitting at an intersection in the near-dark, ten seconds, twenty seconds – what does he call the rapturous seizure he feels as he counts off on his fingers the essential description of where he is in the world? *Here I am, but no one knows my location at this moment. No one knows my eyes are blinking, adjusting, making leaps, asking the question inside the question inside the question—*

And what's the word for that spasm of panic that strikes Larry as he unlocks his back door on a winter night? He enters with his house keys in one hand, a boxed pizza or a bag of takeout chicken in the other. In the tiny linoleum-floored vestibule he stamps the snow off his boots, and stoops to remove them, feeling as he leans forward that the air has dangerously thinned and that he could easily topple over dead on the spot.

He hums Michael Jackson's 'Billy Jean' to scatter the silence, an aerosol spray. The silence contributes to his plummeting faith in his own arrangements. Still air, empty rooms. It was as though he and Dorrie had never embarked on a life of house and children but had been brought to this spiritless edge by force. The walls, the kitchen floor, the tight circle of second-hand appliances, the tiny corner table with its chairs pushed neatly in – these objects refuse to acknowledge him, though he's the one – isn't he? – who brought the scene into being, and who is now trapped in the bubble of his own dread. He ought to rejoice in the settledness of this room, but he doesn't. He should see it as a sequestered cave hidden away in the tall immensity of winter. What is the word for the slow, airless, unrelieved absence he feels? It's coming to him, this word, winging its way as though guided by radar, but it hasn't quite arrived.

Dorrie will be home from her sales job at Manitoba Motors in ten minutes, after she picks up Ryan from daycare. Her mouth will bear a mere trace of her Frankly Fuchsia lipstick. Her quick kiss against his cheek delivers the smallest of electric shocks. A shock of this order doesn't really hurt, but then it doesn't feel good either. Is there a word for a sensation as fleeting and as useless as this?

It strikes Larry that language may not yet have evolved to the point where it represents the world fully.

Recognising this gap brings him a rush of anxiety. Perhaps we're waiting, all of us, he thinks, longing to hear 'something' but not knowing what it is.

Down at Flowercity a guy's come in and ordered an immense gift-bouquet of cut flowers for his aged aunt, and on the card he wants the words: Happy Spring!

And today *is* spring, 21 March, the equinox. The strengthening sun, the melting snow. Everything on earth testifies to the newly arrived season, but Larry's been too sunk in gloom to notice. Things couldn't be worse at home. Dorrie's hardly spoken to him in the last month except to grump about the draft from the north wall of the kitchen. And the lack of closet space. And how she hates their hellhole of a house.

Solstice, equinox. He loves the sound of those words, and remembers how a teacher back in high school once wrote them on the blackboard, putting a slash across the middle of *equinox*, equal nights, night and day. What beautiful logic. The twice-yearly miracle. And here it is. Today. The vernal equinox. About time.

'Larry Weller?'

'Yes?'

'Larry. This is Lucy calling. Lucy Warkenten.'

'Lucy!'

Larry's next-door neighbour, Lucy Warkenten, has never phoned him at work before. He and his latest trainee from Red River College, Bob Buxtead, are standing at the work counter doing centerpieces for a Lions' banquet. They've decided to go for a spring theme, even though the snow's still hanging on here and there, and the daffodils that arrived from British Columbia this morning look faintly puckered at the base of the petals.

Lucy sounds worried, and also excited. 'I hope I'm not interrupting you,' she tells Larry carefully.

'No, not at all.'

'I was just wondering—'

'Yes?'

'Well, I was looking out my window just now, just a few minutes ago, and I was wondering about your maze, Larry. If you've changed your mind or something.'

'About what?'

'If you, you know, decided to start over or something? With a new design. A new concept?'

'No,' Larry said, baffled, fiddling with a pile of bear grass on his work counter, their sharp green edges. 'No, I'm thinking of maybe putting in a new node in the south-east corner when the weather breaks, something a little fancier that I've been working out, but for now—'

'Larry, listen.' He heard her take a long breath before continuing. 'Larry, there's a bulldozer in your yard. Or a, what d'ya call it? – one of those machines. It's been there for about fifteen minutes.'

'A what? Did you say a bulldozer?'

'It's already – I'm so sorry to have to tell you this' – another sharp breath, a trembling inhalation – 'but it, this machine, it's already dug up the whole front part of—'

'Never mind, Lucy. I'll be right there.'

Traffic was bad, even in the dead middle of a Monday afternoon. It was twenty minutes before Larry pulled up in front of his house on Lipton Street.

He saw the ruin of his front yard, the plowed-up furrows of mud and snow, the leveled ground, and the thrusting image of his wooden front steps, suddenly, grotesquely, revealed. A yellow back-hoe, not a bulldozer but just as purposeful, sat silent at the side of the house, and directly in front of it stood the wobbly stick figure of Lucy Warkenten in her flowered parka and purple skirt and boots, her arms held straight out sideways like a crossing guard at attention, the cold spring wind booming off her anxious face. Her posture was defiant and disturbed, as if she were a crazy woman, semaphoring for help.

He remembered later how he shut his eyes against Lucy, and against the pale sunlight coloring the flattened yard. It was not disbelief that assaulted him; on the contrary, he believed at once. He comprehended. He knew. What he felt was the steady, tough pummeling of words against his body: *knowledge*, *pain*, *shame*, *emptiness*, *sorrow*, and, curiously, like rain falling on the other side of the city, that oxygen-laden word *relief*. A portion of what he knew was over. *The end*.

Lucy was moving toward him then, the late afternoon sun striking her face, her eyes, her working lips and teeth. Sorry, sorry, she seemed to be saying through the width of empty air.

And Larry himself, stunned, battered, and opening his mouth at last, giving way not to speech, but to language's smashed, broken syllables and attenuated vowel sounds: the piercing cries and howls of a man injured beyond words.

Set in Stone

Pat Knight

First Day

Have decided to keep diary. Feel it is important to record our daily life so that future generations understand how we lived. Unfortunately pen and paper not yet invented so have to hack words onto cave walls with flint. This is a protracted process so entries will have to be short and to the point (joke).

Og brought me here from my parents' cave. I'd have been happy to stay near them, but naturally Og wouldn't hear of it. As a consequence I was like a Tyrannosaurus Regina with a sore head for days after he dragged me here. I mean, wouldn't anyone be? The journey played havoc with my hairstyle and my bottom was really grazed. Of course Og wasn't bothered. He said I was making a fuss about nothing. He said that he'd dragged his first female nearly three times as far and she'd never complained. Mind, she'd died quite shortly afterwards, but he put this down to depression caused by 'women's troubles', nothing to do with the multiple internal injuries she'd sustained.

Anyway Og kept on about how much I'd like it once we were settled in and had got to know the neighbours, but as far as I can tell they're a common lot with no conversation. I said as much to Og, but he wouldn't listen, just grunted in that prehistoric way of his and shrugged his shoulders. And that's another thing, I didn't realise how hairy he was. I'm sorry, but I just can't fancy a man with a hairy back; and front; and legs; and arms; not to mention hands, feet and face. I'm sorry, but there it is. So not a good start to years of marital bliss.

Second Day

Diary took hours yesterday as having to get used to writing on upright wall and flint kept going blunt. Decided I needed some sort of sharpener to speed up process. Found an old file in pile of Og's junk where I'd found the flint and did my best with it, but couldn't get it right and flint was left with very jagged edges. What a nuisance.

Anyway thought I'd begin by explaining how we divide the daily chores between Og and me. Basically I do *all* the chores and Og spends his time with his mates *allegedly* bringing home the bacon. (Joke, bacon not yet invented.) As I mentioned, I don't fancy Og. And to be perfectly truthful I think this rankles with him as he often makes quite pointed remarks and sometimes tries to push me down on the heap of festering skins in the corner that he likes to call a bed. But I say I can't as the moon is in the wrong quarter. I have no idea what this means, but it does the trick. He just sighs and turns over.

Third Day

When Og got home yesterday he was in a very bad mood. Seems he'd spent all day tracking a dinosaur only to find it was a Brontosaurus which we won't touch since the BSE scare. Had to make do with a salad of roots and berries which he can't stand. Calls it rabbit food, although how he knows what they eat when they haven't evolved yet is a mystery to me. Also he found I'd been using his flint for my writing. It turns out, wouldn't you know it, that this flint is his very, very best flint, one he's had since he was a baby, which he only uses for very, very, very special purposes and that is totally irreplaceable. I must say I was quite offended the way he went on. He couldn't seem to grasp that I'm writing for posterity.

Fourth Day

Feeling very fed up today. Og is still going on about precious flint. Honestly anyone would think I'd done it out of spite. And he implied I was wasting my time with diary. Says it's practically impossible to get published if you're a newcomer to carving, and it may be centuries before my potential is discovered, by which time it'll be too late for me obviously. Also very sniffy about my not having scrubbed cave floor or got any dinner ready. I said I had brushed the floor, but he'd trodden in the heap of dust from my carving when he came in, and if only he'd look where he was walking it would save us both a lot of trouble. He stormed out in huff saying he'd get his own dinner. Heard terrible howl from outside some time later so presume he fell out of tree chasing Pterodactyl.

Fifth Day
A factor I hadn't taken account of when I started this diary is how much space it would take up. I've used up the wall by the cave-mouth already and the light isn't so good further in. I think Og thought he might get round me when he suggested putting in electric light. I said 'and how long will that take? Years and years, I imagine.' Of course he had no answer to that, just stood there looking pathetic. Men! Have also found that the chiselling makes my wrist ache and leaves me too tired to do chores.

Sixth Day
Don't think much of yesterday's entry, tells nothing of daily life. Will try to be more observant in future. Have decided that what I need is a change of routine. Suggested to Og that I went out chasing dinosaurs and he stayed home in cave and did chores. He went ape (Joke, apes etc., etc.,) and said it was man's role to be breadwinner. I said I didn't know what he meant by bread, as we haven't even discovered agriculture yet, still being in the hunter-gatherer phase of our evolution. He got all hoity-toity and called me his little woman. I hit him over head with the first thing that came to hand. His precious flint. I hate being patronised.

Seventh Day
Og regained consciousness at sunset. Complained about fractured skull and loss of blood. Honestly, don't men make a fuss? I told him he

should try childbirth if he wanted to know what real pain felt like. He grunted something incomprehensible (he has a very limited vocabulary), and lurched off, taking his flint with him. I think he said something about going down the pub and realise this could take a while for obvious reasons. But I'm not bothered. I'm sick of being stuck in this bloody cave trying to scrape a living whilst he's out acting the Troglodyte. He needn't think he can lumber back here when he's managed to invent the wheel or something, and expect me to be impressed. Have met sensitive Homo-Sapiens New Man who promises to show me a different way of making ends meet. For this reason have decided to postpone further diary entries for time-being, which, as luck would have it, coincides with fact that as yet there are only seven days on the calendar.

Biographical Notes

Judith Amanthis has lived in London for nearly thirty years. She has two grown-up sons, has published numerous short stories and articles and is writing a novel. She is also preoccupied with African liberation politics.

Deborah Bosley was born in South London in 1965. Her first work of fiction, *Let Me Count the Ways*, was published in 1996 to huge critical acclaim and short-listed for the Romantic Novelists Award. Deborah has travelled extensively and wrote the original Rough Guides to California and San Francisco. She now lives on the Berkshire Downs with her partner and young son, and has written for several publications, including the *Observer, Evening Standard* and *Literary Review*.

Patrice Chaplin has had sixteen works published, including a biography of Modigliani's mistress, *Into the Darkness Laughing*, which has been dramatised for radio and more recently the stage; and *Siesta*, which was made into a film starring Ellen Barkin and Jodie Foster. She has contributed to numerous short story collections and written extensively for radio, newspapers and magazines. Her latest novel, *The Pond People*, will be published by Macmillan.

Agatha Christie is the creator of Hercule Poirot and Miss Marple. She has sold millions of books all over the world and been the inspiration behind numerous films and television series.

Clare Colvin has published two novels, *A Fatal Season* and *Masque of the Gonzagas*. She is also a well-known journalist and short story writer. Her stories have appeared in a number of anthologies, including Constable's *Winter's Tales*, and have been translated in Europe.

Amanda Craig was born in South Africa in 1959 to journalist parents. She later came to England to boarding school and subsequently read English at Cambridge, taking a year out to work for Mother Theresa. After jobs in advertising and as Terence Conran's PR, she became a journalist, winning the Catherine Packenham Award. After this, Amanda turned to fiction, writing *Foreign Bodies, A Private Place* and *A Vicious Circle*. She lives in London with her husband and two children.

Vicky Grut was born in South Africa in 1961 and lived in Madagascar and Italy before moving to England in 1980 to do a fine art degree at Goldsmiths College. Her short stories have been published in various magazines and anthologies since 1994, and in 1999 she was a winner of both The Asham and Ian St James story awards. Until recently she worked for the *New Yorker* magazine in London. She has just completed her first novel and now works as a freelance editor. She lives in London with her partner and their eight-year-old son.

Pauline Holdstock was born in Kent and educated at the Brentwood Ursuline Convent High School. She received a BA degree from London University at Bournemouth. Her novel, *The Blackbird's Song*, was shortlisted for the W.H. Smith/Books in Canada First Novel Award. She has since published four novels and a collection of short fiction in Canada, the UK and Germany, and is currently working on a screenplay and a new novel set in Italy. She has lived in Canada since 1974.

Pat Knight lives in Greater London with her second husband, fourth dog and fifth cat. She likes camping, walking and reading, dislikes housework and gardening, is afraid of heights, but not spiders. An escapee from the Civil Service, her real interest lies in writing poetry and fiction – she has recently completed her first novel, entitled *Much Improved by Death*.

Norma Meacock was born in 1934. She studied English at London University. She has had numerous short stories published and has tutored writing workshops in London and Knighton, Wales. She lives in London and Shropshire.

Alice Munro grew up in Ontario, Canada and attended the University of Western Ontario. She has published nine collections of stories as well as a novel, *Lives of Girls and Women*. During her distinguished career she has been the recipient of many awards and prizes, including three prestigious Governor General's Literary Awards; the Lannan Literary Award; and the 1995 W.H. Smith Literary Award. Her stories have appeared in *The New Yorker*, the *Atlantic Monthly*, *The Paris Review*, and other publications, and her collections have been translated into thirteen languages. She and her husband divide their time between Clinton, Ontario and Comox, British Columbia.

Twice nominated for the Nobel Prize in literature, **Joyce Carol Oates** is one of America's most versatile, serious writers. In addition to numerous novels and short story collections, she has published several volumes of poetry, several books of plays, five books of literary criticism, and the book length essay *On Boxing*. She lives in Princeton where she is the Roger S. Berlind Distinguished Professor of Humanities at Princeton University.

Sylvia Petter has had short stories published in Europe, Australia, New Zealand, Japan and the US, as well as broadcast on the BBC World Service. She is a member of the Geneva Writer's Group in Switzerland and of Boot Camp, an online writing group in cyberspace. Born in Vienna and brought up in Australia, she now lives in France with her husband and daughter, and is working on her second novel and a short story collection.

Jean Pickering has published short stories in North American literary journals, as well as articles on Doris Lessing and Margaret Drabble. Her non-fiction work, *Understanding Doris Lessing*, is published by the University of South Carolina Press, and she is a co-editor of and contributor to *Nostalgia, Gender and Nationalism*, New York University Press/Macmillan UK.

Carol Shields' other novels include *The Stone Diaries* (1993), winner of the Pulitzer Prize and short-listed for the Booker Prize; *The Republic of Love* (1992), *Happenstance* (1991) and *Mary Swann* (1990). *Various Miracles*, a collection of short stories, was published in 1994 and *Dressing Up for the Carnival* is to be published by Fourth Estate in February 2000. Born and brought up in Chicago, Carol Shields has lived in Canada since 1957. She is the Chancellor of the University of Winnipeg.

Shelley Weiner was born in South Africa in 1949. She worked as a journalist for many years before turning to fiction in 1991. Her published writing includes three novels (*A Sister's Tale, The Last Honeymoon* and *The Joker*) and short stories in anthologies such as *Winter's Tales* and *The Slow Mirror*. She holds an MA in English Literature from King's College, London and combines research and writing with teaching. She is married, lives in London, and has a son and a daughter.

Fay Weldon was born in England, raised in New Zealand and received an MA in economics and psychology from St. Andrews University in Scotland. She is the author of twenty-two novels, including *The Life and Loves of a She-Devil, The Hearts and Lives of Men* and *Big Women*, as well as several collections of short stories and books of non-fiction. She lives in London.

Jane Barker Wright is the author of two novels, *The Tasmanian Tiger* and *Mother of Thousands*. She was educated at Queen's University at Kingston and now lives in Vancouver, British Columbia with her husband and three children.